Terror

MANCHESTER
1824
Manchester University Press

Terror

When images become weapons

Charlotte Klonk

Translated from the German by
Martina Dervis and Margaret Hiley

Manchester University Press

Published by S. Fischer Verlag 2017

First English-language edition published in 2020 by
Manchester University Press
Altrincham Street, Manchester M1 7JA
www.manchesteruniversitypress.co.uk

British Library Cataloguing-in-Publication Data
A catalogue record for this book is available from the British Library

ISBN 978 1 5261 4713 4 hardback

Typeset by
Servis Filmsetting Ltd, Stockport, Cheshire
Printed in Great Britain by
Bell & Bain Ltd, Glasgow

But what is at issue is a subject so crucial to me that I still do not know whether I can develop it with sufficient freedom, given the current stage of my thinking and provided that I can succeed in elucidating it at all.

Walter Benjamin to Gershom Scholem, 26 March 1921

Contents

List of figures

Acknowledgements

On a grey winter's day at the beginning of 2005, I was standing in the exhibition *Regarding Terror – The RAF-Exhibition* at the Kunst-Werke Institute for Contemporary Art in Berlin when I suddenly saw a face from long-forgotten times. It belonged to Hanns Martin Schleyer, the President of the Confederation of German Employers' Associations, who had been kidnapped by the Red Army Faction (RAF) in the autumn of 1977. As far as I can remember, I was not consciously aware of the images and videos that the RAF circulated when I was a child. Nevertheless, the encounter in 2005 was more than a lesson in history. To this day I do not know why seeing the face of Hanns Martin Schleyer in captivity, almost thirty years after images of it were first released, was so disturbing for me.

The following summer something similar happened in England, where I then lived. After the first bomb attacks on the London Underground on 7 July 2005 and the failed attacks a fortnight later, the city was in a state of emergency that is difficult to describe. I had never experienced anything like it, not when I was at secondary school in the 1970s in the Federal Republic of Germany, nor as a student in the UK in the late 1980s and early 1990s when IRA bombings were

still a very real threat. Again, it was one particular image that confused me. On the evening of 29 July 2005, with my mind on other things, I glanced at the evening news on TV and saw a video of the arrest of two of the failed attackers. It stopped me in my tracks. It must have been then that I first realised that the extraordinary effect of images of terror was something that I could not explain to myself and that I needed to understand.

It was a long path from there to the publication of this book, with several detours and wrong turnings. Many people accompanied me along the way with support and advice, above all Jenno Fulde, who throughout those years provided valuable information, reading suggestions, ideas and much more. At an early stage, when I began to study images of the RAF, my conversations with David Gugerli and Michael Hagner, as well as extremely helpful correspondence with Petra Terhoeven, did much to steer me in the right direction. Later, I learned much at conferences held by the British research network Terrorist Transgressions, led by Sue Malvern and Gabriel Koureas. And later still, a research fellowship at the Clark Art Institute in Williamstown gave me the opportunity to step back calmly and concentrate on finding a structure for the book. This is when I began to compare notes with James Elkins. This exchange has continued and given me much food for thought. I am also grateful to Carolin Behrmann, Horst Bredekamp, Stefan Grundmann, Herfried Münkler, Christian Saehrendt and Annette Vowinckel for their advice and many valuable suggestions. Finally, Jens Eder made sure that I looked beyond the confines of my own discipline and took account of research in media studies. Without the inspiration of all of these people, this book might never have been written.

I have been able to publish some provisional results from my research in various papers and journals. More than once their editors saved me from errors. I have also benefitted tremendously from discussions, some of them quite intense, after talks and events in cities including Berlin, Florence, Frankfurt, Cologne, London, New York, Oslo and Stockholm. Above all, I owe enormous thanks to Julia Voss, who has enabled me to publish articles on this subject in the *Frankfurter Allgemeine Zeitung* over several years. Like a good fairy she stood by my side from the start, offering help, advice and corrections at crucial moments.

During the final year of writing the book, my colleague Stefanie Gerke, as well as Professor Kai Kappel and the late Professor Michaela Marek, the Departmental Chairs of the Institute of Art and Visual History at the Humboldt University of Berlin at the time, have made sure that I was free of other obligations. This is not something to be taken for granted, and I was very fortunate to have their collegiality and support. I am grateful to Isabelle Graw and Andreas Kablitz for their insightful comments on parts of the manuscript, and to Nina Bergeest and Dortje Fink for extremely careful editing and indefatigable help with picture research. Verena Straub has not only read the whole manuscript and commented on it, but also made many valuable suggestions over several years. I owe a special debt of gratitude to Miloš Vec. He was the driving force behind the book and encouraged me to write and to carry on writing. On several occasions his comments, corrections and ideas not only steered me in the right direction, but also prevented grave errors. I also owe much to Dieter Grimm. His comments on the first drafts have helped me to improve both the content and the style of the text. Moreover, the last chapter would not have been possible without his input and ideas, although I am

sure he would have written it entirely differently. But even with the support and advice of so many people, some errors may remain, for which of course I alone am responsible.

It cannot have been easy for my daughter Leah to square the subject of her mother's research with her own bedtime reading of Astrid Lindgren's books. I am moved to find that now she is an adult and pursues very different professional interests, she continues to engage with the concerns that are at the heart of this book. It is difficult to find words for the role that my father Walter Klonk had in the genesis of this manuscript. My siblings and I were brought up in a very different world from the friend-or-foe schema that determines terror and the generation and instrumentalisation of its images. Despite this, he read every word and, as is typical for him, commented generously. But above all, he always provided a special place of peace and calm, so I could retain my sanity, despite some disturbing moments while I was doing the research for the book.

I am grateful to Alexander Roesler and S. Fischer Verlag for publishing the German version of the book in 2017 and to Thomas Dark and Manchester University Press for taking on the English translation with such enthusiasm. Two anonymous readers reviewed the German book for MUP and provided many helpful suggestions for improvements. My final thanks, however, must go to Martina Dervis and Margaret Hiley. I consider myself lucky to have found in them translators whose efforts went well beyond duty.

Introduction

On the evening of 13 June 2016, a French policeman was stabbed to death in a street in the Paris suburb of Magnanville. His assailant subsequently managed to gain access to the victim's flat, where he murdered the policeman's partner in front of their three-year-old son. While negotiating with members of the special forces, the murderer posted live footage of himself and his victims on Facebook. Acting in the name of the so-called Islamic State (IS), the Magnanville perpetrator, who would later be shot and killed, single-handedly applied one of the fundamental tenets of modern terrorism: it is not the act of violence itself that counts, but the images of it that are brought into circulation.

On 15 March 2019, the mass murderer of fifty worshippers in Christchurch, New Zealand took self-publicity on social media to a new level. Not only did he live-stream his attack on Facebook in the manner of a first-person shooter computer game, he announced it in advance on the darknet. A few minutes before the start of the massacre, he also emailed a long 'statement' – a mixture of far-right symbols, texts and references – to the Prime Minister's office and to media outlets. Facebook and other social media platforms had difficulty preventing its circulation.

What is the correct way to deal with images such as these? This question was relevant long before the advent of the internet. Traditional media have always conveyed more than pure information. When a group that is militarily inferior challenges a state's superior power, the actual number of deaths caused by an attack is less significant than the terror it produces and the perpetrators' potential renown among like-minded individuals. The more intense the media's production of images, the greater the perpetrators' initial success.

This confronts spectators with an unsolvable dilemma. Since we remain physically unharmed when looking at the images, we are soon gripped by a subliminal feeling of *Angstlust*. As Hans Magnus Enzensberger put it: 'If the terror of images doesn't turn you into a terrorist, it will turn you into a voyeur.'[1] The deflection of fear becomes voyeuristic curiosity and vice versa. This makes the path from victim to perpetrator inevitable: curiosity fuels the visual machinery of terror, and the deflection of fear generates counter-images. Following a terror attack, stereotypical images of the 'enemy' are swiftly circulated in order to restore a sense of security. Even before the perpetrators have been caught, the horror is assigned a face, and vague fear is expressed in images – a face and a form that can be used to symbolically denigrate the enemies and dispose of them, even though they may not have been arrested yet. The images amplify the event and produce further visual events, which in turn generate actions and facts that may lead to more lives being lost.[2] In this sense, as the political theorist Herfried Münkler summarises, terrorism is 'a form of warfare in which combat with weapons functions as the drive wheel for the real combat with images'.[3]

This raises the question of whether there is a correct position for media producers and consumers. Are we personally responsible for the way we deal with images of terror? The present book is an attempt to find an answer to this question. Rather than trying to define the causes of violence and find ways of protecting ourselves from it – an endeavour that other, far more qualified, authors have undertaken in recent decades[4] – it seeks to investigate the dynamics of image and counter-image that unfold in the Western media as soon as an attack occurs. Whether and how we arrive at a moral assessment crucially depends, as Judith Butler has emphasised, 'upon a certain field of perceptible reality having already been established'.[5] The following chapters will explore the patterns and strategies that have defined photojournalistic coverage of terror since the late nineteenth century. It is this historical context of image production in the media that we have to understand before we can consider the ethics underpinning our way of dealing with these images.

Image patterns

Butler speaks of 'frames that govern the perceptible, that exercise a delimiting function, bringing an image into focus on condition that some portion of the visual field is ruled out'.[6] The term 'framing', which is commonly used in media and communication studies,[7] refers to repeatable structural devices that predetermine the way in which the media present events and frame their meaning. In what follows, I will speak of patterns rather than frames or framing, because the term 'pattern' conveys two meanings that express the issues at stake in this book more accurately. Patterns are not just templates that determine how each

new event is represented; they are also regularly recurring representations within a specific field. The image patterns used in reports on bombings and hostage-takings and in visualisations of perpetrators may differ, but they often appear together and merge in our mind when we look at the circumstances of a given crime.

What all images in the context of terror share, however, is something that the art and cultural historian Aby Warburg attempted to describe with his concept of *Pathosformel* ('pathos formula'): they evoke and process primeval emotions such as fear, dread, revenge and desire for fame. Studying images from the Renaissance, Warburg identified examples of an intense emotional charge that found expression in a repertoire of forms and figures from classical antiquity.[8] Much the same is true for images of acts of terror. In times of heightened danger, emotional tension is diffused through recourse to well-established patterns. Warburg himself looked for and found the 'pathos formula' primarily in individual images. He argued that agitation is expressed in iconographic figurations handed down from antiquity. In the context of news images, however, a conscious or unconscious reference to individual models is rather rare and difficult to prove. Emotional tension is usually not regulated by individual images but by established patterns of series of images. The calming, civilising effect develops especially through repetition, through the unchanging sequence of images and counter-images that follows a familiar schema of good and evil, friend and foe.

Of course, the selection of images and events discussed here cannot claim to be comprehensive. The phenomenon of modern terror has become too heterogeneous, too global and ubiquitous since its emergence at the end of the nineteenth century.[9] I will therefore focus on Western media

events and images, including images that have become canonical[10] and which, according to the historian Gerhard Paul, have 'themselves made history and simultaneously shaped the memory of that history'.[11] Yet this rather narrow scope does not mean to imply that terror acts of violence are only worthy of consideration if they manage to attract the attention of Western audiences. Far from it: for Western viewers, many attacks are devoid of images and lie outside the sphere covered by their media. We still have virtually no images of the atrocities committed by the radical Islamic group Boko Haram in north-eastern Nigeria, even though its members uploaded videos onto internet platforms such as YouTube which are accessible to the Western world, and activists attempt to remind us of the more than 200 girls who were abducted from a school in Borno State on 14 April 2014, only some of whom had been reunited with their families by 2018.[12]

I have chosen to focus on Western media events and images not only because of the linguistic and cultural accessibility of the sources, but also as a consequence of the ethical issues explored in the final chapter. Since this book is concerned above all with our personal responsibility when faced with the ambivalence of images of terror, I have given prominence to events that have attracted significant attention in the industrialised nations of the Western world.

The meaning of 'terror'

But what exactly does the term 'terror' mean? Can we usefully speak of 'terrorism' and 'terrorists'? These terms are such common currency today that the question might seem unnecessary. Yet a glance at the quite substantial body of research on terrorism shows that scholars agree on only one

thing: that there is neither a generally binding definition nor a comprehensive interpretative approach to the phenomena described by these words.[13] This problem is already evident in the history of its usage. The modern word 'terrorism' initially referred to the state terror that marked the second stage of the French Revolution, when it was deemed necessary to create fear and terror in the population to consolidate the new democracy that the Revolution aimed to establish. The Jacobins spoke of 'la Terreur' in a positive sense.[14] For precisely this reason, the British philosopher and politician Edmund Burke attributed negative values to it. In his 1790 *Reflections on the Revolution in France*, Burke uses the term only to discredit the French regime of terror.[15] Since then, it has developed into a blanket term epitomising absolute evil. As the sociologist Henner Hess points out, it could be expected that the 'causes and goals' of this evil 'are not really worthy of discussion ... Like the pirates of old, the terrorist becomes *hostis humani generis*, the enemy of humanity.'[16] Thus it is hardly surprising that members of violent organisations tend to object strongly to being called 'terrorists'. Matters become even more complex when we consider that some of them have ended up as leaders of the same states that had previously branded them terrorists. The best-known examples for this are Fidel Castro in Cuba and Nelson Mandela in South Africa. The actors themselves usually prefer terms such as resistance, freedom or guerrilla fighters.

Similarly, the totalitarian states of the first half of the twentieth century are generally referred to as terror regimes,[17] but their governments were no more ready to accept the label than non-governmental groups. Although many states are known to have engineered or supported acts of terror through their secret services – Libya, Syria, South

Yemen, Iraq and Iran are frequently mentioned examples, as is East Germany – of course none of them has publicly acknowledged that it sponsored terrorism.[18] Furthermore, the logic with which the terrorism label has been applied can hardly be called consistent. The examples cited by Henner Hess demonstrate this:

> For German politicians and courts, the RAF members arrested in Yugoslavia were terrorists, but the members of the Croatian Ustaše whose extradition Yugoslavia demanded were not. Palestinian aeroplane hijackings and attacks on kibbutzim were terrorist acts, but the massacres perpetrated by the Israeli air force in Palestinian refugee camps were not.[19]

For this reason, I have largely avoided the word 'terrorism' and used 'terror' instead. 'Terror' has the great advantage of denoting only the effects of the acts rather than implying some form of movement of like-minded fanatics. It refers solely to the act and its impact, the dread and fear that are to be sown in the population through the dissemination of dramatic images. We have a plethora of terms for the perpetrators themselves, such as politically motivated assassins, kidnappers or murderers. Unlike 'terrorist', these words define quite precisely what individuals and groups are prepared to do under certain circumstances to achieve their goals. Using 'terror' rather than 'terrorism' and 'terrorist' also allows us to consider the often terror-inducing reactions of states. The history of the fight against terror shows that to avert attacks, states have sometimes deployed secret services and military operations that at least came close to acts of terror. One recent example is the assassination of Osama bin Laden on 2 May 2011 in Pakistan by a special unit of the US Navy – a contentious act from the perspective of international law.[20]

Defining terror as a new form of warfare, as Münkler and others have done, is equally controversial.[21] Although the boundaries between war and terror have become increasingly blurred, it is important to note that wars still need to be declared and that the international law of armed conflict prohibits any involvement of the civilian population in the combat. Terror attacks are characterised precisely by the fact that they only partially adhere to these rules. Many perpetrators consider it at least acceptable to injure and kill non-combatants, and the covert and unpredictable nature of their operations is what makes them so successful. States or communities of states do not always respond to these acts with military force. Nor is there always a declaration of war (such as bin Laden's declaration following the 1998 embassy bombings in East Africa), and the aim is never military victory over the enemy. The perpetrators themselves, for example the Red Army Faction (RAF) in Germany in the 1970s, have often sought to present their attacks as acts of war in order to acquire guerrilla fighter status, which is recognised and regulated under international law, and to force the challenged states to mobilise their military forces. This is what happened in the so-called 'war on terror' launched by the US government under George W. Bush in response to the attacks of 11 September 2001 (known as '9/11'), whereas the Federal Republic of Germany rejected such an approach in its fight against the RAF. The West German authorities consistently denied the members of the RAF recognition as soldiers and prisoners of war, using not the military but the police and secret services to combat them. According to the historian Matthias Dahlke, one logical consequence of defining terror as war would be that terrorists might have to be recognised as war criminals and war criminals as terrorists.[22] It therefore seems advisable to use

the word 'terror' with caution and not hastily equate acts of terror with acts of war.[23]

Since 11 September 2001, there has been an exponential increase in the number of publications on 'terrorism'. While academic research in the 1970s mostly explored left-wing terror from the perspective of the social sciences,[24] during the 1980s international terror networks and their links to states on both sides of the Iron Curtain became the centre of attention.[25] Since the 1990s and especially since 9/11, terrorism studies have increasingly focused on religiously motivated terror.[26] Each new approach has shifted the focus, emphasising certain phenomena and neglecting others.

The approach taken in this book is based on the wave model that the political scientist David C. Rapoport introduced in 2001 in an attempt to systematise the different forms and social foundations of modern terror perpetrated by non-state groups. He distinguishes four waves: a first, anarchist wave beginning in the 1880s; an anticolonial wave that formed in the 1920s; a 'New Left' wave that started in the 1960s; and finally a religious wave that emerged in the 1970s and continues to the present day. According to Rapoport, the premises and manifestations of each of these waves are so diverse that it is hard to subsume them under a single umbrella term. There are also a number of activities that this model fails to account for, such as the ongoing conflicts in India. For the purpose of this book, however, the decisive issue is that each of the sometimes overlapping phases Rapoport identified was shaped by characteristic technological and political conditions, and that the groups active within them depended strongly on transnational and international cooperation with other organisations.[27] The first wave of anarchist

terror, for example, was determined by the transformation of modern communications:

> The telegraph, daily mass newspapers, and railroads flourished during the last quarter of the nineteenth century. Events in one country were known elsewhere in a day or so. Prominent Russian anarchists travelled extensively, helping to inspire sympathies and groups elsewhere; sometimes, as the journeys of Peter Prodhoun [sic] indicate, they had more influence abroad than at home. Mass transportation made large-scale emigrations possible and created diaspora communities, which then became significant in the politics of both their 'new' and 'old' countries.[28]

These transformations also played a major role in the third wave: the rapid expansion of aviation, for example, led to a rise in aeroplane hijackings during the 1970s, and facilitated further attacks because it provided easy access to international networks and remote hinterlands. Yet the strategies were markedly different from those of the first phase. Hostage-taking rose in significance, and attacks pursued a new goal:

> A first-wave victim was assassinated because he or she held a public office. New Left-wave assassinations more often were 'punishments'. Jordan's prime minister and king had forced the PLO out of their country in a savage battle. Similarly, the attempt against British Prime Minister Margaret Thatcher occurred because she was 'responsible' for the death of nine IRA hunger strikers who refused to be treated as criminals. [The politician] Aldo Moro was assassinated because the Italian government refused to enter hostage negotiations.[29]

Rapoport's model, which highlights the changing technological conditions for terror attacks, provides a useful starting point for the present study. Politically motivated acts of violence committed by individuals or small groups

within a state have occurred since antiquity,[30] but the late nineteenth-century anarchist movement was the first consciously to use the amplifying effect of the new illustrated mass media to reach a far greater audience than would have been possible through traditional means of agitation. Researchers have thus long argued that modern terror's use of violence has one primary goal: to spread fear and terror through maximum exposure in the mass media. As Brian Jenkins, a pioneer of terror research, observed in 1974: 'Terrorism is aimed at people watching ... Terrorism is theatre.'[31] Today, there is a growing consensus that the attacks that anarchist groups carried out in the late nineteenth century marked the beginning of modern terror in this sense.

Images and evidence

By focusing on media images produced following terror attacks, this book aims to make a contribution to an approach informed by communication theory, which now dominates research in the field,[32] thus inevitably reproducing some of its blind spots. As Dahlke rightly points out: 'Communication theory researchers working on terrorism are often misled by their own perception':

> They usually depend on images spread by the media. This suggests that attacks they do not know about do not have any wider impact and thus fail to achieve the effect the terrorists want ... Conversely, this means that studying only attacks communicated by the media ignores a large proportion of terrorist activity. What about terrorists' secret campaigns to blackmail state actors into freeing their comrades, where the aim is precisely not to achieve publicity, as in The Hague in 1974? What if the aim of an attack really is to destroy an arms factory or pipeline and not to create headlines about

> it, as in the Netherlands and Austria in 1972? What if, as in the attack on the 1975 OPEC conference in Vienna, the demand that a text be read out in the Austrian media is just a pretext?[33]

By exploring photographic coverage of attacks in Western media, I will inevitably leave out many events or only look at them from a narrow perspective. Prominence is given to internationally active or transnationally networked groups, such as the anarchists and predecessors of the Irish Republican Army (IRA) in the United Kingdom in the late nineteenth century, the far-left RAF in West Germany, the Marxist-Leninist Popular Front for the Liberation of Palestine (PFLP) in the 1970s, militant Shia organisations in Lebanon in the 1980s, and Al-Qaida and IS at the start of the twenty-first century. This book covers three of the four waves Rapoport describes, but not the anticolonial uprisings that started in the 1920s, nor the equally effective images produced by groups fighting for national recognition or independence during the latter half of the twentieth century; for example, in Algeria, South Africa and Cyprus, or in Spain, Colombia and Sri Lanka. These struggles usually were and still are concerned with controlling territories. In visual terms, poster campaigns, murals and graffiti (which have recently begun to attract the attention of researchers) thus play a more important role than images in the international media.[34] By contrast, the anarchists in St Petersburg, London and Paris, the IRA when carrying out attacks in England, Palestinian organisations when acting internationally, the far-left 'urban guerrillas' of the 1970s and the jihadists in the West in the early twenty-first century – all of whom were underground fighters and avoided military confrontation – were not concerned with occupying a territory. What mattered to them were the intimidating psychological effects

their acts produced.[35] The terror that IS perpetrated has a foot in both camps in this regard, aiming both to capture and occupy territory in Iraq and Syria and to threaten and intimidate the Western world.

Readers looking for a comprehensive reconstruction of photographic coverage of modern terror since the late nineteenth century will therefore be disappointed. This book will mention neither spectacular attacks such as the 1975 Vienna Organization of the Petroleum Exporting Countries (OPEC) conference siege, nor the series of IRA bombings in England in the 1970s, nor the far-right terror that has recently attracted increased attention but – for reasons that have not yet been sufficiently researched – received far less media coverage than its left-wing counterparts.[36] It is noticeable, for example, that the Christchurch massacre disappeared from the headlines far sooner than similar attacks in recent years carried out by members of Islamic State. A keyword analysis of nine leading terror research journals by the sociologist Bart Schuurman has shown that non-jihadist attacks perpetrated by right-wing extremists have been systematically underplayed in recent times.[37]

As the present study is limited to selected examples of widely publicised acts of terror, far-right attacks are unfortunately beyond its scope. A detailed analysis of well-known attacks and their available visual coverage has the advantage that it is able to reveal patterns and strategies that have gone largely unnoticed until now, despite the general consensus on the 'symbiotic relationship' between terror and the media.[38] A historical perspective that sees photojournalism as more than just a reaction triggered by violent actors is long overdue. For it is certainly not the case, as Münkler and others assume, that the media merely convey the message of the militarily inferior insurgents, whose

actions the victim states only counter with their police or military forces.[39] So far, no government has been able to resist the war of images set in motion by acts of terror. In most cases, like has been repaid with like. Visual coverage of attacks has always concluded by depicting the perpetrators' arrest or execution, making it possible for the state to demonstrate that it has regained its sovereignty. Recent history contains numerous examples of this reciprocally waged struggle.[40]

At a press conference in Baghdad in June 2006, for example, a US military command presented a framed large-scale photograph of Abu Musab Al Zarqawi, the alleged leader of Al-Qaida in Iraq. Al Zarqawi had just been killed, and the photo showed his face covered in blood. For the US government, the image was a trophy that marked a first success in the 'war on terror' declared by President George W. Bush after the 9/11 attacks – a military struggle that had remained without significant victories for five years, with no prospect of capturing Osama bin Laden. The Americans thus triumphantly displayed the picture of the dead Al Zarqawi. Yet exactly the same photograph could soon be seen on radical jihadists' websites, where it was used as evidence of Al Zarqawi's glorious martyrdom.[41]

A battle of images is above all a psychological struggle and thus is even more difficult to control than its physical counterpart. Unintended consequences are the rule rather than the exception. Despite being launched with clear intentions, images usually only reach their target for a short time and often turn against their creators, foiling their designs with catastrophic results. Al Zarqawi's own brutal strategy of spreading videos of the beheadings of American, Korean and British hostages online was eventually turned against him: instead of winning the Iraqi population to his

insurgent movement through a shocking show of violence, the videos caused widespread alienation, and even prompted Al-Qaida's leadership to distance itself from him.[42]

As this example shows, terror is concerned especially with 'revenge, renown and reaction', to use the words of political scientist Louise Richardson.[43] Contrary to popular notions, images contain little actual information, yet their affective and appellative content is considerable. As art historian Ernst Gombrich has pointed out, we use exactly the same faculties to see both real objects and images (perceiving both as phenomena that have a form, a colour and a spatial dimension), and this may be the reason we tend to attribute greater evidentiary value to images than to verbal communication.[44] Nevertheless, significant codes are at work within these supposedly objective images, an aspect that will be discussed in greater detail in the final chapter. Here, two examples should suffice to demonstrate that even photographs issued to provide evidence do not simply reveal facts.[45] What we see in them depends crucially on the contexts in which they are shown, looked at and instrumentalised. Not the images as such but their context endows them with the power to act as evidence – or not, as the following case will show.

On 27 November 2009, the *Frankfurter Allgemeine Zeitung* published a photograph (Figure 1) on its front page that was supposed to provide information on a controversial airstrike that had been carried out twenty-seven days previously in north Afghanistan, killing over one hundred people.[46] On 3 September, Taliban fighters had hijacked two North Atlantic Treaty Organization (NATO) tankers south of the city of Kunduz. Two US bombers detected the convoy and sent the video material to the German troops who were responsible for the region in question. During

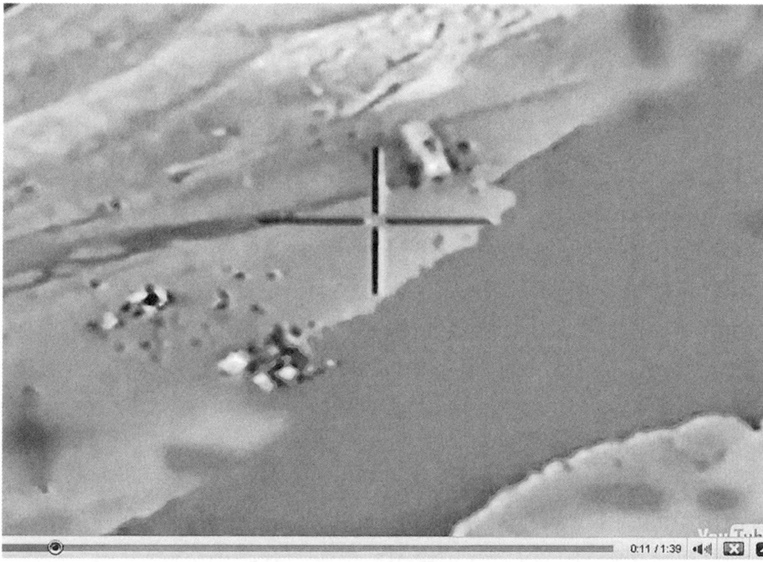

Figure 1 Still from a video sent from a US fighter plane to the German military command in Mazar-i-Sharif on the night of 4 September 2009.

the proceedings later initiated by the German Federal Prosecutor General, the officer in command, Colonel Georg Klein, stated that an informant on the ground had told him that the persons visible around the vehicles in the video were all insurgents. This turned out to be untrue. The Taliban had abandoned the tankers to civilian looters from the surrounding area after getting stuck in muddy ground when trying to cross a river.

The image on the front page of the *Frankfurter Allgemeine Zeitung* was a still from the video that the German commander had watched before giving the order to drop a 500 lb bomb (the video eventually ended up on YouTube). Upon which information, which knowledge, which assumptions did the colonel base his order to strike? This was

the question the image seemed to ask. Neither tankers nor Taliban fighters nor civilians are visible. The only sharply defined object is the crosshairs standing out against an otherwise blurred, black-and-white snapshot. The grainy live video was recorded by a circling US F-15E fighter jet and transferred onto a screen in the German military base about seven kilometres away. It showed numerous black dots around larger structures which can also be seen on the still – a thermal image that was not clear enough to verify whether the persons visible were armed or unarmed. Thus the image on its own provided no indication of how the colonel's decision should be judged. It is not possible to identify any clear features, and it is unclear which conclusions the public, to whom this image was presented in the run-up to the trial, were supposed to draw from it.

On 3 May 2011, the day after Al-Qaida leader Osama bin Laden was killed, newspaper readers might have been equally puzzled when they saw a blurred, orange-brown photo appearing on the front pages of many international newspapers (Figure 2). Hardly anything was recognisable apart from the headline 'ABC News Exclusive'. The picture was taken from footage filmed by elite soldiers as they stormed bin Laden's hideaway in Abbottabad. It was the news commentaries and newspaper captions that informed viewers what they were actually looking at: the room where the Al-Qaida leader was hunted down and shot by special units of the US military. The *Frankfurter Allgemeine Zeitung* also drew attention to the gaping hole in the back wall,[47] but who or what caused this hole remains unexplained to this day.

Much like the previous example, this image neither confirmed nor proved anything. Above all, it did not show what actually happened during the night of 2 May 2011 in

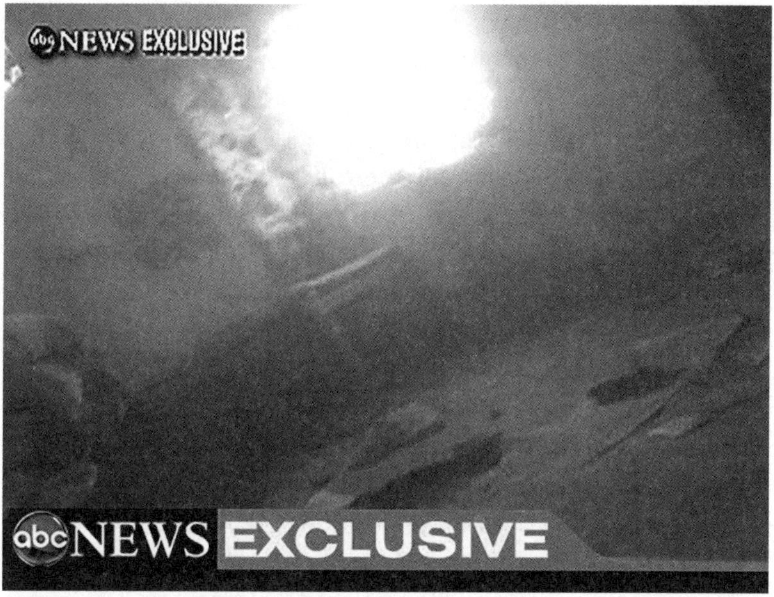

Figure 2 Still from a video recorded by US elite troops when storming Osama bin Laden's house in Abbottabad.

Abbottabad – the death of bin Laden. Although it is well known that photographs can be manipulated rapidly, easily and almost without trace in this digital age, and fake images of the shot Al-Qaida leader were circulating online soon after the compound in Pakistan had been stormed, there were calls for the US government to release a photograph of his corpse as proof in the days following bin Laden's assassination.[48] Both border controls and courtrooms now regard other methods as more reliable evidence of a person's identity, such as DNA samples or storing and comparing biometric data. Accordingly, the US government referred to a DNA test that was supposed to show that the Navy Sea, Air and Land teams (SEALs) had indeed shot none other than Osama bin Laden. Soon it became clear that

demands for the image to be published were actually concerned with something else. The government should finally release the image, argued Eugene Robinson in his blog for the *Washington Post*, as only this would show that the criminal had received his just deserts.[49] What people wanted was not proof of the arch-enemy's death. They wanted their pent-up desire for revenge to be satisfied.

In the context of terror, visual evidence or factual information is rarely what matters most. Although the restoration of public order is always the main focus following an attack, the visual machinery is driven first and foremost by the desire for renown and revenge on both sides. It is a process that is difficult to control. Nothing and no one can eradicate images once they have entered circulation. Whoever hopes for victory and defeat, as in physical warfare, will inevitably fail, for no image is able to destroy what has previously been released. Like the walking dead, these images continue to appear long after the events in question are over. It is a battle that knows no winners and hence no ceasefire either.

Chapter 1

Close-up: assassinations and bomb attacks in the late nineteenth and early twenty-first centuries

Following the attacks of 11 September 2001 and the destruction of the World Trade Center in New York, the President of the United States, George W. Bush, spoke of an event that 'changed our world'.[1] At the time many people shared this opinion. Never before had the media reported on terror in such breadth and intensity and never before had there been such a thorough scholarly debate.[2] But over time, people's perspectives changed.

There is no doubt that the scale of 9/11 was unprecedented. The number of casualties – almost 3,000 – was nearly ten times higher than in any former terror attack. To use planes as bombs, crashing them into the tallest buildings in Manhattan against a clear blue sky during prime viewing time, like a scene from a disaster film, was almost beyond comprehension. The images which subsequently went around the world prompted the composer Karlheinz Stockhausen to speak of a 'work of art' executed with diabolical precision, and the art historian Karl Otto Werckmeister referred to a new 'aesthetic of the apocalypse'.[3] Yet statements like these, some made in the immediate aftermath of 9/11, neglected the fact that the number of casualties and the scale of destruction are not the measure by which

the cruelty of shock and horror can be quantified. For every family that loses even a single person, the suffering is immeasurable.

That the perpetrators used the latest technologies and chose a highly symbolic target was hardly new, nor was the fact that these were religiously motivated suicide attacks. The only novelty was the location: never before had the United States been attacked on its own soil on this scale. The response was drastic. It led to a misguided war in Iraq and a traumatic military intervention in Afghanistan. According to Louise Richardson, the fears provoked by this attack were disproportionate to the actual threat:

> At home Americans became convinced that it was unsafe to fly, even though the facts clearly indicated otherwise. For the ten years from 1992 through 2001, including the deaths on 9/11, the risk of death while flying in the US was one in ten million or one in every 15 billion kilometres travelled. Instead Americans took to their cars, an altogether more dangerous form of transport. Economists have calculated that among the uncounted casualties of 9/11 are the extra 1,200 fatalities on the road occasioned by the diversion from air to road transport after 9/11 … The enormous scale of the atrocity seemed to merit a powerful response and the US replied with the most potent weapon in its armoury, a declaration of war.[4]

It is characteristic of terror attacks that they hardly ever miss their targets. Again and again, they plunge societies into fear and horror, and the governments of the respective states find themselves forced to take drastic measures. It is irrelevant in this context how well the attacks are organised. It does not matter whether nineteen young men carry out a technically sophisticated, well-coordinated plot planned long in advance (as on 11 September 2001) or two individual attackers target the Boston Marathon in a more

or less improvised fashion (as on 15 April 2013) using homemade bombs that caused relatively little damage considering the size of the sports event and the number of people attending. Every attack preoccupies the media for days or weeks, perpetuating the impression that something extraordinary has happened. Yet, as this chapter will show, the visual representation of events in the media usually follows the same patterns, according to a predictable sequence of representation that started to emerge towards the end of the nineteenth century.[5] In this respect 9/11, despite the spectacular images, is no exception.

Self-proclaimed terrorists of the first hour: the attack on Tsar Alexander II

In 1881, a shocking piece of news spread like wildfire through the daily papers of the Western world: the Russian Tsar Alexander II had been murdered on 13 March on his way to the Winter Palace in St Petersburg. More precise information was not available at the time of the first reports, but the perpetrators had already been named. There had been several failed attempts to kill the Tsar in the past, plotted by a group of revolutionaries who at that time were often referred to as nihilists. It was thought that this same group was behind the new attack.[6] However, the assassins did not use the term nihilists: they explicitly called themselves terrorists.[7] That word had not yet acquired solely negative connotations, allowing those in the group to distance themselves from common criminals.[8] The activists were part of Narodnaya Volya ('The people's will'), an anarchist organisation that had been founded in 1876 with the express aim of toppling the repressive and authoritarian Tsarist regime.[9] Around 1870, leading figures of the anarchist movement

in Europe, including the Russians Peter Kropotkin and Mikhail Bakunin who were living in exile in Switzerland, had endorsed violence as a revolutionary means. 'Ideas result from deeds, not the latter from the former', the Italian radical Carlo Pisacane had argued two decades earlier, declaring that the people would not attain freedom through education but would become educated once they were free.[10] Narodnaya Volya was the first organisation to follow Pisacane's call for 'propaganda of the deed' and started putting this into practice with the help of the latest technological invention, Alfred Nobel's dynamite.

The murder of the Tsar in the 1881 war was the group's biggest success, but also its last. As reported among others by the *Illustrated London News*, the empire under his rule may have been brutal and repressive, but he had recently introduced a promising programme of reforms. 'The lamentable death of Alexander II will not probably – certainly not immediately – conduce to the alteration of this bureaucratic régime. It has been a profound mistake of the Nihilists to suppose that it would do so', the newspaper predicted shortly after his assassination.[11] It would be proved right. After the Tsar's son, Alexander III, had ascended to the throne, he promptly revoked all liberal reforms his father had introduced and immediately established a ruthless secret police that was feared throughout Europe.[12] Within a month, all leading members of Narodnaya Volya were arrested, the assassins sentenced to death and their sympathisers banished to labour camps in Siberia.

In some respects, the murder of the Tsar still followed the centuries-old tradition of tyrannicide: in contrast to later terror attacks, it was the targeted killing of a ruler that mattered, not the symbolic effect of the act. Yet unlike previous assassinations, this one had repercussions that, due to the by

then efficient networks of the international press, reached far beyond Russia. The assassination was covered by all the leading European dailies, and the illustrated press – still in its infancy – offered its readers a wealth of visual material. The *Illustrated London News*, which had been pioneering this form of illustrated reporting since its foundation in 1842,[13] followed the events for weeks. Its counterparts in Germany and France, the Leipzig *Illustrirte Zeitung* and the Paris weekly *L'Illustration*, dedicated several issues and illustrated reports to the attack. Wherever publishers could afford it, they sent an artist to St Petersburg to sketch the incident according to eyewitness reports. The drawings were then turned into prints back home.

On the basis of such a sketch, the *Illustrated London News* initially published a reconstruction of the assassination (Figure 3). The artist had chosen the brief moment between the explosion of the first bomb and the throwing of the second that led to the monarch's death. The carefully annotated illustration shows the ruler still alive in the door of his carriage, which is shrouded in clouds of smoke. In the foreground on the left lie a murdered young courier and a Chechen from the Tsar's bodyguard. Next to them is an officer, mortally wounded but still standing, while in the middle ground a policeman is rushing to the scene. The two assassins, who consciously risked losing their own lives in the attack, are not visible.

This reconstruction was followed by images of a horrified crowd running to the location of the murder (Figure 4). After the depiction of the act itself, they contained a particularly important message. Contrary to the name that the rebels gave themselves, the assassination was shown to be the work of a small number of fanatics who did not represent the people's will. A further illustration displaying

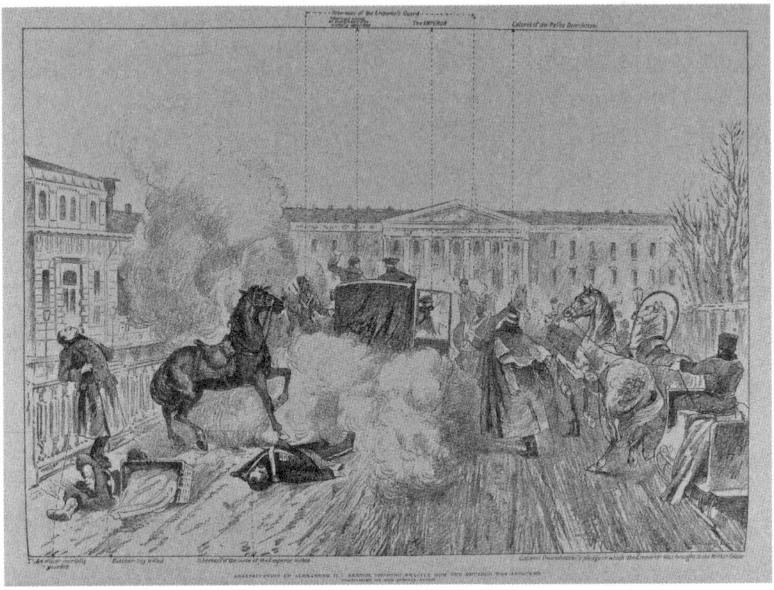

Figure 3 The assassination of Tsar Alexander II on 13 March 1881.

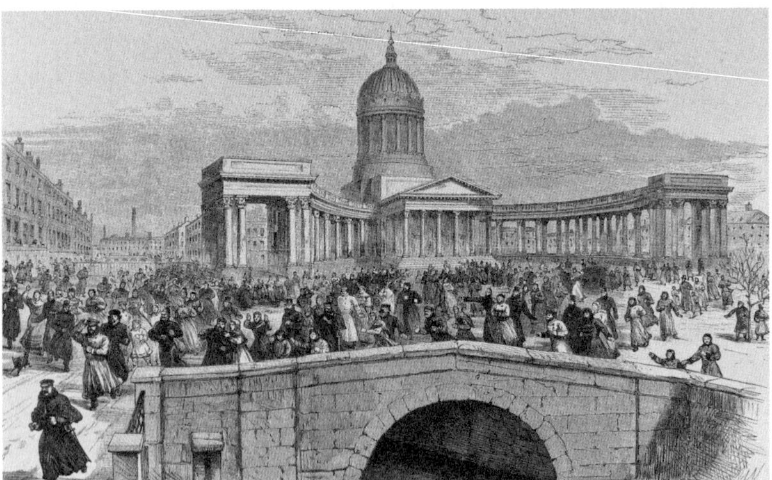

Figure 4 A crowd running to the place where the Tsar was murdered in St Petersburg.

the burnt-out carriage (Figure 5) was succeeded by a number of images showing the Tsar lying in state (Figure 6) and finally his burial and the coronation of the new Tsar, leaving no room to doubt the unbroken power of the state. Among the numerous pictures in the *Illustrated London News*, only the violent death of the Tsar remained imageless. In fact, the depiction of his lying in state expressed the exact opposite: it showed the physically intact body of a peacefully deceased ruler who seemed unmarked by his cruel death.

When the assassins were executed a month later in front of hundreds of spectators, the state could finally display its undiminished power to the public, and that is how this scene was depicted (Figure 7). The four men and one woman are shown still alive, at the moment when – visibly against their wishes – they are receiving the last rites from

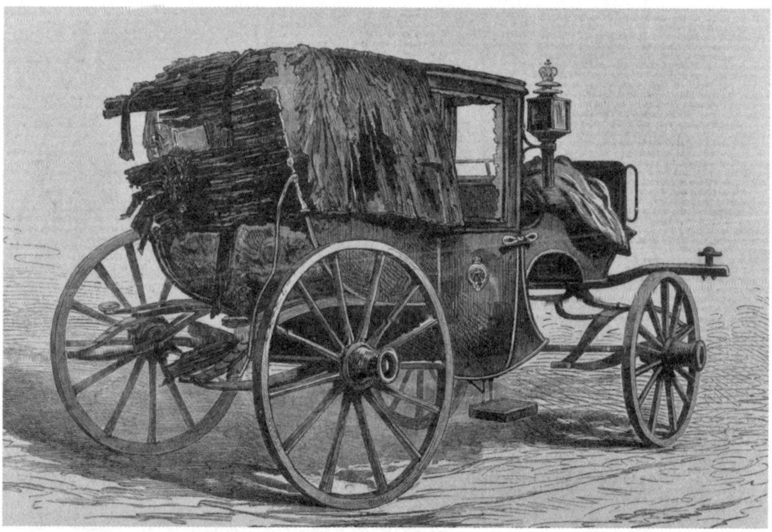

Figure 5 The Tsar's destroyed carriage after the bomb attack of 13 March 1881.

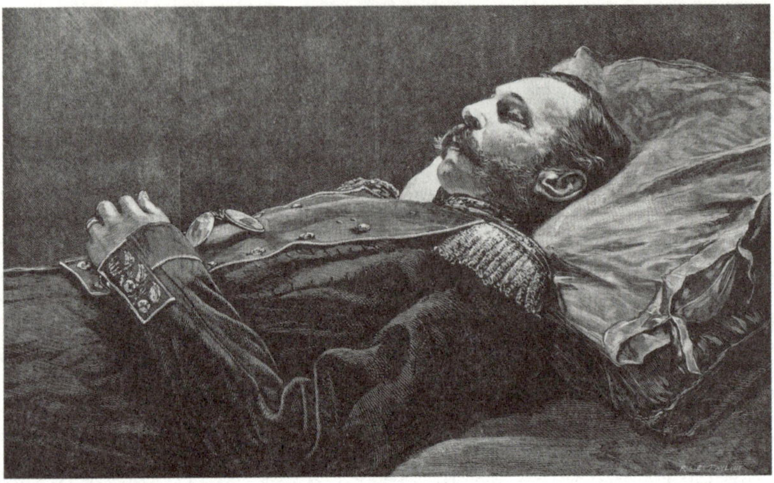

Figure 6 Tsar Alexander II lying in state.

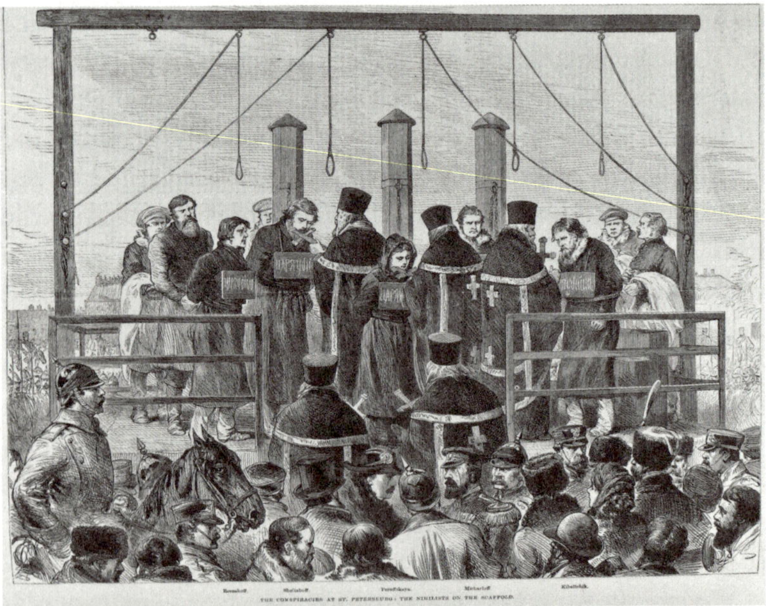

Figure 7 The execution of the assassins in St Petersburg on 15 April 1881.

two priests. The assassins are depicted carrying placards inscribed with the name of their crime, 'Tsaricide', as if they had been branded. The horror of their act is mirrored in their resistance to any kind of religious intervention, however merciful the priests' intentions.

This sequence, which began with the visualisation of the attack according to eyewitness accounts and ended with the sentencing and execution of the perpetrators, follows a pattern that was subsequently repeated in the Western illustrated press whenever those responsible for a terror attack could be arrested. *Illustrirte Zeitung* and *L'Illustration* also depicted the aftermath of the attack on the Tsar, and some of the images were identical to those in the *Illustrated London News*. This suggests that many of them, including those that show the monarch lying in state and the execution of the perpetrators, were supplied by Russian news services.[14] The first depiction, however, was always based on a sketch by a named draughtsman – *Illustrirte Zeitung* credited the artist (Gustav Broling), the *Illustrated London News* had the by-line 'forwarded by our special artist', and *L'Illustration* 'D'après un croquis de notre correspondent particulier' (after a sketch by our own correspondent). In each case, the first reaction to the shocking news was to try to visualise the attack as accurately and vividly as possible. The next step, however, was to reaffirm the state's inviolability by a display of its indomitable power. Drawing on the unambiguous images of friend and foe supplied by Russian news services, the press thus sought to push away the horror or to shift the terror back to its creators.

We can draw certain conclusions about readers' expectations from the fact that these illustrated papers, which were among the leading publications in Western Europe, share

the same image patterns. But it is difficult to tell whether it was the images that shaped the public's imagination or vice versa, for relevant sources and historical studies are not available. Yet the differences in the first depictions produced by different artists commissioned by the newspapers are striking, and significant for the subsequent development of media coverage. Contrary to the careful reconstruction of the site of the attack in the *Illustrated London News*, *L'Illustration*, for example, published a dramatic visualisation of the explosion, and *Illustrirte Zeitung* even depicted the mangled body of the Tsar, still alive at the time (Figures 8 and 9). The source of these drawings is unclear, but it is unlikely that they were based on direct eyewitness reports, since the Tsar was taken away directly after the attack.

Even more spectacular were the illustrations in newspapers which – unlike the *Illustrated London News*,

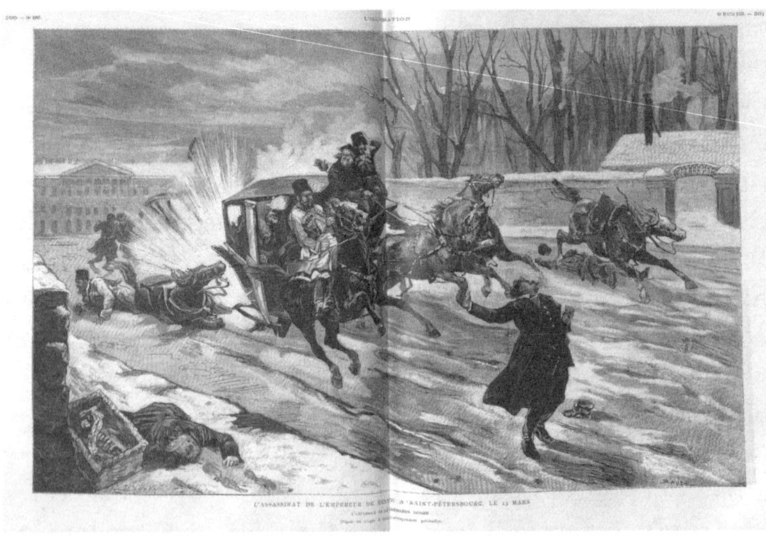

Figure 8 The assassination in *L'Illustration* of 26 March 1881.

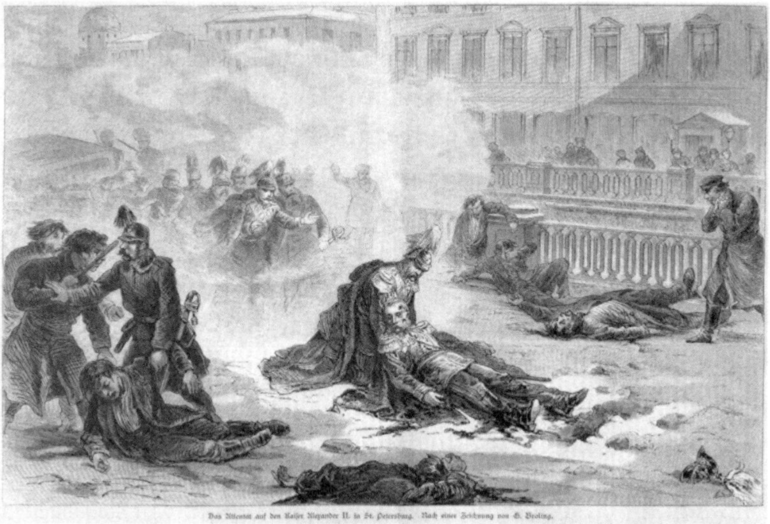

Figure 9 The assassination in the Leipzig *Illustrirte Zeitung* of 2 April 1881.

Illustrirte Zeitung and *L'Illustration* – did not exclusively target an educated middle class, but sought to address a broader readership.[15] The French weekly *L'Univers illustré*, for example, printed a highly dramatic visualisation of the explosion itself (Figure 10). In the bright light of the flames, the Tsar is falling to the ground, while in the background the horses of the carriage are shying. In the foreground the first casualties are already visible. What is understated in the English paper is intensified in the representation in *L'Univers illustré*, as if it were a live report.

This difference, which had less to do with the places of publication than with the different types of readership, persisted during the following decades, even when terror attacks no longer targeted individuals in positions of power but could potentially hit anybody who happened to be in a public place in a European capital. The organisation

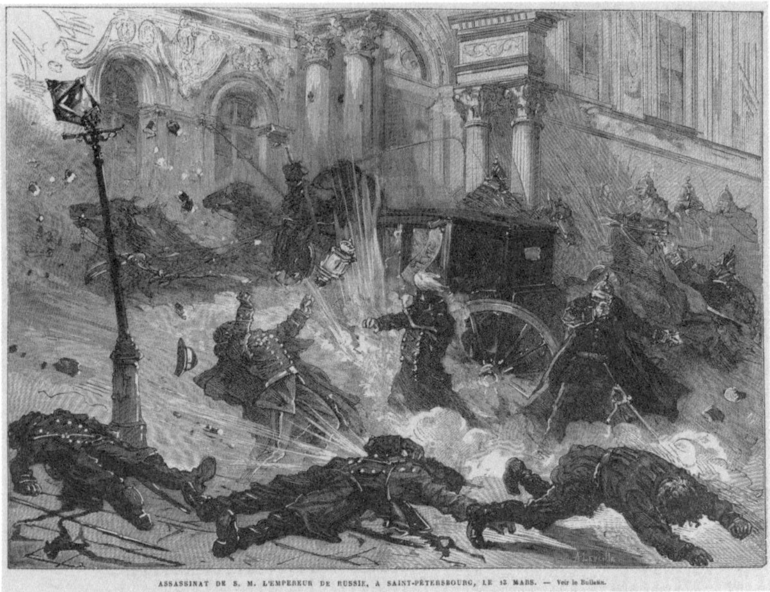

Figure 10 The assassination in *L'Univers illustré* of 19 March 1881.

and the political outcome of the Tsar's murder may have been a catastrophe for the conspirators, but measured by its media coverage the assassination was clearly a great success. While it was hardly surprising that an event like this received enormous attention, its visualisation in such intricate detail in the international illustrated press was new. It tapped the possibilities that the illustrated press offered politically motivated perpetrators of violence. While the Russian Narodnaya Volya was still primarily concerned with the act itself rather than the production of images, it was not long before a new generation of activists emerged who recognised that images could fulfil a major goal of their actions – to spread fear among the population.

The first serial attacks in history: Irish terror in London

During the same year that saw the murder of the Tsar, a group of Irish Republicans who called themselves Clan na Gael or United Irishmen began a long series of 'propaganda of the deed' attacks on English soil.

Throughout the nineteenth century, there had been repeated attempts at an armed uprising in Ireland to end British rule, but none of these had come even remotely close to achieving the desired aim.[16] In England, too, there had been attacks prior to 1881, but each time the goal was direct and functional: to free comrades from English jails.[17] In contrast to this, the attacks by Clan na Gael, which were organised and financed by Irish exiles in the United States between 1881 and 1885, sought above all to destabilise public life in England and thus weaken public support for British rule. These bombings already bore all the hallmarks of later series of twentieth-century terror attacks. What mattered was not the actual number of casualties, but the destruction of landmark sites whose symbolic value would cause a stir in the press.

The first attack of this kind had taken place three months before the Tsar's assassination. On 14 January 1891, just before 6 p.m., the Salford Infantry Barracks in Manchester was blown up by a charge of dynamite. Three people were killed instantly; a boy died later in hospital.[18] The location was no random choice. Three Irish independence fighters – the so-called Manchester Martyrs – had been executed in the barracks in 1867.[19] Strikingly, the report in the *Illustrated London News* once again did not show any victims. The only image was a depiction of the destroyed snow-covered barracks being quietly examined after the event by a single walker – a placeholder for the viewer (Figure 11).

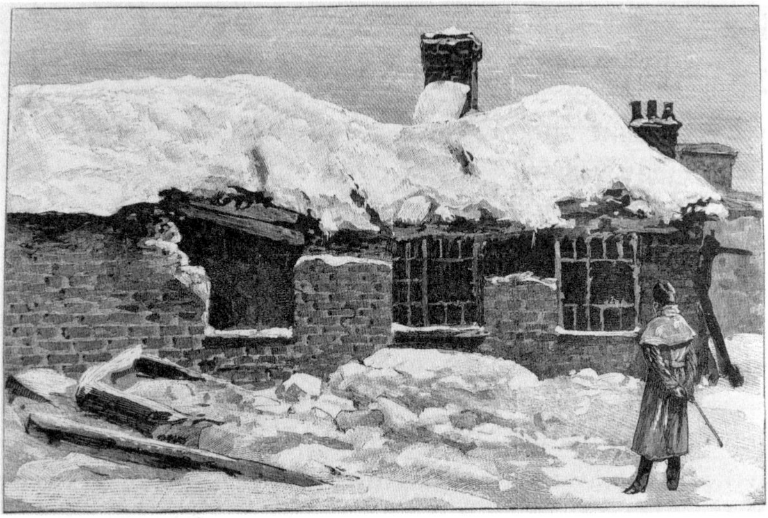

Figure 11 The Salford Infantry Barracks in Manchester after the bomb explosion on 14 January 1881.

When Clan na Gael struck again two years later, on 15 March 1883 in London's Whitehall, there was a real risk that people would lose their lives. For the first time in history, simultaneous attacks, as we know them today from Al-Qaida and IS, destroyed government offices in Charles Street in Westminster as well as the offices of *The Times* on Printing House Square. The Irish terror campaign was starting to have an impact. The *Illustrated London News* found itself compelled to make a defensive statement:

> the hasty remarks of some of the foreign newspapers that John Bull is panic-stricken are singularly misplaced. Any people might well be alarmed at the discovery … of a widespread conspiracy of a wholesale massacre …[20]

The report went on to say that John Bull would not allow himself to be terrorised.

The images in the *Illustrated London News*, however, told a different story. Not only did the first page show the destruction of government buildings – which was particularly disturbing because at the time of the explosion Parliament was sitting – but on another page it also offered the first, and for the time being the last, visualisation of the explosion itself as it was experienced by a patrolling policeman (Figure 12). Dramatic images of this kind primarily served the purpose of making the scale of the attack comprehensible. All the more important was the news, three weeks later, that four people had been arrested in Birmingham in connection with the explosion.[21] This news report also featured illustrations whose clear lines and well-ordered layout provided what were almost counter-images to the preceding depictions of the terrible event (Figure 13). The profiles and names of the arrested attackers shown on the bottom right helped to give a face to the horror, in an attempt to personify and thus banish it.

Despite this success for the police, another attack followed six months later. On 30 October 1883, two bombs exploded for the first – but not the last – time in the London Underground. An explosive detonated around 8 p.m. on the tracks in the tunnel between Charing Cross and Westminster stations. There was no train in the tunnel at the time, but the force of the blast was so powerful that people waiting in both stations were covered in glass shards and dust. Three minutes later a second bomb went off in the tunnel near Praed Street station, injuring sixty people, some seriously. The *Illustrated London News* reported this without showing any images, as if these attacks, the worst to date with the highest number of injured people, had finally managed to frighten John Bull after all.[22] It is certainly true that the attack in the dark tunnel would not have been easy

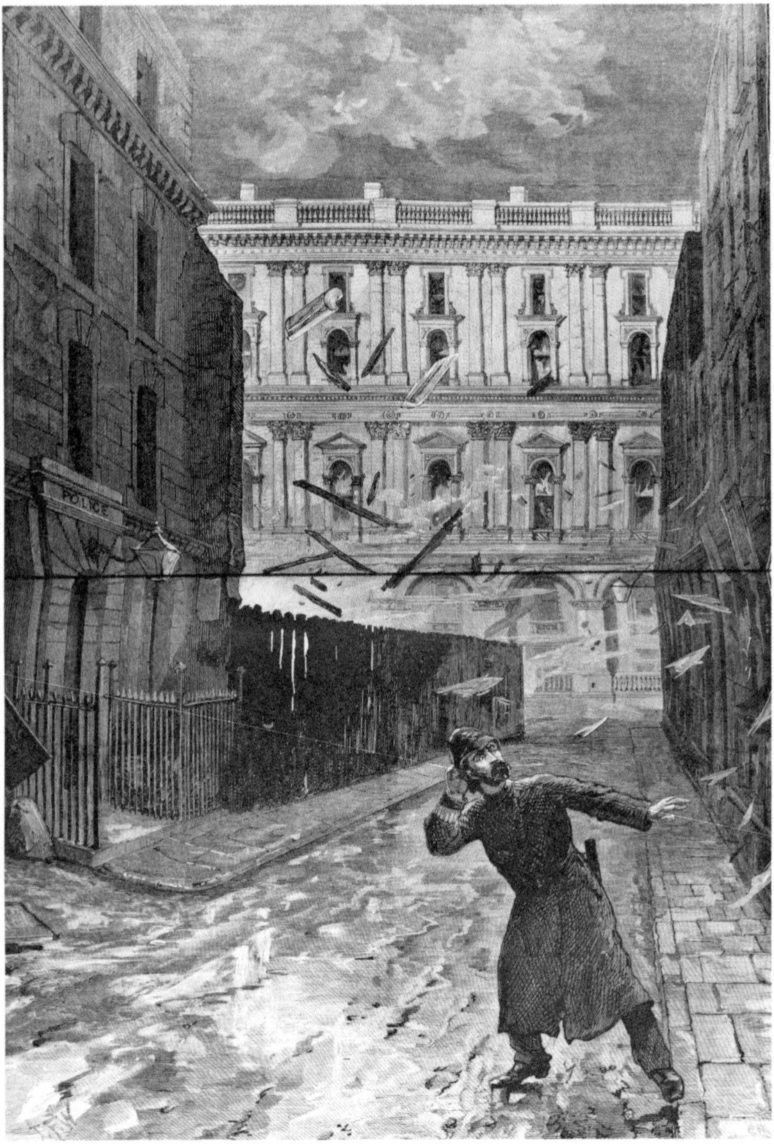

Figure 12 Bomb explosion in Whitehall on 15 March 1883.

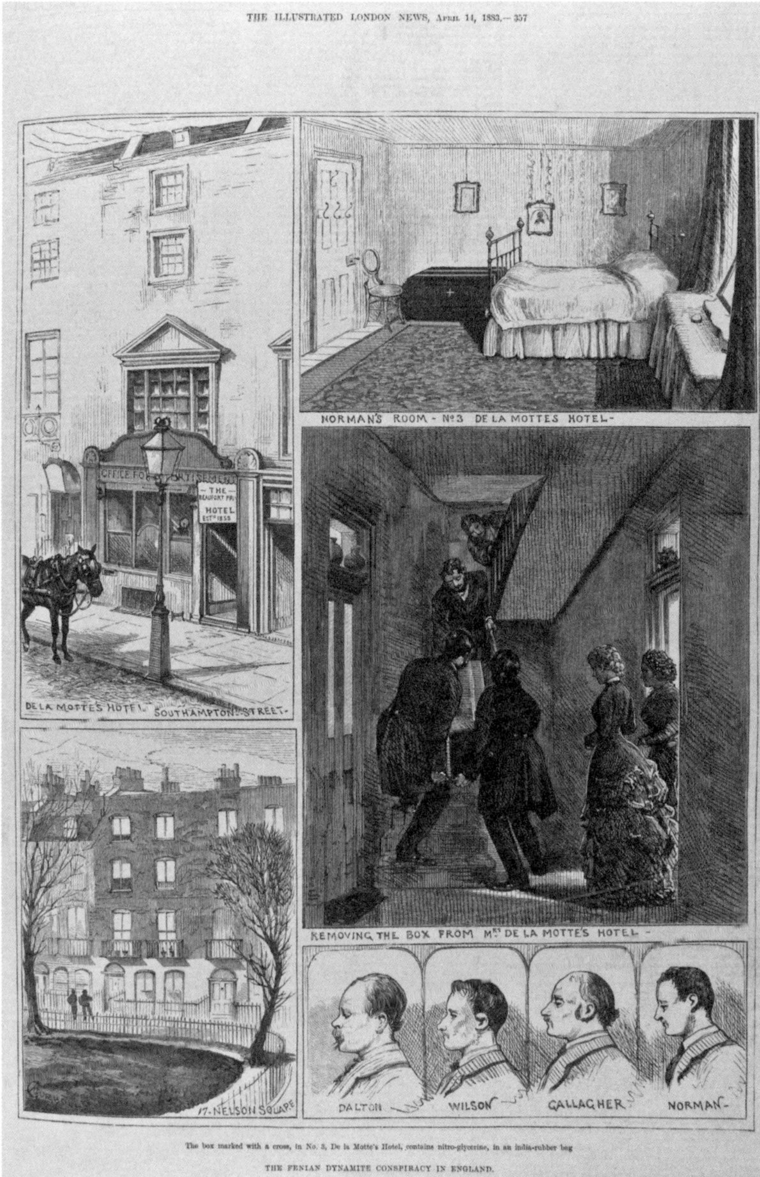

Figure 13 The discovery of the conspirators' HQ in Birmingham.

to visualise, but the reluctance of the *Illustrated London News* to depict the victims is again notable and has to be understood as a conscious media strategy.

When Clan na Gael staged another attack four months later and nobody was injured, the paper returned to its old habit and published detailed illustrations.[23] The bomb exploded during the night of 25 February 1884 in Victoria railway station and destroyed the central departures and arrivals hall. Initially only a diagram of the site was published, but a depiction of the damage soon followed (Figure 14). It showed the wrecked first-class waiting room and the collapsed roof of the station entrance behind it. Once again, it was not long before news came of the arrest of a suspect and the discovery of the conspirators' HQ and dynamite store in a house near Birmingham. The *Illustrated London News* showed the building together with a crowd of

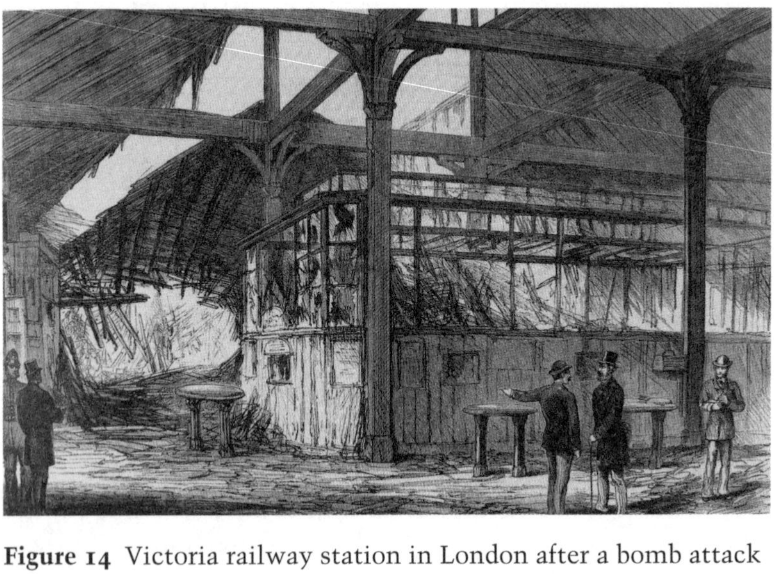

Figure 14 Victoria railway station in London after a bomb attack on 25 February 1884.

onlookers and policemen searching for bombs (Figure 15). By then, the Special Irish Branch of the British police had successfully infiltrated Clan na Gael and its sister organisation in Ireland, the Irish Republican Brotherhood, so that swift arrests could be made, although this did not prevent further attacks. Two months later bombs destroyed part of the police headquarters at Scotland Yard,[24] and in the following year there were again several explosions in London, among others in the House of Commons in Westminster, the Tower of London and the Admiralty in Whitehall.[25]

The numerous attacks by Clan na Gael between 1881 and 1885 marked a dramatic new development in the history of politically motivated violence. Instead of assassinations targeting important government officials or even a head of state, or serving to free supporters, there was now a continuous campaign of serial attacks whose aim was to instil permanent fear in the population.[26]

Yet in contrast to the secular Palestinian groups in the late twentieth century and radical Islamic suicide attackers of the early twenty-first century, neither Clan na Gael nor the later IRA nor the radical left-wing terror groups of the 1970s intended to endanger civilians. The bombs mostly exploded during the evening or night, at a time when there was little traffic, and later these groups also issued warnings to news channels or press agencies just before an attack. In this sense, the Irish Republicans at the end of the nineteenth century and most of the left-wing terror groups of the 1970s understood themselves as warring parties, which even before the Hague Convention of 1899 and subsequent international legal agreements distinguished between combatants and non-combatants. The British government, however, consistently refused to recognise this self-proclamation and in doing so also

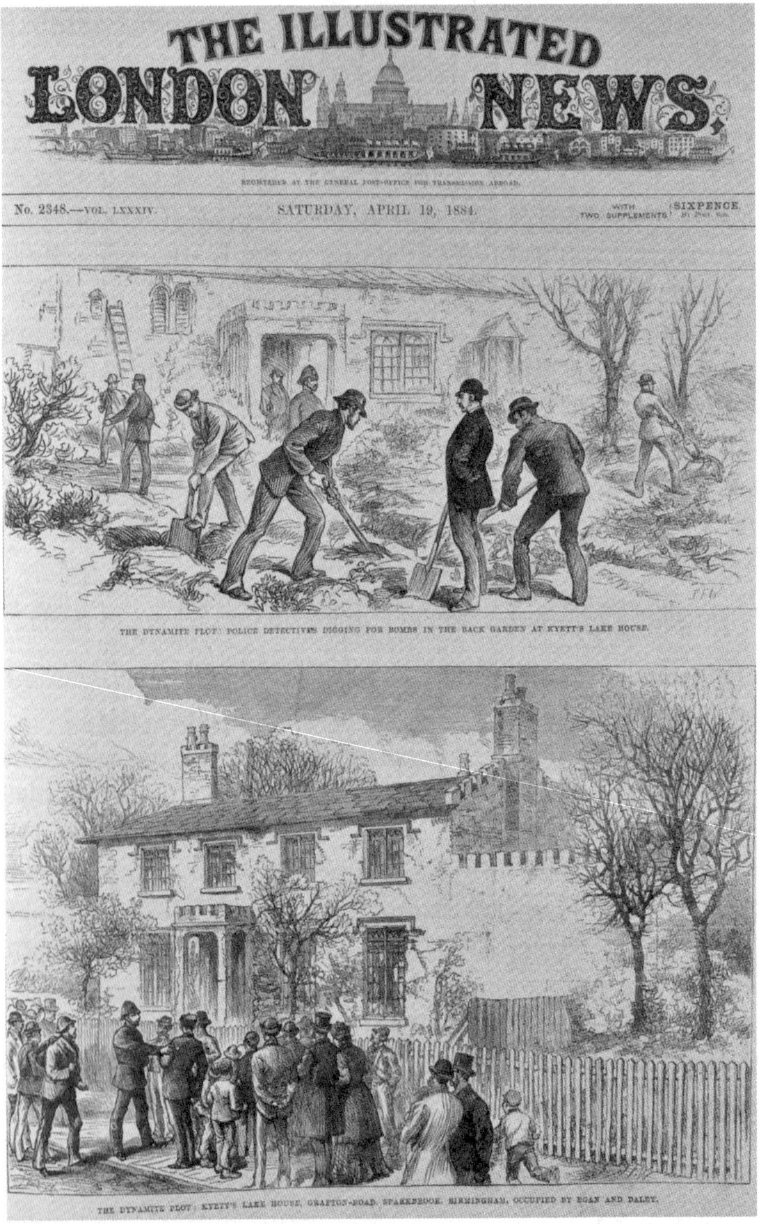

THE ILLUSTRATED LONDON NEWS,

REGISTERED AT THE GENERAL POST-OFFICE FOR TRANSMISSION ABROAD.

No. 2348.—VOL. LXXXIV. SATURDAY, APRIL 19, 1884. WITH TWO SUPPLEMENTS | SIXPENCE

THE DYNAMITE PLOT: POLICE DETECTIVES DIGGING FOR BOMBS IN THE BACK GARDEN AT KYETT'S LAKE HOUSE.

THE DYNAMITE PLOT: KYETT'S LAKE HOUSE, GRAFTON-ROAD, SPARKBROOK, BIRMINGHAM, OCCUPIED BY EGAN AND DALEY.

Figure 15 Police searching a dynamite factory in Birmingham.

invoked international law, which assumes that conflicts are between states and fought by their armies.

Yet not all politically motivated groups condoning violence at the end of the nineteenth century distinguished between combatants and non-combatants. Attacks carried out in the 1890s by anarchist assassins on the European continent intentionally targeted bourgeois society as such, and not just its government and communications infrastructure. In the eyes of these attackers, every tax-paying citizen was responsible for the unjust government they aimed to overthrow. At the beginning of the twenty-first century, Osama bin Laden shared this view, declaring that every tax-paying citizen of the United States was an enemy of Al-Qaida.[27]

Targeting bourgeois society: anarchist attackers in Paris

The Paris attacks in the early 1890s were unprecedented, especially because their targets included the civilian population. They began in March 1892 with an act of revenge by the French anarchist François-Claudius Koenigstein, known as Ravachol.[28] In response to the imprisonment a year earlier of two anarchists who had been involved in a violent clash with police, Ravachol detonated two bombs, with an interval of two weeks, in the houses of the judge and public prosecutor who had led the case. A month later he placed a bomb in the Lobau barracks in Paris to avenge the murder of nine unarmed factory workers by troops in the town of Fourmies. In both cases there was substantial damage but – more by chance than design – nobody was killed. This changed when Ravachol was sentenced to death; not for these attacks but because of a previous murder. The anarchist press made him a martyr who had selflessly sacrificed

his life for the poor and the outcast.[29] On the day he received his sentence, a bomb exploded in the café where he had been arrested after a tip-off from a waiter. The explosion killed two people and badly injured many others. About six months later, on 8 November 1892, another bomb detonated, this time in a police station in rue des Bons-Enfants, causing five casualties. On this occasion the perpetrator, Émile Henry, was able to escape unharmed. On 9 December 1893, a bomb exploded in the Palais Bourbon, the seat of the National Assembly. Fifty people were wounded, including the attacker Auguste Vaillant, who was arrested at the scene. A few weeks after Vaillant's execution, on 12 February 1894, a bomb destroyed the Café Terminus near Gare St Lazare. A policeman lost his life and many other people were seriously injured.[30] In the following years there were further attacks of this kind.

The images published by the French press after each of these events were shocking. While *L'Illustration* mostly just printed views of the scale of the destruction (Figure 16), pictures in the popular press evoked an immediacy that anticipated later live reports. *Le Petit Journal*, for example, showed the moment of the explosion in colour on the cover of its illustrated supplement (Figure 17), and just a little later *L'Univers illustré* featured as many as three images of the attack on the Café Terminus, which followed its stages in an almost cinematic way (Figure 18). The upper half shows the explosion itself, which happened at a time when the café was busy and the orchestra, depicted on the left, had just started playing. The lower half shows the arrest of the attacker, who was caught in the street after a dramatic chase and several shots fired at a policeman. A small, circular image in the centre right finally shows the perpetrator in a strikingly relaxed pose at the police station. The terror

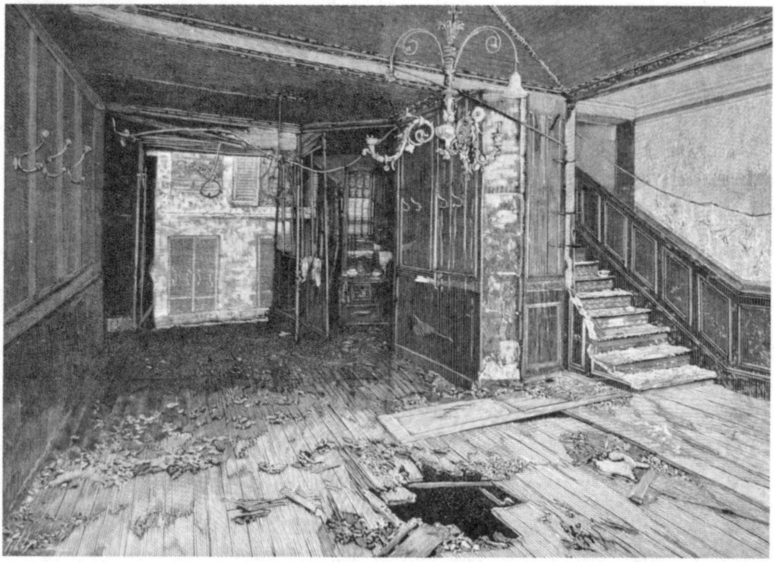

Figure 16 The Café Véry in Paris after a bomb explosion on 25 April 1892.

of the deed is thus immediately complemented by an image of order, although during the later court case this was put into question by the accused himself, Émile Henry. Like Ravachol before him, Henry used the courtroom to publicly proclaim his political motives. Asked by the public prosecutor why he had killed innocent people, he answered in a calm, composed manner that in his opinion there was no innocent bourgeois.[31]

During the years that followed, the security services, partly thanks to more efficient cooperation, increasingly managed to prevent attacks in Europe and the United States.[32] Even so, since every single attack was immediately reported around the world, people gained the impression that a large conspiratorial and above all transnational operation was under way, which could launch surprise attacks

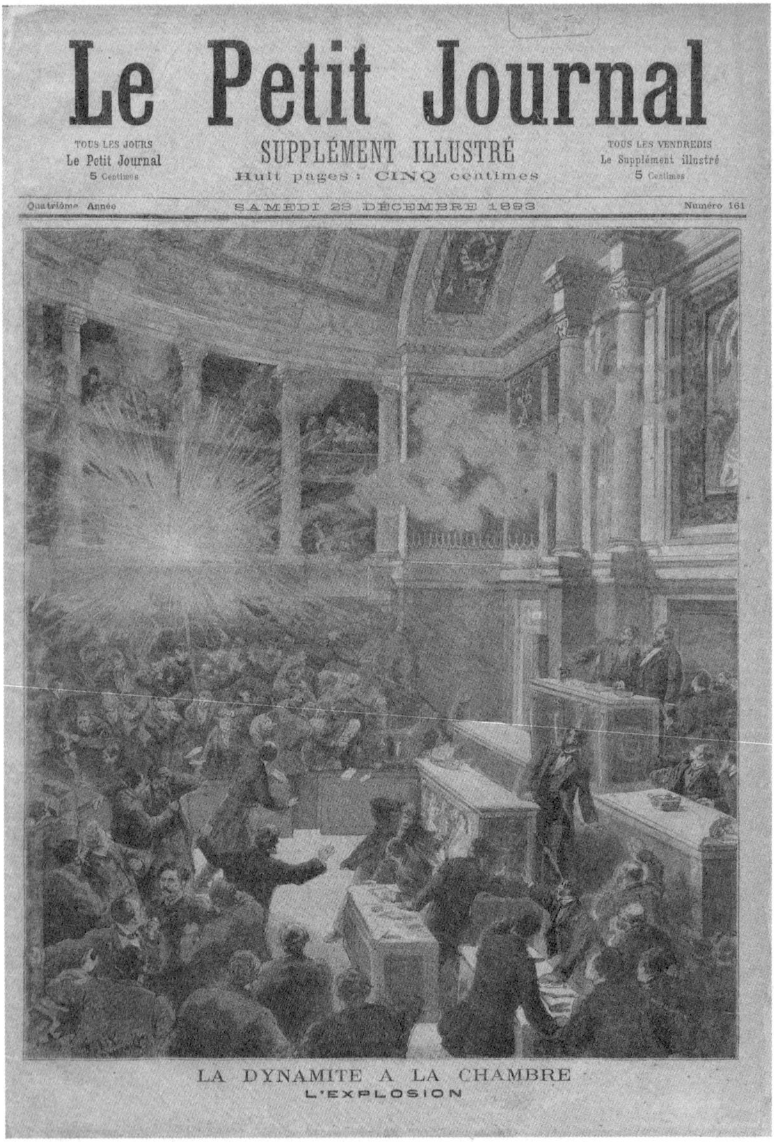
Le Petit Journal

TOUS LES JOURS
Le Petit Journal
5 Centimes

SUPPLÉMENT ILLUSTRÉ
Huit pages : CINQ centimes

TOUS LES VENDREDIS
Le Supplément illustré
5 Centimes

Quatrième Année — SAMEDI 23 DÉCEMBRE 1893 — Numéro 161

LA DYNAMITE A LA CHAMBRE
L'EXPLOSION

Figure 17 Bomb explosion in the French National Assembly on 9 December 1893.

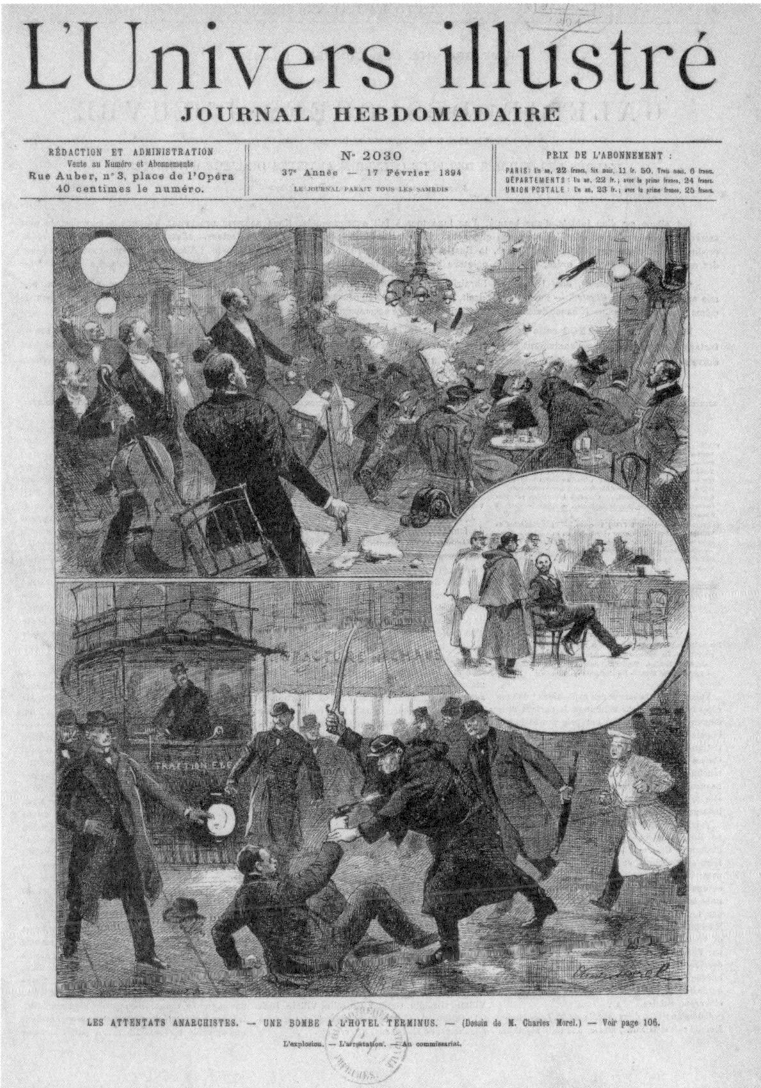

Figure 18 Attack on the Café Terminus in Paris on 12 February 1894.

that would result in many casualties and paralyse the vital infrastructure of large metropoles.[33] The number of casualties was in fact often quite low – Henry's bombing of the Café Terminus, for example, had killed just one person. Yet the images that subsequently appeared in the illustrated press expressed something else: namely, that there could have been many more victims and might well be in the future.

Tactics and strategies at the end of the nineteenth century

By the end of the nineteenth century, terrorists had adopted a number of different tactics and strategies which have since become characteristic of modern terror.[34] One of these was the use of a relatively safe place abroad from which the attack could be planned and where attackers could hide. After he bombed the police station in rue des Bons-Enfants, Henry briefly went into hiding in the London anarchist underground, and Clan na Gael operated mainly from the United States.[35] The Irish attacks in England brought other innovations, such as the use of time-delay bombs and the targeting of particular sites because of their powerful symbolic value, as well as the focus on maximum disruption to everyday urban life by serial explosions. And finally, there was the assumption that the media would amplify the attacks. The basis for this was created by the emergence of the illustrated press around the mid-century.

Initially, illustrated reports of terror attacks always tried to depict the attack itself in as much detail as possible, even if at the time of going to press they had no other evidence than eyewitness reports of varying reliability. The proportions of necessary information, terrifying images and sheer sensation-mongering were fluid from the very

beginning and, like today, they were tailored to different readerships. The middle-class *Illustrated London News*, for example, usually refrained from publishing images of attacks from the 1880s onwards – there were none after the bombings in the London Underground and none during the anarchist dynamite attacks in France. More popular publications, on the other hand, like *L'Univers illustré* and *Le Petit Journal*, always tried to reconstruct the events as dramatically as possible, to give readers the impression they had been at the scene.

There is one other rule which was applied then and can still be seen today: the media generally did not show images of their own country's injured and dead, although they were less sensitive when it came to their enemies.[36] The more unlikely it was that a similar attack could occur in their own country, the fewer the inhibitions over what was shown. The victims of the Paris attacks were usually not pictured in French newspapers. In Germany, where this kind of attack was not yet known, *Illustrirte Zeitung*, for example, printed an image of the destruction wreaked at the police station in rue des Bons-Enfant, in which battered bodies and severed limbs were clearly visible in the debris (Figure 19). In *L'Illustration*, on the other hand, all that could be seen were firemen clearing up the damage (Figure 20). This iconography was an early part of the sequence of reporting on terror. The first pictures of the destruction (with or without victims) were swiftly followed by images that showed active reactions to the horror and were thus meant to reassure: the deployment of police and rescue workers and the grieving of survivors and families. The reportage only came to an end when the perpetrator had been arrested and sentenced. There are images of Ravachol and Henry, for example, showing them during their arrest, in the courtroom and under the

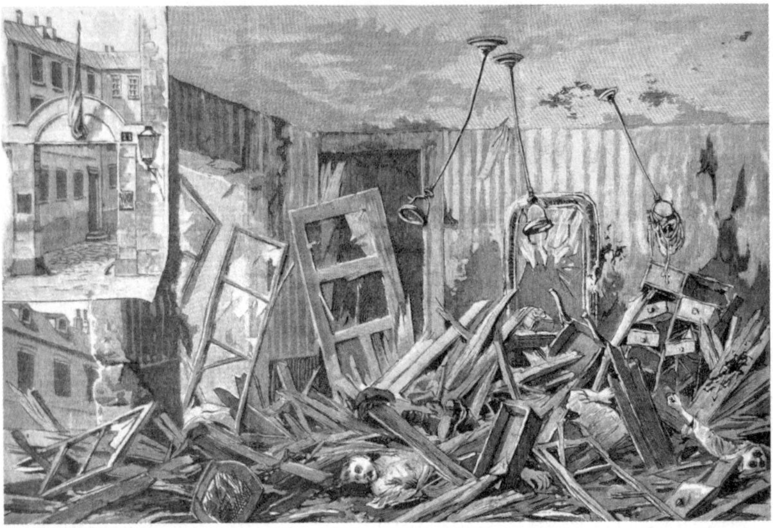

Figure 19 The police station in rue des Bons-Enfants after a bomb explosion on 8 November 1892.

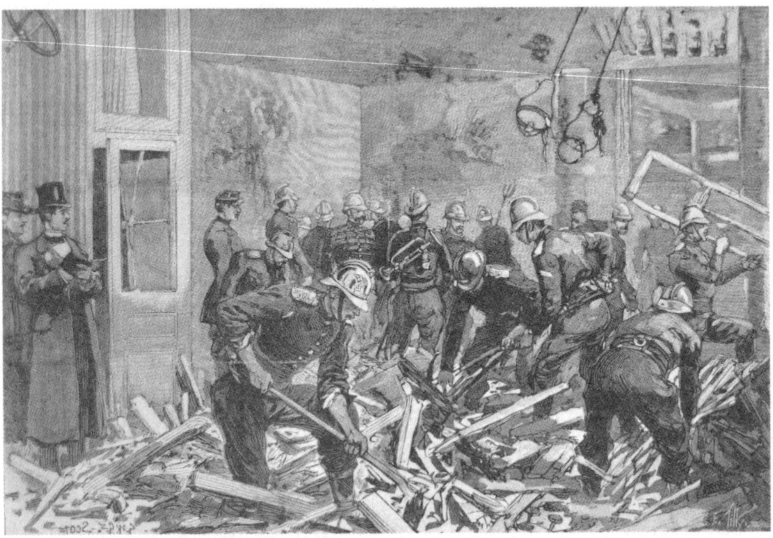

Figure 20 Clearing up debris in the police station in rue des Bons-Enfants.

guillotine (see Chapter 3). Thus evil acquired a face and was kept in check, and the threat could be confined to the past. Or at least, this was the hope that was nurtured by these final images of the attackers.

The literature on the numerous illustrated man-made catastrophes of the nineteenth century tends to focus on the pictorial strategies of individual images. The argument is that by drawing on formal categories such as the picturesque or the sublime, these images offer a visual framework that reintegrates shocking events into a known, reassuring aesthetic order.[37] This does not, however, necessarily apply to images of terror. Initially, each individual image of an attack induces fear. Here, only the full sequence, the succession of images following the same pattern, conveys the comforting impression that everything is under control, that order has been re-established, and that the attacked state has retained its monopoly of power.

In the late nineteenth century, the first pictures following an attack owed much of their shock effect to the fact that they were based on drawings that had been created from eyewitness reports and then transferred to wood or steel engravings. Scenes of destruction could thus be shown alongside visualisations of the explosions themselves. With the widespread introduction of photography in the early twentieth century, this visual proximity to events was no longer possible.[38] It is one of the characteristics of terror attacks that they are carried out suddenly and unexpectedly. Since exposure times were still relatively long and photographic equipment quite cumbersome, it was impossible for photographers at the scene to capture more than debris and destruction. Only live television transmissions, from the 1970s onwards, provided the possibility for an attack to unfold in real time in front of a running camera. The first

example of this, the attack by the Palestinian terror group Black September on Israeli athletes in the Olympic Village in Munich in the summer of 1972, will be discussed in Chapter 3. Al-Qaida directly picked up on this, as is shown in a statement by Abu Ubeid al-Quarishi, a leading member of the organisation, shortly after the attack on the World Trade Center in New York:

> Munich was ... a great propaganda strike. Four thousand journalists and radio personnel and two thousand commentators and television technicians were there to cover the Olympic Games; suddenly, they were broadcasting the suffering of the Palestinian people. Thus, 900 million people in 100 countries were witness to the operation by means of the television screens. This meant that at least a quarter of the world knew what was going on at Munich; after this, they could no longer ignore the Palestinian tragedy.
>
> The September 11 [operation] was an even greater propaganda coup. It may be said that it broke a record in propaganda dissemination.[39]

The Western world as the enemy: the attack on the World Trade Center in New York

There is no doubt that serial images express emotions rather differently from individual images, and that the impact of photographs is different from that of wood and steel engravings. Even though we know that photographic images can be manipulated, they always have a stronger link to reality than other media, as will be discussed in the final chapter. It is all the more significant, then, that the act of terror itself ceased to be depicted once photography had come to be the dominant visual medium of press reporting. A live film recording, however, directly involves every viewer from the very beginning. Yet even here a high degree of

mediation is at play, although we are only partly aware of it.[40] If images are replayed in an endless loop, as they were on 11 September 2001, the result is 'a loss of reality, not because we know too little, but because we know too much without being able to control any of it', as Alexander Kluge had already noted in 1985.[41] Ever since 9/11, scholars have repeatedly emphasised that it is impossible to view images of the event without preconceptions.[42] Disaster films, from *King Kong* in the 1930s to *Towering Inferno* in 1974 and Michael Bay's 1998 *Armageddon*, had introduced an iconography of Manhattan as the scene of an inferno by imagining a threat coming from the skies. Some commentators argued that the attackers were thus simply following a cinematic script when they flew the planes into the Twin Towers on 11 September 2001.[43]

We will probably never be able to ascertain whether this was indeed the case. What we do know is that huge numbers of people all across the world were watching television that day. The vast majority reacted to the images 'with a combination of disgust and horror and simultaneous fascination'.[44] And while the first attack on the North Tower at 8:46 a.m. was recorded more or less by chance by a single camera on the ground, by the time the second aeroplane hit the South Tower at 9:03 a.m., numerous television teams and photographers were present at the scene, recording the events live and capturing them from several different angles, although international TV stations initially used only the footage shared by CNN.[45] In the hours and days that followed, many people filmed and photographed what was happening on the streets of Lower Manhattan. As early as late September 2001, a fundraising exhibition in a mall displayed several thousand images by professional and amateur photographers that could be purchased for twenty-five

dollars each as computer printouts. Proceeds went towards supporting children orphaned by the attack.[46]

It is thus all the more surprising that today only a very circumscribed set of images are reproduced and remembered in connection with 9/11. Our memory of the third plane, which hit the Pentagon, the main seat of the American Ministry of Defence in Arlington, Virginia, and of a fourth aircraft that crashed near Shanksville in Pennsylvania, is virtually imageless.[47] The first and prime image to appear in history books and general accounts is nearly always one of the burning towers against a bright blue sky, with no sign of human life or human suffering.[48] The day after the attacks, a surprising number of international newspapers ran the same picture. In vividly contrasting colours, it showed a black cloud of smoke drifting skyward from one of the towers, while orange flames billowed from the upper third of the other (Figure 21). As the photography historian Clément Chéroux has shown, 95 per cent of American, and only a slightly lower proportion of European, newspapers used precisely this image on their front pages.[49] The photograph was taken by Spencer Platt, who sent it to the Getty photo agency shortly after the attacks. For many editors around the world, it seemed to encapsulate perfectly what many people were feeling: something incomprehensible had occurred out of nowhere, something that seemed even more incredible against the backdrop of a calm and idyllic late summer morning. The towers are still standing proudly above the city, with no sign that they would collapse so dramatically only a short time later. The buildings and streets below are mostly outside the frame, making this image almost abstract in its stark contrasts.

'The familiarity with certain photos builds our sense of the present and immediate past', writes Susan Sontag. In

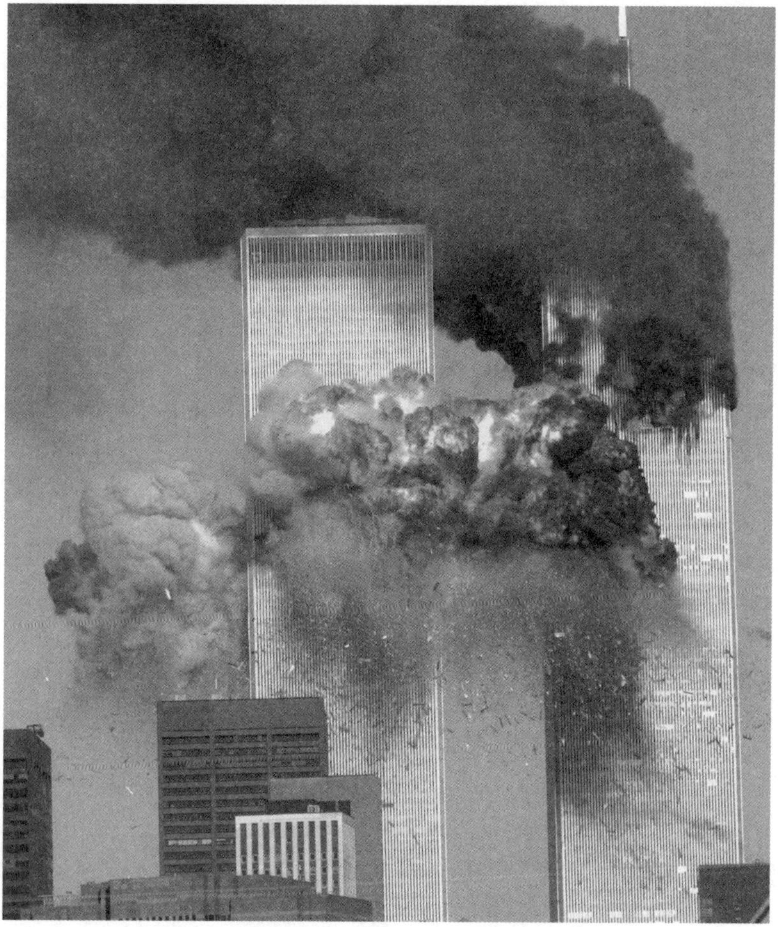

Figure 21 Spencer Platt, *New York – September 11, 2001*.

her book *Regarding the Pain of Others*, she describes such images' social function as follows:

> Photographs lay down routes of reference, and serve as totems of causes: sentiment is more likely to crystallize around a photograph than around a verbal slogan. And photographs help construct – and revise – our sense of a more

> distant past … Photographs that everyone recognizes are now a constituent part of what a society chooses to think about, or declares that it has chosen to think about. It calls these ideas 'memories', and that is, over the long run, a fiction.[50]

Which images of the 9/11 attacks have become iconic is thus a significant question.[51] The people who were there at the time may be unable to forget the other, more traumatic, scenes imprinted on their minds. Yet Platt's photograph or variants of it have imprinted an image of one thing above all on the minds of global audiences: an attack that occurred quite literally 'out of the blue'. Although terror attacks usually happen unexpectedly, this impression neglects the fact that there had actually been advance warnings that were ignored by the security forces, including bin Laden's 1998 declaration of war.[52] It also marginalises the unspeakable suffering that took place in front of the towers and in the streets below in the hours following the attacks, for these condensed iconic images reproduce not just memories, but also blind spots.

Even at the time of the attacks, the suffering on the ground was barely visible in the media.[53] A detailed analysis of the CNN news broadcasts showed that on the day of the attack and those that followed, the same loops were shown over and over again. These loops were made up of montages that all followed the same pattern: footage of the planes hitting the towers and the towers burning, then images of the towers collapsing and shots showing the huge amount of dust and debris in the streets of Manhattan. People covered in dust could be seen fleeing as clouds of black smoke spread behind them. Right at the end of the loop, viewers saw images of the rescue services on the scene.[54]

What was left out were those who died in front of the towers, and the more than one hundred desperate people

who jumped from the towers to their deaths. During the live commentary, a camera zoomed in briefly on a dark, moving speck in free fall. But once the camera people realised what they were filming, they immediately zoomed out again without further comment.[55] Given the large number of people who died in this horrible way, it is surprising how little coverage there was of their deaths. There is one exception to which I will return in more detail in the final chapter, precisely because it broke this taboo: Richard Drew's photo 'Falling Man', which was circulated via Associated Press. *The New York Times* and other American papers printed it shortly after the attacks[56] – but only once and never again. Following a public outcry, the photograph was excluded from the intense memory work of these events. 'On this day saturated with graphic photos and images, the falling bodies became the only taboo image', the media scholars Brooke Barnett and Amy Reynolds note, continuing:

> In commemorations of the attacks, the images of falling people were either left out or reduced to just one image from a distant focal point. These images are still readily available, but now on sites that featured autopsy photos of Nicole Brown Simpson and videotapes of executions.[57]

However incredible the attacks of 11 September 2001 were, and however unprecedented their scale, their coverage in the media followed traditional patterns.[58] Even the next day's *New York Times* front page only showed pictures of the burning skyscrapers, an army of firefighters in the towers' ruins, and a survivor being aided by rescue workers (Figure 22). At the moment when the threat was greatest, most images focused on showing that civil society was still functioning, just as they had done in the late nineteenth century.

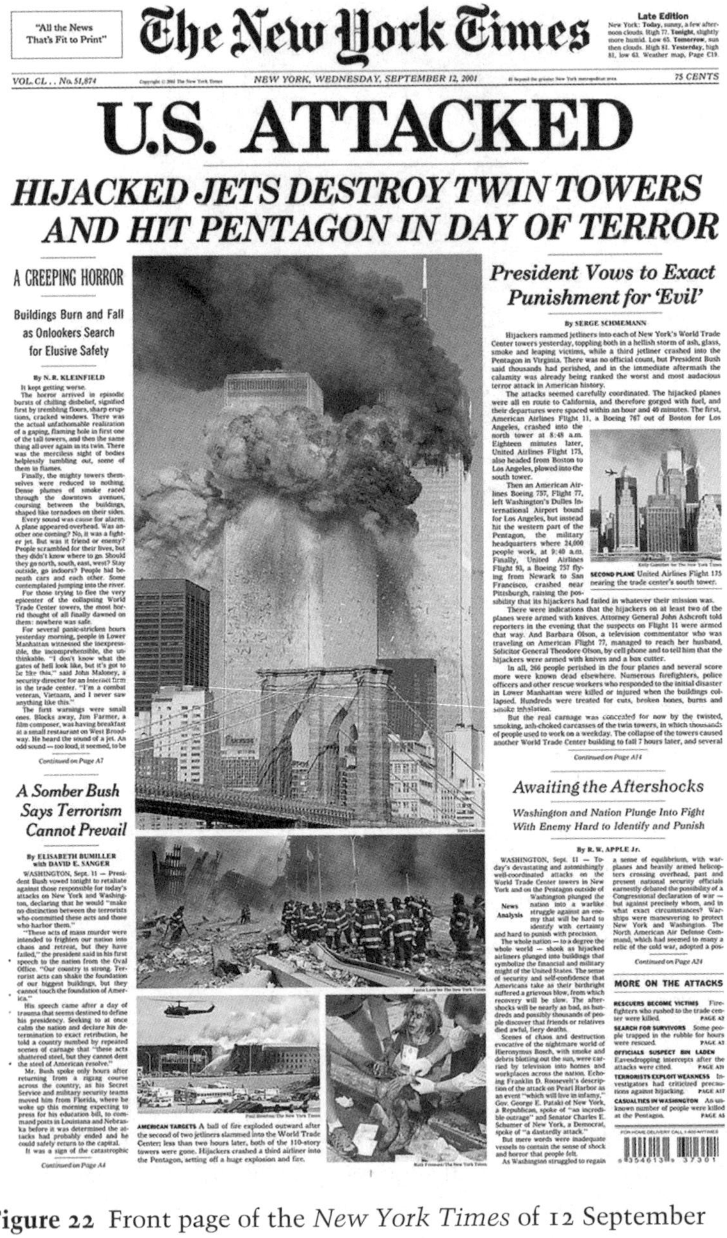

"All the News That's Fit to Print"

The New York Times

Late Edition
New York: Today, sunny, a few afternoon clouds. High 77. Tonight, slightly more humid. Low 65. Tomorrow, sun then clouds. High 81. Yesterday, high 81, low 63. Weather map, Page C19.

VOL. CL . . No. 51,874 — NEW YORK, WEDNESDAY, SEPTEMBER 12, 2001 — 75 CENTS

U.S. ATTACKED

HIJACKED JETS DESTROY TWIN TOWERS AND HIT PENTAGON IN DAY OF TERROR

A CREEPING HORROR

Buildings Burn and Fall as Onlookers Search for Elusive Safety

By N. R. KLEINFIELD

It kept getting worse.

The horror arrived in episodic bursts of chilling disbelief, signified first by trembling floors, sharp eruptions, cracked windows. There was the actual unfathomable realization of a gaping, flaming hole in first one of the tall towers, and then the same thing all over again in its twin. There was the merciless sight of bodies helplessly tumbling out, some of them in flames.

Finally, the mighty towers themselves were reduced to nothing. Dense plumes of smoke raced through the downtown avenues, coursing between the buildings, shaped like tornadoes on their sides.

Every sound was cause for alarm. A plane appeared overhead. Was another one coming? No, it was a fighter jet. But was it friend or enemy? People scrambled for their lives, but they didn't know where to go. Should they go north, south, east, west? Stay outside, go indoors? People hid beneath cars and each other. Some contemplated jumping into the river.

For those trying to flee the very epicenter of the collapsing World Trade Center towers, the most horrid thought of all finally dawned on them: nowhere was safe.

For several panic-stricken hours yesterday morning, people in Lower Manhattan witnessed the inexpressible, the incomprehensible, the unthinkable. "I don't know what the gates of hell look like, but it's got to be like this," said John Maloney, a security director for an Internet firm in the trade center. "I'm a combat veteran, Vietnam, and I never saw anything like this."

The first warnings were small ones. Blocks away, Jim Farmer, a film composer, was having breakfast at a small restaurant on West Broadway. He heard the sound of a jet. An odd sound — too loud, it seemed, to be

Continued on Page A7

A Somber Bush Says Terrorism Cannot Prevail

By ELISABETH BUMILLER with DAVID E. SANGER

WASHINGTON, Sept. 11 — President Bush vowed tonight to retaliate against those responsible for today's attacks on New York and Washington, declaring that he would "make no distinction between the terrorists who committed these acts and those who harbor them."

"These acts of mass murder were intended to frighten our nation into chaos and retreat, but they have failed," the president said in his first speech to the nation from the Oval Office. "Our country is strong. Terrorist acts can shake the foundation of our biggest buildings, but they cannot touch the foundation of America."

His speech came after a day of trauma that seems destined to define his presidency. Seeking to at once calm the nation and declare his determination to exact retribution, he told a country numbed by repeated scenes of carnage that "these acts shattered steel, but they cannot dent the steel of American resolve."

Mr. Bush spoke only hours after returning from a zigzag course across the country, as his Secret Service and military security teams moved him from Florida, where he woke up this morning expecting to press for his education bill, to command posts in Louisiana and Nebraska before it was determined the attacks had probably ended and he could safely return to the capital.

It was a sign of the catastrophic

Continued on Page A4

AMERICAN TARGETS A ball of fire exploded outward after the second of two jetliners slammed into the World Trade Center; less than two hours later, both of the 110-story towers were gone. Hijackers crashed a third airliner into the Pentagon, setting off a huge explosion and fire.

President Vows to Exact Punishment for 'Evil'

By SERGE SCHMEMANN

Hijackers rammed jetliners into each of New York's World Trade Center towers yesterday, toppling both in a hellish storm of ash, glass, smoke and leaping victims, while a third jetliner crashed into the Pentagon in Virginia. There was no official count, but President Bush said thousands had perished, and in the immediate aftermath the calamity was already being ranked the worst and most audacious terror attack in American history.

The attacks seemed carefully coordinated. The hijacked planes were all en route to California, and therefore gorged with fuel, and their departures were spaced within an hour and 40 minutes. The first, American Airlines Flight 11, a Boeing 767 out of Boston for Los Angeles, crashed into the north tower at 8:48 a.m. Eighteen minutes later, United Airlines Flight 175, also headed from Boston to Los Angeles, plowed into the south tower.

Then an American Airlines Boeing 757, Flight 77, left Washington's Dulles International Airport bound for Los Angeles, but instead hit the western part of the Pentagon, the military headquarters where 24,000 people work, at 9:40 a.m. Finally, United Airlines Flight 93, a Boeing 757 flying from Newark to San Francisco, crashed near Pittsburgh, raising the possibility that its hijackers had failed in whatever their mission was.

SECOND PLANE United Airlines Flight 175 nearing the trade center's south tower.

There were indications that the hijackers on at least two of the planes were armed with knives. Attorney General John Ashcroft told reporters in the evening that the suspects on Flight 11 were armed that way. And Barbara Olson, a television commentator who was traveling on American Flight 77, managed to reach her husband, Solicitor General Theodore Olson, by cell phone and to tell him that the hijackers were armed with knives and a box cutter.

In all, 266 people perished in the four planes and several score more were known dead elsewhere. Numerous firefighters, police officers and other rescue workers who responded to the initial disaster in Lower Manhattan were killed or injured when the buildings collapsed. Hundreds were treated for cuts, broken bones, burns and smoke inhalation.

But the real carnage was concealed for now by the twisted, smoking, ash-choked carcasses of the twin towers, in which thousands of people used to work on a weekday. The collapse of the towers caused another World Trade Center building to fall 7 hours later, and several

Continued on Page A14

Awaiting the Aftershocks

Washington and Nation Plunge Into Fight With Enemy Hard to Identify and Punish

By R. W. APPLE Jr.

News Analysis

WASHINGTON, Sept. 11 — Today's devastating and astonishingly well-coordinated attacks on the World Trade Center towers in New York and on the Pentagon outside of Washington plunged the nation into a warlike struggle against an enemy that will be hard to identify with certainty and hard to punish with precision.

The whole nation — to a degree the whole world — shook as hijacked airliners plunged into buildings that symbolize the financial and military might of the United States. The sense of security and self-confidence that Americans take as their birthright suffered a grievous blow, from which recovery will be slow. The aftershocks will be nearly as bad, as hundreds and possibly thousands of people discover that friends or relatives died awful, fiery deaths.

Scenes of chaos and destruction evocative of the nightmare world of Hieronymus Bosch, with smoke and debris blotting out the sun, were carried by television into homes and workplaces across the nation. Echoing Franklin D. Roosevelt's description of the attack on Pearl Harbor as an event "which will live in infamy," Gov. George E. Pataki of New York, a Republican, spoke of "an incredible outrage" and Senator Charles E. Schumer of New York, a Democrat, spoke of "a dastardly attack."

But mere words were inadequate vessels to contain the sense of shock and horror that people felt.

As Washington struggled to regain a sense of equilibrium, with warplanes and heavily armed helicopters crossing overhead, past and present national security officials earnestly debated the possibility of a Congressional declaration of war — but against precisely whom, and in what exact circumstances? Warships were maneuvering to protect New York and Washington. The North American Air Defense Command, which had seemed to many a relic of the cold war, adopted a pos-

Continued on Page A24

MORE ON THE ATTACKS

RESCUERS BECOME VICTIMS Firefighters who rushed to the trade center were killed. PAGE A3

SEARCH FOR SURVIVORS Some people trapped in the rubble for hours were rescued. PAGE A3

OFFICIALS SUSPECT BIN LADEN Eavesdropping intercepts after the attacks were cited. PAGE A21

TERRORISTS EXPLOIT WEAKNESS Investigators had criticized precautions against hijacking. PAGE A17

CASUALTIES IN WASHINGTON An unknown number of people were killed at the Pentagon. PAGE A5

Figure 22 Front page of the *New York Times* of 12 September 2001.

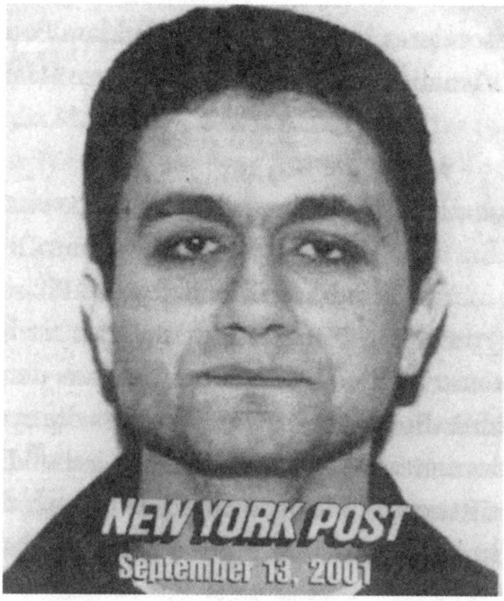

Figure 23 Mohammed Atta on the front page of the *New York Post* of 13 September 2001.

One way of doing this was to release photos of the attackers as quickly as possible. The Federal Bureau of Investigation (FBI) was already circulating images of this kind a few hours after the attacks. The face of the suspected leader of the group, Mohammed Atta, became particularly famous; it featured on the front page of the *New York Post* as 'The face of utter hatred' (Figure 23). The picture was taken from the murderer's Florida state driving licence. Bin Laden's name and image were likewise in circulation only a few hours after the attack, allowing Bush to declare six days later, in an allusion to the 'wanted' posters of the Wild West, that bin Laden was an enemy of the state 'wanted dead or alive'.[59] As Chapter 3 will show, none of these photographs was really a suitable image of the enemy. Nevertheless, they all met the urgent need to personify the horror and thus render it tangible.

These images have frequently been reproduced and discussed,[60] but there are other iconic photographs that have decisively shaped the memory of 9/11 since then. Perhaps the most important of these, besides Platt's frequently reproduced burning skyscrapers against the blue sky, is Stan Honda's so-called 'Dust Lady', who was later identified as Marcy Borders (Figure 24). This photo, which Honda submitted to Agence France Presse and which has since appeared in *Time Magazine*'s list of twenty-five most influential images,[61] shows a young woman completely covered in dust, illuminated by the yellow glow of that day's surreal light. We see someone who is a victim in need but nevertheless a survivor, her stance and her clothing dignified

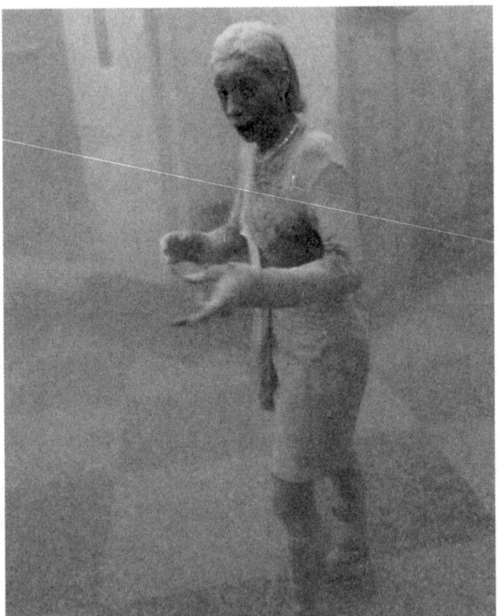

Figure 24 Stan Honda, *Dust Lady*, New York, 11 September 2001.

even though she is coated in dust. Borders was among the few people able to escape from the North Tower's 81st floor. What the photograph shares with Platt's burning skyscrapers and, as we will see in the final chapter, Drew's 'Falling Man' is something that is characteristic of many media icons: it condenses the tragedy of events by visualising it through a powerful contrast. The dust makes the smartly dressed young and slim woman look years older, and her movements seem frozen. Yet we know that she is alive and this creates a dynamic that ultimately cuts through the filtered yellow tint and dissolves it. We already know that the 'dust lady' will step from the cabinet of horrors out into normal daylight, which changes this depiction of a victim into an image of self-affirmation.

Another media icon of 11 September 2001 went one step further. Thomas E. Franklin's photo of three firefighters raising the Stars and Stripes in front of the World Trade Center's grey ruins ultimately translates civil society's gesture of self-assertion in the face of trauma into a patriotic narrative (Figure 25).[62] The photograph, which was circulated through Associated Press, also featured on the front pages of numerous American newspapers the day after the attack. In the days and weeks that followed, it was reproduced all over the world.[63] Unlike the other media icons of 9/11, it did not become famous because it presented the incomprehensibility of the events through a striking formal contrast, but because it quoted an iconic photograph that was firmly rooted in the American memory: Joe Rosenthal's shot of three Marines raising the American flag on the island of Iwo Jima, which had just been recaptured from the Japanese (Figure 26).

This image, which was printed on stamps and later even carved in stone and cast in bronze, was the prime symbol of

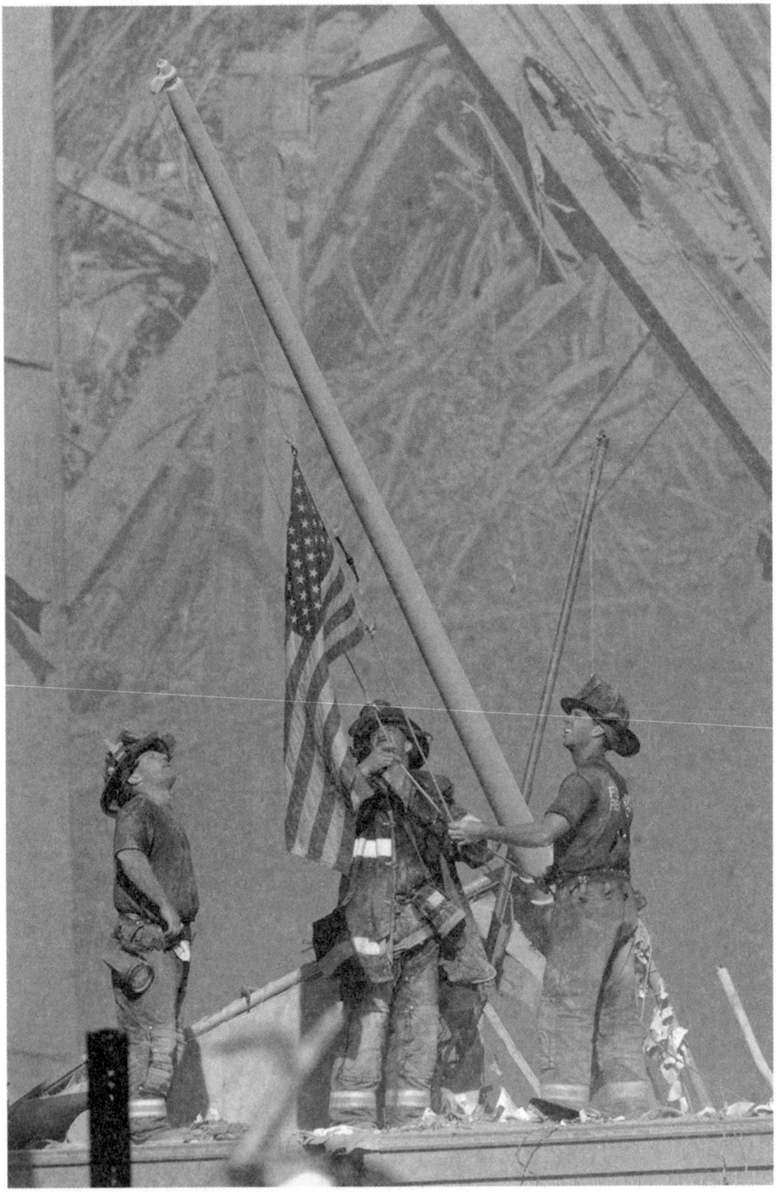

Figure 25 Thomas E. Franklin, *Raising the Flag at Ground Zero*, New York, 11 September 2001.

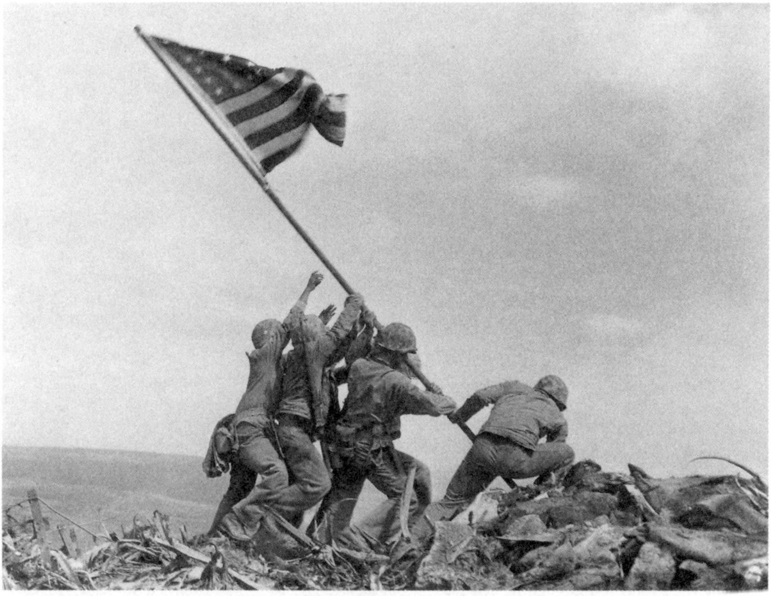

Figure 26 Joe Rosenthal, *Raising the Flag on Iwo Jima*, Mount Suribachi, Iwo Jima, 23 February 1945.

American self-confidence regained after the trauma of Pearl Harbor.[64] Franklin's photographic quote of 11 September 2001, found more or less by chance, provided a similar counter-image that was immediately comprehensible and, according to Gerhard Paul, expressed 'the Americans' patriotic will to win against unknown evil'.[65] By quoting a previous image from a context of war between two countries, it not only transformed the civilian rescue workers into heroes in the tradition of images of soldiers, but inevitably contributed to the country's military mobilisation, which finally became political reality with Bush's famous 'War on Terror' speech of 20 September 2001.

With hindsight, we can see that it was not the apocalyptic images themselves that were unique, as some

commentators assumed at the time,[66] but the rhetoric of war in which they were cast. Images of an attack are always witnesses to traumatic events, and neither the weapons nor the choice of target were unprecedented. Aeroplanes in the hands of terrorists were hardly new (see Chapter 2), and five years earlier jihadists had already carried out a bomb attack on the World Trade Center, although by pure chance no more than six people had died. Attacks on supposed centres of the capitalist world had taken place since the nineteenth century, starting with Clan na Gael's series of explosions in 1885, and again a hundred years later when Irish Republicans bombed the London Stock Exchange.[67] However, the language of war adopted in the written, spoken and visual reactions to the 9/11 attacks was indeed unprecedented.

Since then, only the French president François Hollande has adopted this rhetoric, in the aftermath of the Paris attacks of 13 November 2015. Yet, as most of the attackers came from France or from neighbouring Belgium (unlike the 9/11 murderers who were foreign nationals), Hollande's declaration of war missed its mark.[68] While IS (who claimed responsibility) could be fought with military means in Syria, this was out of the question when the perpetrators were French or citizens of a friendly nation. Accordingly, patriotic self-affirmation was expressed not through symbols or metaphors of war, but through images of the Eiffel Tower lit up in the national colours (see Chapter 3). Other European governments have so far avoided the rhetoric of war in reaction to attacks on their soil. What this reticence means for the images that circulate after an attack was particularly evident following the bombings carried out by Al-Qaida or groups close to it on 11 March 2004 in Madrid and 7 July 2005 in London.[69]

An attack without icons and the triumph of charity: bombings in Madrid and London

On 11 March 2004, ten explosive devices went off in various Madrid train stations between 7:39 and 7:42 a.m. local time, killing 191 people and injuring 2,051. Once again, there were many images of the destruction and the emergency services at work. In contrast to the New York attacks, however, most news programmes and newspapers published strikingly gruesome photographs showing not only severely wounded people, but also dead bodies. The front page of the Spanish daily *El Pais* featured one of these photos, which was also published in the British *Guardian* and elsewhere and has since become comparatively well known.[70] It showed not only wounded victims being helped, but corpses and even a severed body part in the foreground. This image was made famous because the *Guardian* shaded the bloody limb grey to make it less obvious. Similarly extreme (albeit unprocessed) images were published in Germany too, including in the *Hamburger Morgenpost*, which ran a picture in which a dead woman's face was clearly visible, with the headline '190 dead – it was Al Qaida'.[71]

Three bombs had exploded in Atocha Station, Madrid's main travel hub, four in a train around 800 metres outside the station, and three in the urban railway stations El Pozo del Tio Raimundo and Santa Eugenia in the southeast of the city. Numerous photographers and camera teams had free access to these locations for several hours, and even today some websites still offer the most shocking images – alongside pornography. In spite of this wealth of photographs, many of them extreme, there is still no real media icon of this event. This lack of an icon is particularly

striking in comparison with the London Underground bombings of 7 July 2005, and is in need of an explanation.

In contrast to Manhattan and Madrid, nearly all the photos in circulation after the London bombings showed the rescue services, without the victims being prominently visible. Once again, the attacks took place almost simultaneously at 8:50 a.m. during the morning rush hour in moving Underground carriages near Liverpool Street and Edgware Road stations and between King's Cross St Pancras and Russell Square. Since the bombs exploded in the tunnels, the British security forces could quickly cordon off the area around the stations. Accordingly, there were very few images of the horror that unfolded below ground, although many eyewitnesses subsequently gave accounts of it.[72] Forty-nine people were killed by three suicide attackers, who had been carrying the bombs in black rucksacks. Thirteen more people died almost an hour later in a fourth explosion on a double-decker bus in Tavistock Square. More than 700 people were injured in total, some of them severely, so that the city's rescue workers were operating in a state of emergency. The four suicide bombers also died in the attack. Yet the only images to circulate in large numbers were of the destroyed bus. They had been taken by press photographers and camera teams once the dead had been recovered and the injured rescued (Figure 27).

It is hardly surprising, then, that the photograph destined to become a media icon showed neither the rescue workers nor the destruction and havoc. Instead, it depicted two people's faces that graphically expressed not only the great suffering of the victims, but also the empathy and assistance of their fellow human beings. This image appeared on the cover pages of numerous British and international newspapers the day after the attack, captured from a range

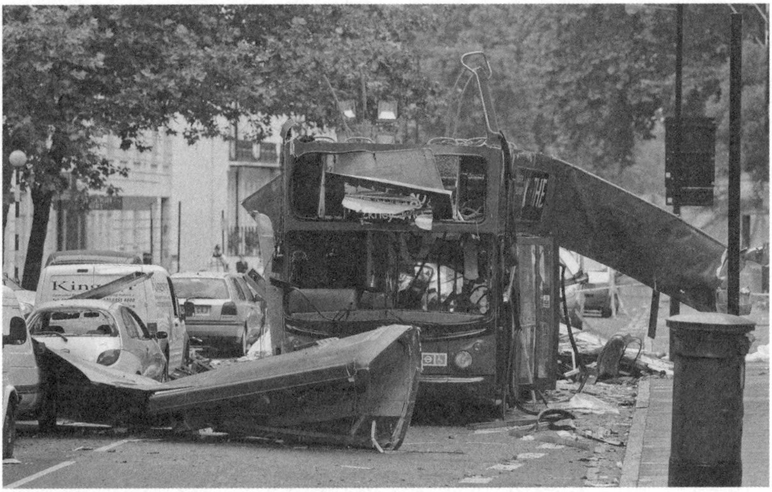

Figure 27 Destroyed double-decker bus, Woburn Place, London, 7 July 2005.

of angles by various photographers.[73] Each version of the photo showed a woman, her face covered by a gauze mask, being led across the road by a volunteer who has his arms wrapped tightly around her (Figure 28). Both the injured woman and the man helping her were later identified. Twenty-four year-old Davinia Turrell had suffered serious injuries and burns in one of the explosions, and former firefighter Paul Dadge had been on his way to work when the first victims emerged from Edgware Road station. Dadge immediately helped to set up an emergency care station and provide first aid. Yet at the time the photo was taken, for the media these two people were simply an anonymous victim and her rescuer. The image thus illustrated what both the media coverage after the attacks and later memorial services have emphasised: the extraordinary humanitarian efforts of not only the rescue workers, but also countless volunteers in the minutes and hours after the explosions.

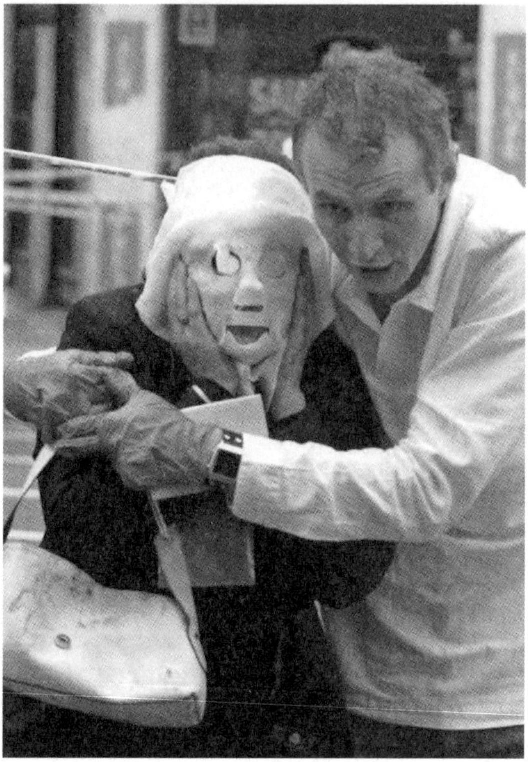

Figure 28 A victim wearing a face mask and her rescuer, Edgware Road underground station, London, 7 July 2005.

The contrast between the rescuer's caring gaze and embrace and the victim's anonymising face mask, which simultaneously expressed the intangible threat of the events, created an image that gave viewers comfort and reassurance. In the face of a homegrown terrorist attack – three of the four perpetrators were British men of Pakistani descent, who had grown up and gone to school in Leeds – the photo of Turrell and Dadge illustrated the indestructible unity of a society that, in its most challenging hour, was capable of exceptional solidarity and charity.[74]

An image pattern and its limits

Like the assassinations in the late nineteenth century, each of the attacks in the early twenty-first century perpetrated by Al-Qaida or groups associated with it struck directly at the vulnerable heart of the cities affected. Attackers selected heavily frequented locations to cause maximum suffering and spread fear in the targeted societies. And each time the media reacted with a predictable logic: photographs of the destroyed locations were immediately followed by images that served to reassure the threatened populace, especially depictions of survivors and of the rescue services at work. This sequence also includes scenes of collective mourning, which were reproduced time and again in different variations. Despite the major twentieth-century developments in technical media – from wood and steel engravings to photographs and live recordings – the pattern stayed the same. The images of mangled corpses reproduced after the Madrid train bombings are in fact surprisingly similar to the engraving printed by *Illustrirte Zeitung* to illustrate the destruction of the Paris police station on 8 November 1891 (see Figure 19). Moreover, media analyses of live broadcasts of 9/11 have shown that 'while the categorisation as a "live broadcast" implies a claim to convey reality directly', the reports themselves followed predictable genre conventions.[75]

Yet very few images also attain the status of media icons. Of the many photos circulating in the hours and days after attacks, only a small number are printed in newspapers and magazines, and of those merely a narrow selection appear with striking frequency. Usually these photographs have succeeded in capturing a formal contrast that visualises the extreme experience of the attack (death and survival, suffering and selfless care). Or, like Franklin's photograph, they

refer to a well-known iconographic model and thus sum up the situation in a way that also suggests a familiar interpretative framework. Moreover, most media icons are able to visualise the self-affirmation of threatened societies in a particularly evocative way. The heroisation of the rescue workers and the patriotic visual rhetoric in the United States after 9/11 made it possible to imagine 'a counterstrike as a concrete course of action',[76] as Paul writes, while in London the self-affirmative images focused on social cohesion, precisely because the enemy was not foreign.[77] In Madrid, by contrast, political confusion reigned. In an attempt to garner support three days before parliamentary elections, the government initially claimed that the Basque terror organisation ETA was behind the attacks. Nevertheless, it soon became known that significant evidence pointed in another direction.[78] Without a clear political stance or a clearly defined enemy, there was ultimately no coherent, identity-establishing narrative and thus no media icon of the events. 'Ideologies create substantiating archives of images,' writes Susan Sontag, 'representative images, which encapsulate common ideas of significance and trigger predictable thoughts, feelings.'[79] It is therefore not insignificant which images we use to remember events, and the archives might one day yield an alternative account.

After the attacks of the early twenty-first century, it became increasingly obvious that the traditional image pattern might already be acquiring a new facet. Yet it was initially not perceived as such. For the first time since the spread of the illustrated press in the late nineteenth century, a new medium had emerged that began to have a significant impact on news reporting. After 11 September 2001 and 7 July 2005, for example, the American and British secret services circulated security camera footage that did

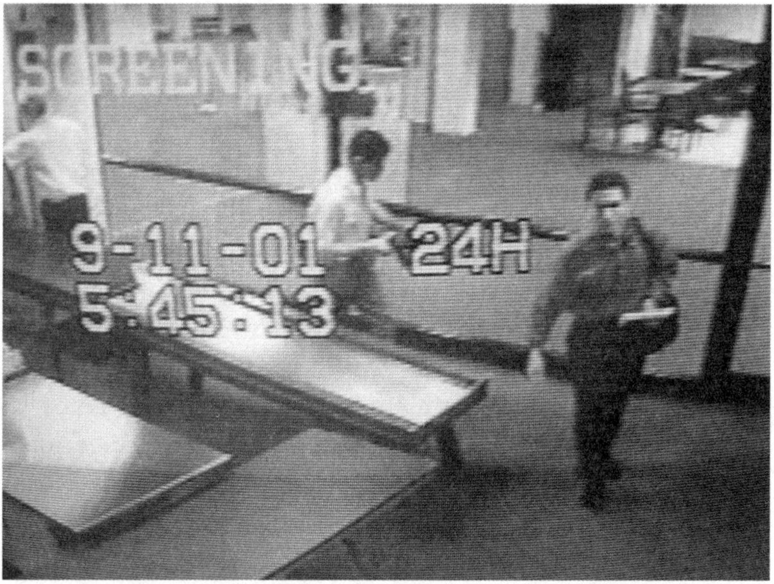

Figure 29 Security camera footage of Mohammed Atta at Portland Airport on 11 September 2001.

not show the perpetrators, as previously, before or after the attack, but in the act of carrying it out. Only a few hours after the destruction of the World Trade Center, the FBI released a video showing Mohammed Atta going through the security gate at Portland Airport on the way to his deadly destination (Figure 29). Of course, this clip was published not to hunt down Atta, who was already dead by then, but to visualise and personify the enemy. Yet the video was even less suited to this purpose than the photo taken from Atta's driving licence. It shows an irritatingly normal-looking young man in a blue shirt calmly walking through the gate with his jacket thrown casually over his shoulder and a plane ticket in his hand. No one could have suspected what his intentions were, and even with hindsight it is

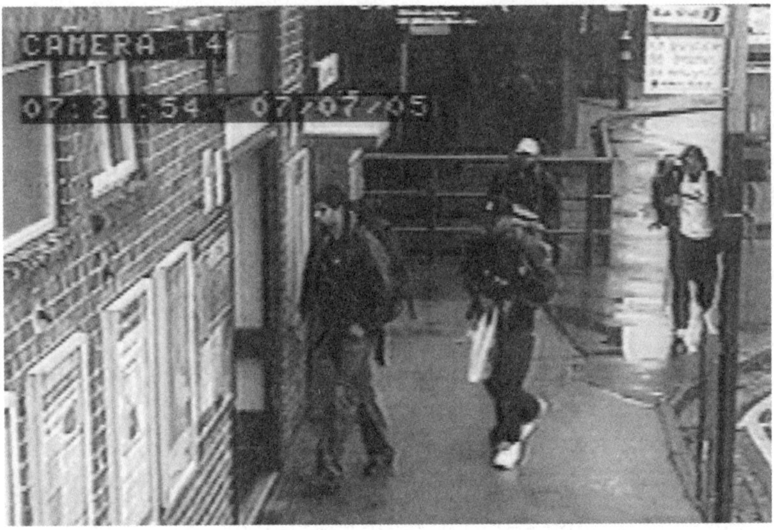

Figure 30 Security camera footage of the London suicide attackers walking into Luton station on 7 July 2005.

impossible to detect any suspicious signs, which makes the image appear both trivial and disturbing at the same time. The same is true for the footage from a security camera that the Metropolitan Police circulated (much more hesitantly) four days after the London attacks. It shows the four suicide attackers walking through Luton Station at 7 a.m. on their way to London (Figure 30). Here too, all that could be seen was four young men exhibiting no outward signs of nervousness, embarking on a journey with rucksacks on their backs, just like many other travellers.

What exactly distinguishes these images from those of other perpetrators? This question requires further analysis, and will be addressed again in Chapter 3. Another image of the London attacks reveals yet another new development, whose problematic nature has only recently become clear. Even though press photographers and camera teams did not

have access to the horror unfolding in the Underground tunnels, people used their mobile phones to capture what they saw, taking numerous photos and films. As there were no professional photos of this kind, the BBC's news desk issued a call for amateur photographs to be submitted so they could be uploaded onto the cooperation's website after being screened by the editors. The call went out on the day of the attack, and a blurred, dark photo taken by Alexander Chadwick with his mobile phone was, among others, subsequently published showing the evacuation in the Underground tunnel. The very next day, this photo appeared on the first page of the *Washington Post* and other newspapers (Figure 31).[80] For the first time in history, a non-professional mobile phone photograph had made it onto the front pages of leading international papers and, a short time later, into news programmes.[81] Yet the picture itself did not

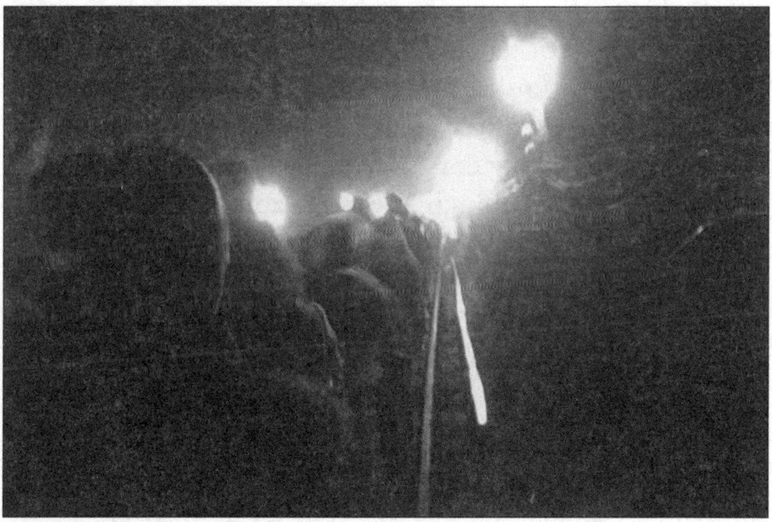

Figure 31 Mobile phone photograph of the evacuation from the tunnels of the London Underground on 7 July 2005.

show very much. Its blurriness conveyed only a sense of the dark and the threatening, confusing situation in the tunnel, reported by many other victims in the aftermath.

Since then, the importance of non-professional photographs showing terror attacks has increased considerably. The images thus entering circulation – often uploaded directly to internet platforms such as Facebook and YouTube without being filtered by news desks – only partly conform to the established image patterns of terror coverage. Their spread raises new issues that need further consideration. For the moment, however, it is sufficient to state that picture and news editors no longer serve as gatekeepers to the images that reach the public. Today, potentially every single person who carries a device with internet access is capable of taking and circulating pictures of disasters.

I will come back to this development in the last chapter. First, however, I will turn to another kind of terror imagery and visual reportage that has developed alongside bomb attacks. It differs from those we have discussed so far in several crucial respects. Besides bomb attacks, one of the most effective strategies used by terror groups to gain media attention has been to take hostages. While photos of attacks bring viewers particularly close to the events, and their content is defined by the political dynamics of the societies affected, images of abductions speak from afar and in the language of the perpetrators. They rarely produce media icons. Yet once they have become public, they too become difficult to forget.

Chapter 2

Distant images: hostage-takings and aircraft hijackings since the 1960s

For governments, the media and indeed the public, abductions and aircraft hijackings pose far greater challenges than bomb attacks. This may seem surprising at first, for devastated railway stations, city-centre cafés and high-rises in which many people may have lost their lives are obviously more terrifying than the news that an individual has been kidnapped in a far-away place and is being held prisoner in an unknown location. But since the outcome of kidnappings and hijackings is always uncertain, everyone involved acts under enormous pressure. While images released immediately after a bomb attack already provide a reassuring framework that helps the public to make sense of what has happened, kidnappings often last for days, weeks or even years, and the situation is much more unpredictable and volatile.

When kidnappers pursue their more or less clearly formulated attempts at extortion, they know that they can fail dramatically. Governments on the other hand, while playing for time and counting on their negotiation skills, must appear uncompromising, for hostage-taking is a criminal offence. After the first great wave of abductions in Latin America in the 1960s, many states adopted the official

policy never to make concessions to kidnappers or to negotiate with them.[1] The media, while following their mission to deliver accurate information as fast as possible, also thrive on shock and drama, and thus often get into conflict with government strategies. In such a situation, the relationship between media and governments can be particularly tense, as the political scientist Christian Buck explains:

> At the outset, the media are a reality that no government can ignore. Empirical research also suggests that government press departments have less control during a crisis situation because the media carry out their own investigations more thoroughly in times like these. Their reports can interfere with government plans, put more pressure on politicians and even lead them to make rash decisions. In a crisis, the media take on a more politically purposeful role than they usually have. Their coverage shapes a part of reality. The realm of the media and the realm of reality become entangled.[2]

The public are caught up in this volatile situation. Torn between the attraction of sensationalism and empathy with the plight of the hostages, people crave more information, but also expect the government to demonstrate its power and leadership qualities. The devastating effect of conflicting interests has rarely been clearer for all involved than during the occupation of the US embassy in Tehran, Iran, when 52 diplomats and staff were held hostage for 444 days.

The student revolutionaries who stormed the embassy on 4 November 1979 had sole control over the images from the very start. Iranian television and press broadcast images of the assault on the embassy (Figure 32) and of the spectacularly staged burning of the American flag (Figure 33). In both images, extreme low-angle shots amplified the impact of the students' victory poses. The Western media, for want of any alternative coverage, adopted both of these, as well

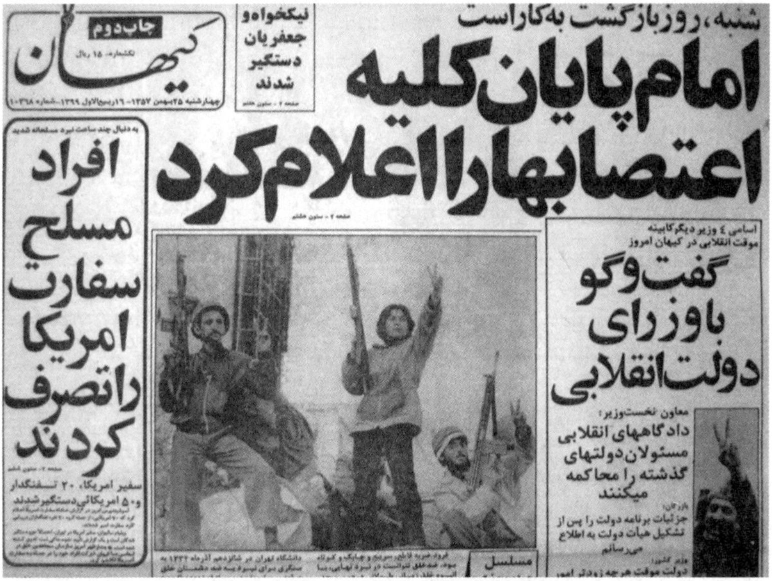

چاپ دوم

کیهان

نیکخواه و جعفریان دستگیر شدند

شنبه، روز بازگشت به کار است

امام پایان کلیه اعتصابها را اعلام کرد

به دنبال چند ساعت نبرد مسلحانه شدید

افراد مسلح سفارت امریکا را تصرف کردند

سفیر امریکا، ۲۰ تفنگدار و ۵۰ امریکائی دستگیر شدند

اسامی ٤ وزیر دیگر کابینه موقت انقلابی در کیهان امروز

گفت وگو با وزرای دولت انقلابی

معاون نخست‌وزیر: دادگاههای انقلابی مسئولان دولتهای گذشته را محاکمه میکنند

بازرگان: جزئیات برنامه دولت را پس از تشکیل هیات دولت به اطلاع میرسانم

Figure 32 Occupation of the US Embassy in Tehran on 4 November 1979.

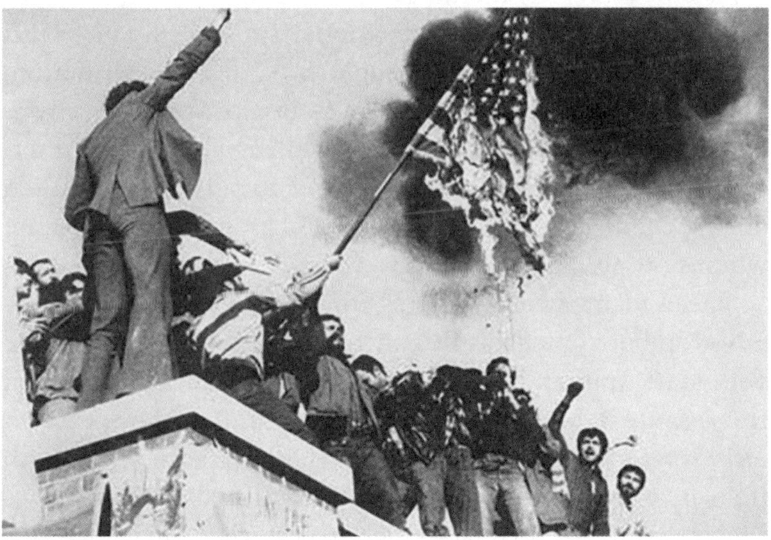

Figure 33 Burning of the US flag.

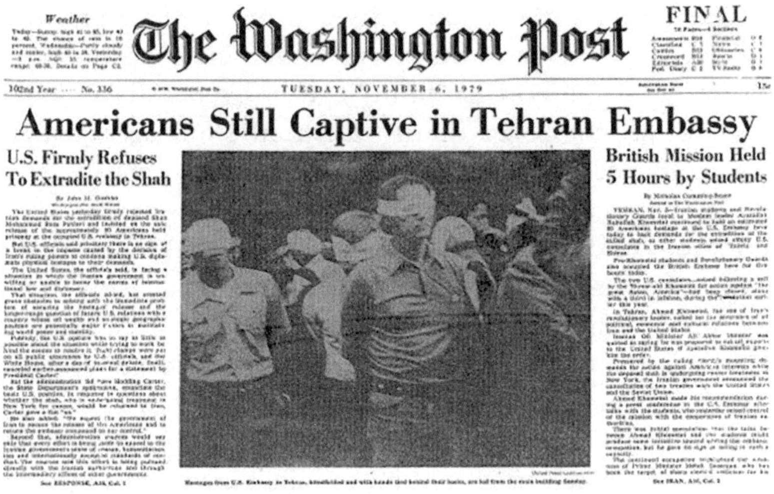
Weather

The Washington Post

FINAL

102nd Year No. 336

TUESDAY, NOVEMBER 6, 1979

Americans Still Captive in Tehran Embassy

U.S. Firmly Refuses To Extradite the Shah

British Mission Held 5 Hours by Students

Figure 34 Parading of the hostages in Tehran in November 1979.

as the picture of the subsequent parading of blindfolded hostages (Figure 34).[3]

The occupiers soon realised that their aim – the extradition of the Shah, who had fled to the United States – could not be adequately conveyed to Western audiences through images and news reports alone. One of the hostage-takers later said that this led them to change their strategy:

> It was not long before the inflow of information from our interviews, and the nature of the coverage we were receiving, convinced us to reconsider our public relations policies. We announced that no interviews would be given to any American television or radio reporter unless it was to be broadcast live and uncensored.[4]

To obtain news and keep contact with the hostages, the US television station NBC agreed to the terms, and on 10 December 1979 it broadcast an uncut statement from the kidnappers followed by an interview with one of the hostages.[5]

The longer the hostage crisis continued, the more the US government came under pressure. Increasingly seen as too weak,[6] President Jimmy Carter eventually ordered a secret military operation to rescue the hostages, which was launched on 24 April 1980. It failed disastrously, and six months later Carter lost the US presidential election.[7] Iran, too, paid a high price for the occupation: the country suffered a long period of political isolation and disastrous economic sanctions, which were only lifted by a United Nations (UN) resolution in 2015. Only the hostages emerged comparatively well from the tragedy. Even though the kidnappers' initial aim, the extradition of the Shah, had not been achieved (and he had died in the meantime), the hostages were released shortly after Ronald Reagan's inauguration.[8] Their return to the United States was widely celebrated in the news, as is customary for hostage-takings with lucky endings. The media, however, remained under fire. They were blamed for everything from restricting the government's room for manoeuvre through excessive use of emotions in their coverage to publication of secret government strategies, and even involuntary complicity with the perpetrators.[9]

There is a growing body of research about the fraught interaction between government and media in the context of political hostage-takings and aircraft hijackings.[10] If images are mentioned at all in these studies, they are mostly treated as merely illustrative of the precarious situation and outcome that in itself is largely determined by other factors.[11] The reason is obvious: photos of hostages are much less spectacular than images of carnage and devastation in cities around the world. All they usually show is the portrait of an individual, often unknown to the general public, who has been abducted to some nameless place and

photographed against an obscure background. Sometimes the logo of the terror organisation claiming responsibility also appears in the picture, but that is all. Since secrecy is essential, the images conceal and confuse more than they reveal. In this respect, the photographs and videos of the hostage-taking in Tehran that appeared in the media are far from representative. The storming of the US embassy and the parading of the hostages could be staged publicly, because the revolutionary regime supported the occupation and thus none of the occupiers had to fear criminal prosecution.[12]

The first significant wave of hostage-taking occurred in Latin America in the 1960s, followed, a decade later, by a number of abductions carried out by the PFLP and far-left groups in Italy and Germany. In the 1980s, numerous kidnappings in Lebanon were covered by the Western media, and in the early twenty-first century abductions and subsequent beheadings by Al-Qaida and IS dominated the news. In most cases the captors, who had largely gone underground, circulated images which deliberately concealed the locations where they held their victims. Although the images that reached the Western media must have seemed like distant echoes of far-away events, they did not fail to be effective. On the contrary: photos of hostages are important factors in the volatile context of kidnapping dramas, and their perception by Western audiences often decisively shapes the course of events. As we will see in what follows, the publication of images can influence the ways in which kidnappers attempt to communicate, ensure that public attention is focused on the plight of the hostages, or even be indirectly complicit with the captors.

It is not always clear at the outset which way the pendulum is going to swing. While images of attacks hardly

ever fail to achieve the shocking effect the perpetrators intend, the intentions of those who release hostage photos do not always match the public's perception of them. The images of the occupation of the US embassy in Tehran are no exception in this respect. They were supposed to demonstrate the popular support for the new regime in Iran and thus strengthen the kidnappers' demand that the Shah be extradited and his assets seized. Yet a study of television news coverage in the United States revealed a very different response. Rather than feeling any sympathy for the Iranian revolution, Americans regarded the photos with suspicion, seeing nothing but a gang of brutal foreigners whose triumphal parading of the hostages was little more than a senseless act of violence that inflicted gratuitous suffering on innocent people.[13]

Since images of aircraft hijackings are considerably less ambivalent, they will be considered separately in the final part of this chapter. The perpetrators only have indirect influence on their circulation and, although the outcome is as open as with other hostage-takings, public perception is largely in the hands of press photographers working for the Western media. Yet these images too are distant: until very recently the actual drama within an aircraft cabin was invisible and could only be conveyed through pictures of planes on anonymous runways during occasional stopovers.

Distance and urgency are intertwined in a strange way in these images too. Walter Benjamin has called this effect a 'peculiar weave of space and time', a unique 'appearance only of distance, however close it may be'.[14] For Benjamin, this was a quality of early portrait photography in the nineteenth century that subsequently got lost: the aura of the images, created by long exposure times and complex equipment, had vanished in the fleeting shots of modern press

photography and been replaced by shock effects.[15] In the disturbing images of hostage-takings and hijackings, however, aura and shock appear together. The shock of accelerated action and perception and the aura of a near distance are both present, in an uncanny way that cannot be found in images of attacks.

New strategies in the 1970s: from the Tupamaros in Uruguay to the RAF in Germany

Politically motivated abductions took place long before the emergence of modern terror. But as the political scientists Norman Antokol and Mayer Nudell have pointed out, people taken hostage before the twentieth century always had some official relationship with the government of the country from which the hostage-takers sought concessions.[16] This changed after the Second World War, when Latin American rebels began abducting private people. Since then, kidnappers who take hostages for political reasons are not primarily concerned with the immediate exchange value of an individual. Like other perpetrators of terror attacks, they fight their battle on a higher, symbolic level. Attracting attention, gaining sympathy and challenging the power of the state are at least as important as direct extortion.

The first big wave of political hostage-taking in the twentieth century started with a surprisingly successful propaganda coup.[17] In 1958, Cuban rebels led by Fidel Castro kidnapped the Argentine racing driver Juan Manuel Fangio, along with 45 North Americans. Since the Cuban government systematically denied that the revolutionaries existed, the group wanted to demonstrate their power to an international public. After extensive worldwide coverage, all hostages were released without the captors having

made any demands. Some ten years later, other rebel groups in Latin America used political hostage-taking as a means to draw attention to their causes, but now often also demanded the release of their comrades held in state prisons. Until the early 1970s, a surprising number of these political abductions were successful, especially in Brazil and the Dominican Republic, where the governments obligingly negotiated with the rebels. However, countries whose governments had adopted a strategy of principled intransigence soon saw the first casualties. On 5 April 1970, the body of the West German ambassador Count Karl von Spreti was recovered from an abandoned house in Guatemala, and four months later Daniel A. Mitrione, a US security adviser, was shot dead in Uruguay.

The Uruguayan rebel group Moviemiento de Liberación Nacional, better known as the Tupamaros, claimed responsibility for Mitrione's murder, but swiftly put the blame on the Uruguayan government which had refused to negotiate. Nevertheless, the murder backfired and proved to be a serious setback for the movement. Like other radical movements in many Latin American countries, the Tupamaros had the support of large parts of the population, but the news of the murder of an innocent person soon changed public opinion. In response, the Tupamaros began releasing images that showed their hostages in good health and in humane conditions. The American agricultural consultant Claude Fly, for example, could be seen reading a book, while other photos showed hostages eating a meal or playing cards (Figure 35). An image of another hostage, the British ambassador Sir Geoffrey Jackson, appeared a little later in *The Times* of 27 March 1971 (Figure 36).

Although these photos initially served as proof to families and governments that the hostages were still alive, the

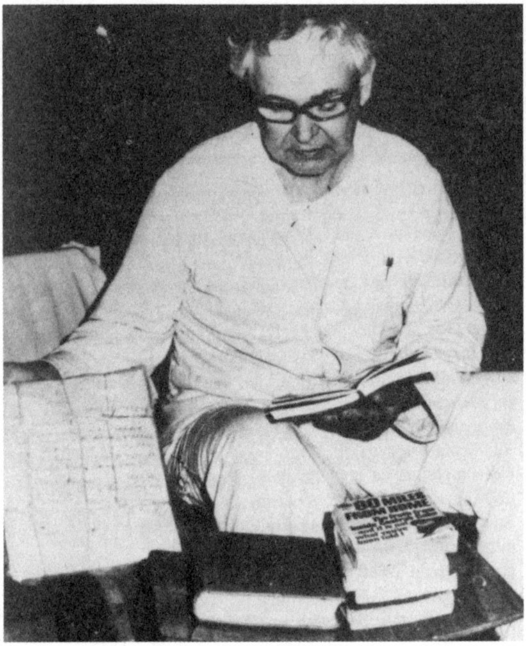

Figure 35 Claude Fly as hostage of the Tupamaros in October 1970.

targets of this new strategy were primarily the people of Uruguay. Instead of impressing sympathisers with brute force, the hostage-takers tried to regain their lost status by demonstrating apparently humane behaviour, although in fact none of the carefully staged photos corresponded to the real situation. As Fly and Jackson reported later, they spent most of their time in dark cellars and underground cages.[18] The only hint of this to be found in the images is the grimly ironic book titles. It was not by chance, for example, that Jackson was photographed reading Gabriel Garcia Marquéz's *One Hundred Years of Solitude*, or that the publication lying on the table in front of Fly bore the clearly visible title *80 Miles from Home*.

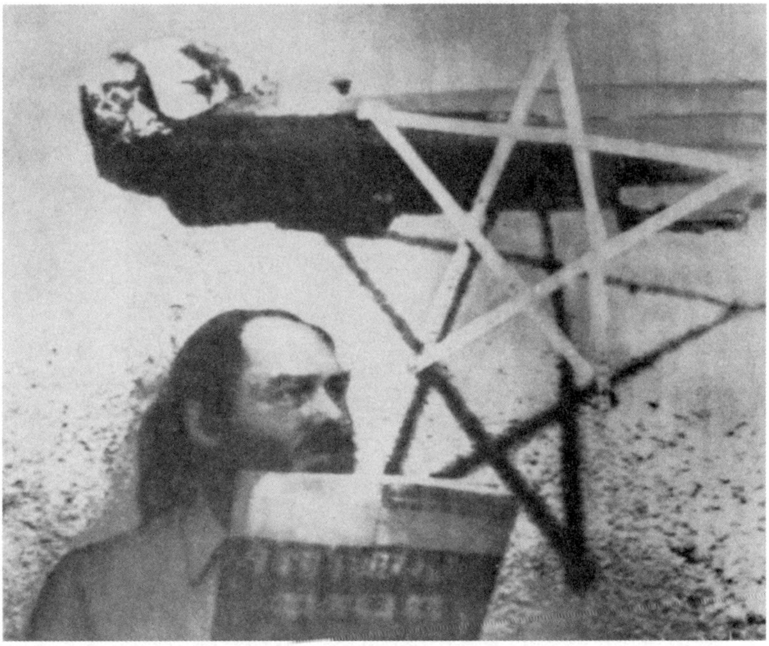

Figure 36 Geoffrey Jackson as hostage of the Tupamaros in March 1971.

The photograph of Jackson contains another element, one that would become quite common in the iconography of hostage photos during the years that followed. On the wall behind the hostage was an improvised version of the Tupamaros' logo made from sticks, a five-sided star which would normally have had a 'T' in the centre – but here the 'T' was unambiguously replaced by a machine gun. To include the logo in the picture, the hostage was positioned with his head lower down, clearly demonstrating the power relations of the situation. With this simple visual language the Tupamaros established a convention that far-left urban guerrillas in Europe would adopt a few years later.[19] By then, things had moved beyond ostentatiously humane photos

of hostages; and in any case, the families of the hostages and the public in the countries they came from had always read these images rather differently. The report in *The Times* that included Jackson's photo, for example, did not utter a word about humane treatment. Expressing sympathy for the suffering of the hostage and his family, it presented the image above all as a sign of Jackson's self-discipline and fortitude.[20]

In this tangled web of relationships, the effect of these images is barely controllable. The various protagonists pursue different aims, so that the meaning of the photos remains contentious. Which way the pendulum will swing is, in the course of abductions, unclear to all involved until the end. Just how much so became particularly evident during the tense autumn of 1977, when the Federal Republic of Germany also experienced a wave of abductions.

When five members of a 'commando unit' of the Red Army Faction (RAF) kidnapped Hanns Martin Schleyer, President of the Confederation of German Employers' Associations, in the early evening of 5 September 1977, few of those involved would have imagined the drama that would unfold in the weeks that followed.[21] Initially, the captors hoped for a swift resolution.[22] A statement from the 'Siegfried Hausner Commando', which reached news agencies a day later, said: 'We presume that [Chancellor Helmut] Schmidt ... will endeavour to clarify his relationship to this fat magnate of the cream of the national economy.'[23] The kidnappers assumed that with Schleyer they had captured an important functionary of the ruling elite who would force the state to negotiate. They demanded the release of eleven imprisoned RAF members, among them leading figures such as Andreas Baader, Gudrun Ensslin and Jan-Carl Raspe. Yet it soon became clear that they had

miscalculated. The fact alone that there were four people dead at the site of the crime – the chauffeur of Schleyer's car and three police escorts – left the government with little scope for manoeuvre. As the journalist and film director Lutz Hachmeister pointed out, there was the risk that it might look as if 'the state can be blackmailed for a chief capitalist while it disregards the execution of low-ranking employees and civil servants as an occupational hazard'.[24]

Two years earlier, the state had agreed to negotiate. When Peter Lorenz, the Christian Democrat (CDU) candidate for mayor of West Berlin, was taken hostage by the 2 June Movement in February 1975, five prisoners were released in exchange, who all immediately went back underground. By April of the same year some of them took part in another hostage-taking, organised by the RAF. This time the government under Chancellor Helmut Schmidt refused to negotiate, and the outcome was tragic. During the occupation of the West German embassy in Stockholm four people lost their lives, among them the military attaché Andreas von Mirbach and the RAF member Siegfried Hausner, who was turned into a martyr by the group when they gave his name to the commando unit that abducted Schleyer.[25]

Horst Herold, President of the Federal Criminal Police Office and, apart from Schmidt, the most important person in the crisis team created after Schleyer's abduction in September 1977, recommended playing for time. The sophisticated new information-gathering system that he had introduced raised hopes that the police might be able to locate the place where Schleyer was being held and free him.[26] But from the very beginning there was a tacit agreement that the government would not give in to the demands of the kidnappers, even though Schleyer had close

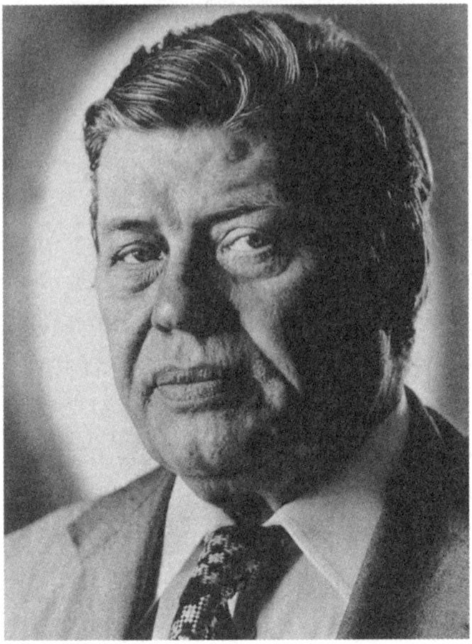

Figure 37 Hanns Martin Schleyer, President of the Confederation of German Employers' Associations from 1973 to 1977.

friends at very high levels in politics and the economy.[27] A member of the board of directors of Daimler-Benz AG, he had been elected in 1973 as president of the Confederation of German Employers' Associations (Figure 37). To the general public he epitomised the figure of an uncompromising capitalist, since he was responsible for the first lockouts during strikes in post-war Germany.[28] One of the kidnappers, Stefan Wisniewski, later said that he had first become aware of Schleyer through a report in *Stern* magazine entitled 'Boss der Bosse' (Boss of the bosses), which also mentioned his Nazi past.[29]

The kidnappers initially relied on an image strategy which, as the historian Petra Terhoeven has shown, had been successfully employed by the Red Brigades in Italy.[30]

Reversing the imagery employed by the Tupamaros, but pursuing the same aim – that is, to win sympathy for their cause – the Red Brigades had sent a photo of the kidnapped Idalgo Macchiarini to the Italian news agency ANSA on 3 April 1972. It showed Macchiarini, a manager from SIT Siemens who was loathed and feared by his employees, crouching anxiously on the floor with pistols pointing at his head (Figure 38). With a statement on the placard that their prisoner was forced to wear around his neck, the Red Brigades claimed responsibility for his abduction and declared that 'no one will go unpunished' and 'all power to the armed people'. All this was no more than a propaganda coup, however. As soon as the picture had been taken and sent to ANSA, Macchiarini was released, to great applause

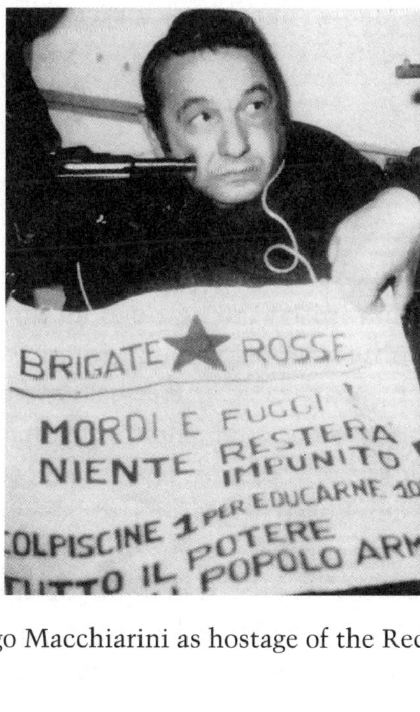

Figure 38 Idalgo Macchiarini as hostage of the Red Brigades on 3 April 1972.

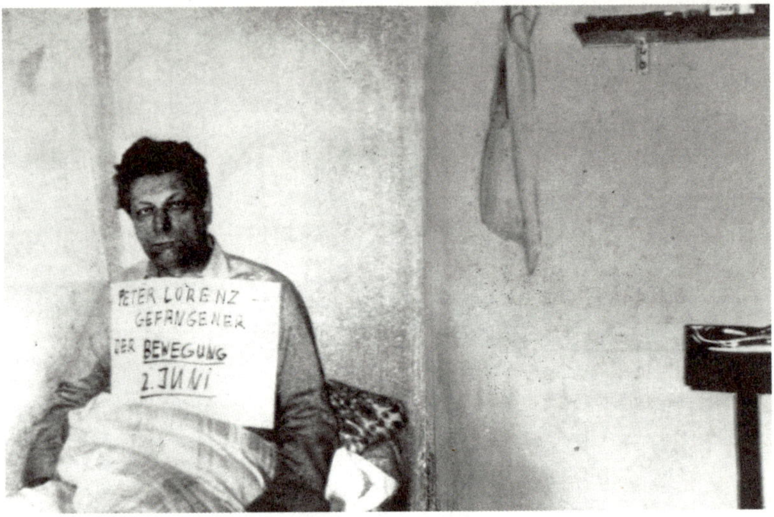

Figure 39 Peter Lorenz as hostage of the 2 June Movement on 27 February 1975.

from the people.[31] A similarly humiliating picture of the politician Peter Lorenz was circulated three years later by the 2 June Movement. Shot from above, it showed their hostage in visible distress, with a hand-written placard on his chest and sitting on a camp bed (Figure 39).

Five years later, the RAF employed a similar strategy of humiliation. The first Polaroid photo, shot on the day after the abduction, shows a haggard, sweating Schleyer clothed in a vest and tracksuit top (Figure 40). Like Lorenz, he holds a hand-written placard, to which the date of the photo has been added. What was new here was that the logo of the RAF could be seen on the wall behind the hostage, a five-pointed star with machine gun and lettering that borrowed from Tupamaros imagery. It seems that the kidnappers hoped not only that this photograph would force the government to act, but that it might also make an impression on the

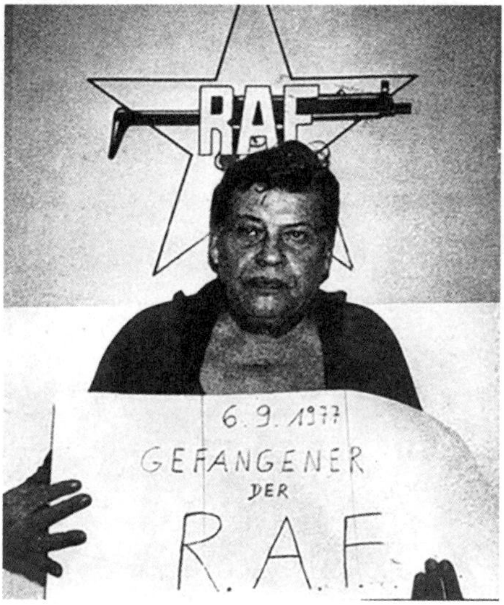

Figure 40 Hanns Martin Schleyer as hostage of the RAF on 6 September 1977.

country's indecisive Left and those workers whom Schleyer had locked out just a few months earlier. A greater contrast to the official images of Schleyer, which showed him as a powerful, calm and authoritative business leader, was hard to imagine.

To the great disappointment of the kidnappers, the image was not immediately made public. When their demand that the images be shown on the ARD's main evening news programme *Tagesschau* at 8 p.m. was not met, the RAF – for the first time in the history of hostage-taking – sent video messages directly to news agencies at home and abroad.[32] In the meantime, the German government had negotiated a similarly unprecedented news blackout with the German Press Council.[33] When the first Polaroid photo appeared in the media despite this restriction, it soon became clear that the kidnapper's strategy had been a miscalculation from

the very start. After the French news agency AFP had published the photograph on 9 September, the German media followed suit. Across the political spectrum, the photo was met with horror: 'An image that makes you want to cry' was the headline of the tabloid newspaper *Bild*, and *Spiegel* magazine also emphasised the physical suffering of the helpless hostage.[34]

This prompted the kidnappers to rethink their strategy. On the second Polaroid photo, which was sent to the French paper *Libération* on 26 September, Schleyer now wears a suit, his hair looks combed and he appears composed (Figure 41). An almost imperceptible change on the placard he is holding also reveals a change of meaning. Large letters

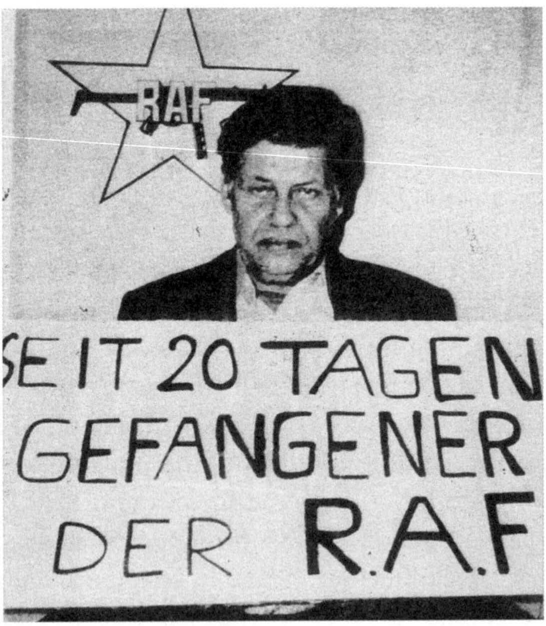

Figure 41 Hanns Martin Schleyer as hostage of the RAF on 26 September 1977.

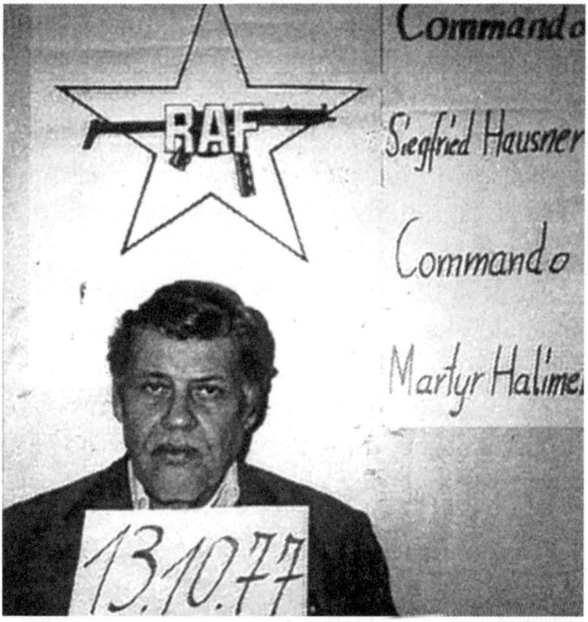

Figure 42 Hanns Martin Schleyer as hostage of the RAF on 13 October 1977.

now list the number of days of his imprisonment, so that the interpretation shifts from a demonstration of power to an accusation of delaying tactics on the part of the government. On the last photo, from 13 October, Schleyer is also seen with a dated placard, but now every explicit allusion to his imprisonment has been dropped (Figure 42). As the added lettering on the wall shows, the image was supposed to establish a link between the hijacking of the Lufthansa plane by the Palestinian Commando Martyr Halimeh and Schleyer's abduction. When it became clear that the government could not be blackmailed, it seemed pointless for the kidnappers to continue trying to win sympathy for their cause. Putting pressure on the government by creating

a wave of public compassion for Schleyer now must have appeared to be the more promising strategy. Yet this was precisely what the government tried to prevent with the news blackout.[35] In fact, only *Bild* printed three photos from the series circulated by the kidnappers on 10 October 1977, while the hostage drama was still ongoing.[36]

This setback led to a remarkable collaboration between the kidnappers and their victim, in which Schleyer apparently even seized the initiative. From the third day of his imprisonment he regularly sent moving appeals to important political friends. On 9 September, he wrote to Eberhard von Brauchitsch, the managing director of Flick KG: 'In my situation, this uncertainty is of course horrible. If Bonn declines they should do it soon, even though a man – as it was in the war – would like to survive.'[37] Three days later he tried to win over Helmut Kohl, the leader of the opposition, with a tape recording. He declared that he had never begged for his life, but what was now going on was nothing less than senseless torture.[38] Schleyer's communications with the outside world became increasingly desperate the longer he was imprisoned. There must have been a moment when his efforts turned into hopelessness. In a last video recording from 13 October, he no longer appeals for his liberation but accuses the state of having sacrificed him:

> I really ask myself in my current situation: does something else have to happen for Bonn to finally reach a decision? After all I have now been imprisoned by the terrorists for five and a half weeks and all that only because I have stood up for this state and its freedom and democracy for years.[39]

Wisniewski later reported that Schleyer gradually realised that he had been abandoned.[40] The kidnappers, however, had not yet given up, for the hijacking of the Lufthansa plane had set negotiations in motion again. When the Palestinian

Commando Martyr Halimeh also failed three days later, all reasons for hope had gone. Soon after this, Schleyer, having been held hostage for one and a half months, was murdered in a forest near the Belgian–French border.[41] His corpse was found on 19 October 1977 in the boot of a car in Mühlhausen.

In the agonising tug-of-war between the RAF and the government in the autumn of 1977, it became clear how unpredictable the influence of images can be in such situations. It seems that with the first humiliating Polaroid shot of Schleyer, the kidnappers did not just intend to blackmail the government, but also expected the public to greet their hostage's plight with glee. When this failed they changed their strategy and started building pressure via a wave of compassion for the victim. Yet each picture that bypassed the news blackout and reached the public had an effect that neither the government nor the kidnappers could control. Rarely did this become clearer than after the release of the last video, an extract of which was exceptionally also broadcast on the ARD's *Tagesschau* at 8 p.m. The kidnappers still clung to the desperate hope that their victim's suffering might move important decision-makers. Schleyer, on the other hand, must have already doubted at this point that his face still had exchange value. In the video that was subsequently released, the intended emotional identification with the victim was thus thwarted by Schleyer's self-abandonment (Figure 43). The result was a kind of non-portrait that makes viewers feel close to the person they see, even though the victim's face remains strangely alien, remote and inaccessible. In hindsight, the fact that we know that Schleyer suffered a violent death probably also contributed to the harrowing effect of the video, but in essence this distressingly alienated presence is typical of all hostage photos.

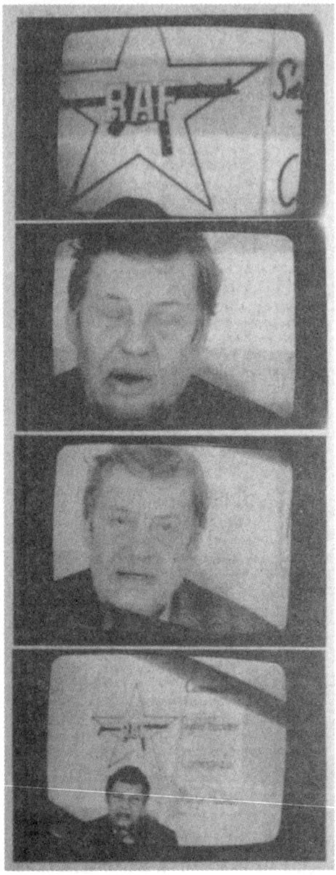

Figure 43 Stills of Hanns Martin Schleyer as hostage of the RAF from a video of 13 October 1977.

None of these images is a media icon of the kind discussed in the previous chapter. They all lack a discernible formal contrast or an iconographic model that would provide an intelligible meaning to a wider public. Nevertheless, even years after a hostage drama, the combination of distance and proximity, which encapsulates the existential suffering of the victims, can still shock. The painfully slow passage of time and the intangibility of space are inscribed forever in these photos. But just as in the attacks, each individual image here only gains its meaning as part of a series. It is not always a change of strategy, as in the Schleyer hostage drama, that constitutes its significance. More often it is

the repetition of similar photos that establishes the meaning. During the longest and largest wave of hostage-takings to date, the numerous abductions of Western citizens in Lebanon between 1982 and 1992, it was precisely the immutability of regularly appearing images that was decisive. Their recurrence seemed to give a sign of hope, one that at the time was of great importance for the victims and their families.

Signs of life in the 1980s: hostage-takings in Lebanon

The events of the autumn of 1977 brought the wave of kidnappings carried out by far-left groups to a close. Only isolated acts were to follow, such as the abduction and murder of the Italian politician Aldo Moro by the Red Brigades in 1978. For the Western media, however, the topic of hostage-takings was far from over.

After Ayatollah Khomeini became the Iranian head of state in 1979, Iran made every effort to export its Islamic Revolution to other Arab countries. Initially it focused on Iraq, but after the Israeli occupation of southern Lebanon in 1982, Iran also supported the Lebanese militia. Forces from the Iranian Revolutionary Guard Corps (IRGC) were sent into Lebanon and the Shi'a group Hezbollah was formed, which over the following years grew into one of the strongest forces in the Lebanese Civil War, not least because of Iran's financial and organisational assistance.[42] Its militia, the Islamic Jihad Organization (IJO), initially attracted international media attention through spectacular suicide attacks using car bombs. The historian Thomas Riegler points out that 'more than 500 people died in the year between November 1982 and November 1983 in a total of five major attacks on American, French and Israeli targets'.[43] The primary goal of

this terror was to force Israel to withdraw from Lebanon, but it also aimed to prevent Western involvement so that Shi'a forces would be able to expand their power within the region. In February 1984, the United States withdrew its troops from Beirut, as did Israel one year later. Despite this, the threat of terror attacks continued unabated. Foreign institutions in Beirut and elsewhere were targeted, the planes of international airlines hijacked and car bombs detonated. Above all, numerous Western citizens were taken hostage.

Today, the kidnappings in Lebanon are almost forgotten, even though they represented the largest wave of hostage-takings in history to date. Between 1982 and 1992, more than thirty Western citizens (mostly American, British and French) were kidnapped by various Shi'a terror groups. As the kidnappers' demands were frequently unclear, many abductions lasted for years. In most cases, their aim was to force the release of Hezbollah activists from Israeli and French prisons.[44] However, as Salah Khalaf, a leading member of the Palestinian Liberation Organisation (PLO), stated on 21 February 1987 in the *Washington Post*, the taking of hostages also served as '"protection" against feared retaliation by the United States, Syria or "any other Arab or non-Arab force"'.[45] The large number of hostages presumably functioned as a shield against possible attacks, as nobody knew exactly where the hostages were hidden and no Western government could risk recklessly jeopardising their lives.

None of the states involved ever officially confirmed that the kidnappers' demands were met. While individual hostages were occasionally released in unexplained circumstances, for many others the agony of imprisonment lasted several years. The American AP correspondent Terry Anderson, for example, was missing for nearly seven years; Thomas Sutherland, dean of the American University

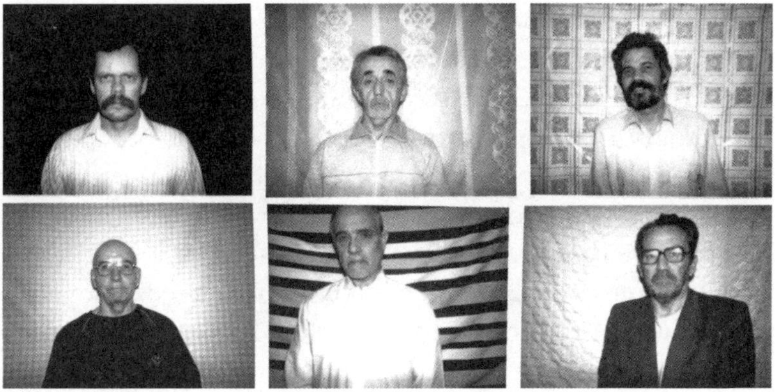

Figure 44 Photos of six hostages, Lebanon, 1985.

of Beirut, for almost as long; the British journalist John McCarthy was held for nearly five years; and the hostage negotiator of the Church of England, Terry Waite, for nearly four. The AP image archives contain a photo of six hostages that was sent to the news services in Beirut in 1985 (Figure 44). Terry Anderson can be seen top left. Below him is the Presbyterian missionary Benjamin Weir, who was released shortly afterwards, as was the priest Lawrence Martin Jenco, whose image appears next to Weir's. In the middle of the top row is the Central Intelligence Agency (CIA) station chief William Buckley, his face already marked by the harsh conditions of his imprisonment and torture; he was to die soon afterwards.[46] To Buckley's right is Thomas Sutherland, and below him David Jacobson, director of the American University Hospital in Beirut. With the exception of Buckley, all the captives look composed, confident, almost defiant, and not as if they had been demonstratively humiliated in front of the camera.

Over the years, images such as these and similarly staged video messages were sent to the media at irregular intervals.

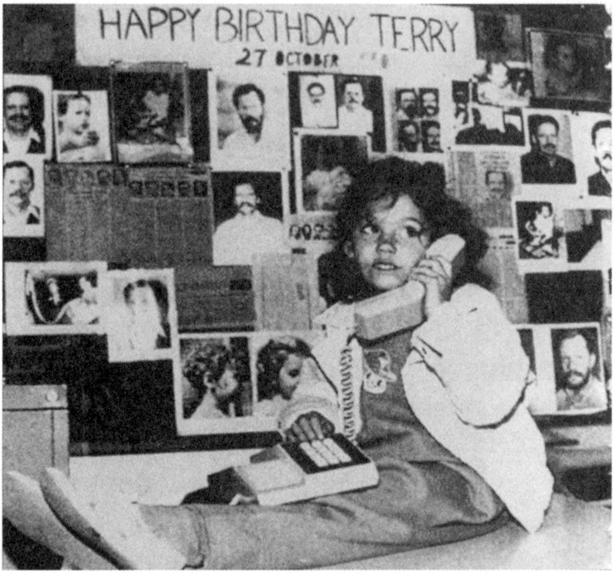

Figure 45 Terry Anderson's daughter in his office in Beirut in 1990.

An image in Anderson's 1993 memoirs reveals how many photographs of him were taken and occasionally published over the long years of his imprisonment.[47] It shows his daughter in front of a pinboard covered with newspaper clippings and photos (Figure 45), a montage created in 1990 to mark his forty-third birthday. It was supposed to convey best wishes to Anderson in his captivity, which at that point had already lasted for five and a half years, and incorporated pictures of the time prior to his kidnapping. Also included are photographs of his daughter as well as at least six newspaper articles – some with, some without images – that discussed the hostages' fate. Anderson does not mention in his memoirs whether this image actually reached him at the time, but that he included it in his autobiography suggests that it did have the desired effect, albeit perhaps retrospectively.

For someone who must have been afraid of being forgotten, even the photographs circulated by the hostage-takers for their own ends constitute important signs of life. As the pinboard in Anderson's office shows, family and friends also valued the images as a means of keeping the memory of the hostages alive.

The appropriation was made possible by the relative neutrality of the photos. Unlike other images of hostages, none of these pictures includes a logo or writing on the wall – a sign that the organisations that carried out the abductions remained ambiguous. Hezbollah, which was actually responsible, denied the kidnappings for political reasons. To obscure any clues to the whereabouts of the hostages, the background is draped with various fabrics. Most crucially, however, all visible signs of humiliation and violence have largely been avoided, even though after their release some prisoners reported having been subjected to such treatment.[48]

In contrast to later terror acts by radical jihadists, hardly any violent images demonstrating the kidnappers' power and cruelty emerged during the civil war years in Lebanon. Exceptions are a photograph released by Islamic Jihad on 10 February 1986 showing the corpse of the French sociologist Michel Seurat, and two months later a photograph of the hanged British journalist Alec Collett. In August 1989, a video appeared of the American colonel William Higgins, also hanged, who had been kidnapped in Tyre on 17 February 1988.[49] After the release of this video, a military strike to avenge Higgins's murder was publicly discussed in the United States.[50] However, the simultaneous appearance of images of hostages who were still alive had created an undercurrent of public concern for their fate, making any military intervention in Lebanon politically unfeasible. The

media were subsequently accused of having turned themselves into the perpetrators' accomplices, betraying the nation's interests by publishing the hostage photographs.[51]

It is undeniable that the publication of the photos from Lebanon served the perpetrators' ends. Yet in some cases, like Schleyer's earlier abduction, it was also in the victims' interests. During the long years of secret negotiations, their fate risked being forgotten. The images offered a way of communicating both to their families and to the public that the hostages were still alive and in the world, even though the message was conveyed according to the terms of the tormentors and in their visual language.[52] Despite this, the media would eventually have lost interest in the comparatively uneventful hostage crisis in Lebanon had it not been for the determined lobbying by family members in all the countries affected. The images circulated by the perpetrators served all of them as a valuable resource in their struggle for attention.[53] Yet in the end, the hostages were freed not because of public pressure on their governments to act, but because Iran had been weakened militarily and financially by its war with Iraq, and Lebanon had become isolated when Syria, too, joined the international coalition against Saddam Hussein in the autumn of 1990. The last hostages, the German citizens Thomas Kemptner and Heinrich Stübig, were released in June 1992.[54]

As the protracted hostage drama in Lebanon shows, photos in the media may deprive governments of scope for action, but in some circumstances they can also serve to keep the victims alive. This is especially the case if they are not produced to humiliate or degrade the hostages. There was certainly no need for US news channels to have shown the video of Higgins's hanging in order to keep public attention focused on the suffering of the other prisoners. The portraits

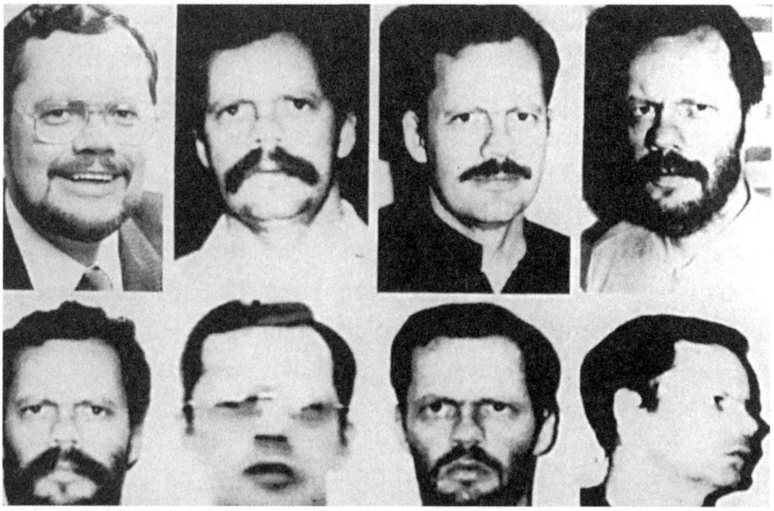

Figure 46 Eight photos of Terry Anderson shortly before and after he was taken hostage in Lebanon between 1985 and 1991.

offer little to curious eyes, but their repeated publication is an indispensable reminder of the abducted individuals' existence. Anderson included a compilation of eight images in his recollections of his captivity, beginning with a photo taken just before his abduction and ending with a hostage photo almost seven years later (Figure 46).[55] Sometimes he is wearing glasses, sometimes not; sometimes he has a beard, sometimes not. Otherwise, the images hardly vary. Even the wall in the background, covered with different fabrics, is scarcely discernible. It is not the changing visual language that is crucial here, as in the Schleyer kidnapping, but the repetition of a recognisable face. It preserves the memory of a person who might otherwise be forgotten with the passing of time. The portraits were able to fulfil this function precisely because all parties had a reasonable interest in the victims' survival – a pact that only ended at the beginning of

the twenty-first century, when radical Sunni organisations abducted people not in order to negotiate, but to kill them in front of the camera.

Involuntary complicity in the early twenty-first century: the decapitation videos of Al-Qaida and IS

In hostage-takings, technical conditions of image production play a much greater part than in other attacks. Already in the 1970s kidnappings, the available technology assumed a crucial role. The invention of the Polaroid camera allowed the perpetrators to circulate images without delay and without the additional risks that elaborate laboratory equipment might involve. Affordable versions became available on the market from 1965 onwards. In the early 1970s, transportable video recorders and players followed, which were first used by the RAF in the abduction of Schleyer. In the early twenty-first century, digital recording devices, the internet and social media finally offered new ways of publishing images. It was not long before radical jihadists embraced these new opportunities, having previously tried in vain to release their images via traditional Western media outlets.

In the 1980s, the Lebanese Islamic Jihad had occasionally released photographs of murdered hostages. Each time, their publication had led to a public outcry in the West and – as in the case of the video of Higgins's hanging – to a highly controversial debate in the media. But when the American-Israeli journalist Daniel Pearl was kidnapped in Pakistan in January 2002 by an organisation associated with Al-Qaida, not a single Western news organisation would broadcast the video. The perpetrators subsequently uploaded it to the internet, so that its content – it showed

the dead man's throat being cut with a kitchen knife – became public after all.

Thomas Riegler notes that videos of particularly excessive violence towards 'unbelievers' were circulated among radical groups in Bosnia, Algeria and Chechnya from the 1980s onwards, yet none of these were ever published or broadcast by Western media, and they were 'usually only available "on the quiet" ... within militant Islamist congregations'.[56] This changed abruptly after the video showing the desecration of Pearl's corpse. From now on perpetrators did not even attempt to reach the Western media, but posted the images directly online. In spring 2004, the first video of this kind appeared in Iraq, after even the news channel Al Jazeera (which at this point still had links to Al-Qaida) had refused to broadcast it.[57] It showed the shooting of Fabrizio Quattrocchi, an officer of an Italian security company, who had been kidnapped by the Muhajideen 'Green Brigade of the Prophet'. The exceptional cruelty arising from the combination of the politically motivated brutal murder of a defenceless civilian and its recording and publication was outdone two months later when the Iraqi Abu Musab Al Zarqawi, associated with Al-Qaida, decapitated the young American Nick Berg with a knife in front of the camera on 11 May 2004. Within six months, seven more videos of beheadings followed, all staged according to the same pattern and uploaded to Al-Qaida's internet page Al Ansar shortly after the act. 'Most of the pictures were blurred', according to Thomas Riegler,

> but otherwise their staging was 'media-compatible': the kidnappers are masked or wearing headscarves, are dressed in black (like executioners) and present their weapons in a stiff, martial manner. Banners are usually displayed in the background, bearing the group's name and thus contributing

> to the formality of the scene. The prisoners are seated or kneel in the foreground; some of them are presented in orange overalls that symbolise the prison uniforms of Guantanamo and the oppression of Muslims by the West. First comes a lengthy recital of 'offences' and 'crimes'. In the case of an execution, the prisoner is given the opportunity for 'last words', or addresses the audience, pleading with them to fulfil the kidnappers' conditions and enable his release.[58]

The Western media only published excerpts of these recordings, omitting the actual killing. Yet, according to the historian Gerhard Paul, so many people tried to access the Al Ansar website to which the videos were uploaded that after Nick Berg's murder, for example, it was inaccessible for several days.[59]

Ten years later, on 20 August 2014, Islamic State tried to build on this dubious success by uploading a video showing the execution of the American journalist James Foley to the video portal YouTube. Most social networks immediately deleted the video and in the United Kingdom it was banned altogether. Moreover, Western media largely published at most a pixelated still. Despite this, a British survey conducted three days after the video's publication revealed that around 2 per cent of the population had searched for, found and watched the video in its entirety.[60] In the United Kingdom alone, where this could have resulted in criminal proceedings, this amounted to more than 1.2 million people.

Dressed in orange overalls, Foley knelt in front of his black-clad, masked killer in a wide desert landscape against a blue sky. The scene was reminiscent of the Hollywood movie *Seven* (1995) and, much like in a Hollywood film, the act of greatest cruelty – the beheading itself – was not shown.[61] While the execution videos from Iraq used the pseudo-authenticity of the blurred hand-held camera image,

the video of Foley's beheading was marked by a filmic perfection that is typical of all IS propaganda images.[62] Further videos of this kind soon followed, culminating in a recording of February 2015, which showed the Jordanian pilot Muath al-Kasasbeh being burned alive in an iron cage.

The journalist Carolin Emcke argues that we need to expose ourselves to such images in order to understand the all-too-human nature of these violent acts.[63] This may apply to exceptional cases in which the photographs or videos came about more or less by chance, but that is decidedly not the case here. There is no stumbling, no clumsiness on the part of the perpetrator in the video of Foley's execution – nothing is shown that does not form part of the faceless murderers' rigorous plan. Far from it: the recording is not a form of expression, but the real reason for the killing. The victim needed to die so that the video could be made. His death is the precondition for its existence. The same goes for each new escalation. Whenever the shock effect threatened to wear off, new, even more drastic violence was required, until the attention threshold had become so high that the only possible course of action was a change in strategy, as pursued by IS in its destruction of ancient monuments in the Syrian oasis town of Palmyra.[64] While other photos of hostages can help to keep the victims alive, the martial act of destruction is the sole purpose of execution videos. The public desecration of the kidnapped individuals' bodies aims only to demonstrate revenge, increasing the perpetrators' fame within their own camp and sowing horror among the enemy. The medieval tradition of *pittura infamante*, defamatory images used to publicly humiliate people, re-emerges with greater cruelty than ever in these videos. Every click on the respective internet pages, each viewing of the recordings, incites more such acts of terror. For this reason, the

present text shows none of these images. They turn their viewers into unwilling accomplices and lead to murder. Yet they too are distant and abstract images – echoes from a no-man's land with masked perpetrators and victims who have become alien, however close and direct the shock of cruelty may be.

Media events: plane hijackings of the Popular Front for the Liberation of Palestine in the 1970s

In the past, images of hostages were often more than a means for the kidnappers to bolster their extortionate demands. They were a sign of life and thus of hope for the victims and their families, reminding the world of the hostages' existence. In the decapitation videos of Al-Qaida and IS, by contrast, the kidnapped person's death is the precondition for the creation of the images. It thus seems more apt to compare execution videos with images of attacks rather than with other photographs of hostages. In this sense they are also similar to the propagandistic aim pursued by the spectacular aircraft hijackings of the 1970s. Here, too, the main focus was maximum visibility in the media and not strategic underground action, as in other hostage-takings.

After the Six-Day War with Israel, it was primarily Palestinian groups that used the general media interest in aeroplane disasters to draw the world's attention to their people's terrible suffering. There had been politically motivated hijackings before – in 1931, during a military putsch in Peru, rebels captured a plane to drop propaganda leaflets across the country, and subsequently air piracy was used mainly in escapes to and from Cuba and from the countries of the Eastern Bloc. Yet according to the cultural historian Annette Vowinckel, none of these hijackings employed 'the

enhancing power of audiovisual coverage' as part of its strategy.[65] This changed on 23 July 1968, when members of the Marxist-Leninist PFLP hijacked an Israeli El-Al plane on its way from Rome to Tel Aviv, forcing it to land in Algeria (then still nominally at war with Israel), where it was met by a television team summoned to the location.

An even more spectacular operation took place two years later, when PFLP members managed to gain control of several airliners simultaneously on 6 and 7 December 1970. Once again, the media had already been notified when two planes – a third followed later – landed at the former British military airport of Dawson's Field in the North Jordan desert. An international press conference was held there the very next morning.[66] Using a loudspeaker, the PFLP's press spokesman Abu Sharif demanded that prisoners be released, and the press were permitted to ask both him and the hostages questions from a distance of twenty metres. On the evening of 12 September, six days after the first hijacking, the evacuated planes were suddenly blown up (Figure 47). News channels had already broadcast special reports soon after the hijackings, but it was only once the British news channel ITN was called to the desert airstrip and filmed the explosions live that the world's attention was drawn to the events. To this day, the images that resulted from the destruction of the three airliners remain the most spectacular in the history of plane hijackings.

However sensational the images were, they remained one-offs. Hijacked planes are airborne most of the time, so camera teams can only film them during stopovers – and even then, they are normally behind barriers and a long way off. Although hijackers do not act covertly, as in other hostage-takings, and leverage the media's interest in current events to draw attention to their political concerns in

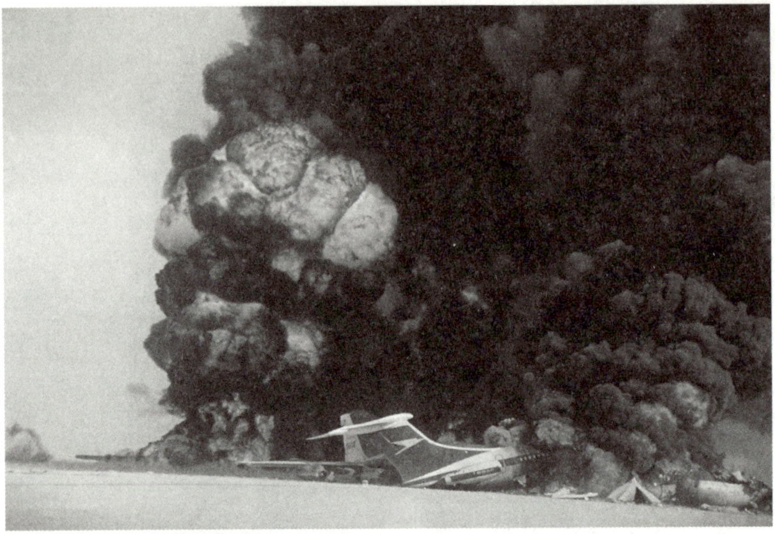

Figure 47 Hijacked aircraft exploding on Dawson's Field in the Jordan desert on 12 September 1970.

order to force governments to act, images of these events are hardly ever dramatic. The fate of the people on board and their suffering remained – until recently – more or less invisible.

A hijacking by the Japanese Red Army six months before the dramatic explosions at Dawson's Field was more typical in this respect. Here, too, the events were partly broadcast live on television, 'with the result that the streets of Japan were', according to Vowinckel, 'as empty as during a major sports event'.[67] Still, many of the pictures that could be seen were unremarkable. One, for example, showed the plane behind a wire-mesh fence during its first stop on the runway at Fukuoka. The exception is a photo taken during the release of the women, children and elderly passengers, which attracted interest mainly because it also showed one of the kidnappers standing in the door of the plane armed

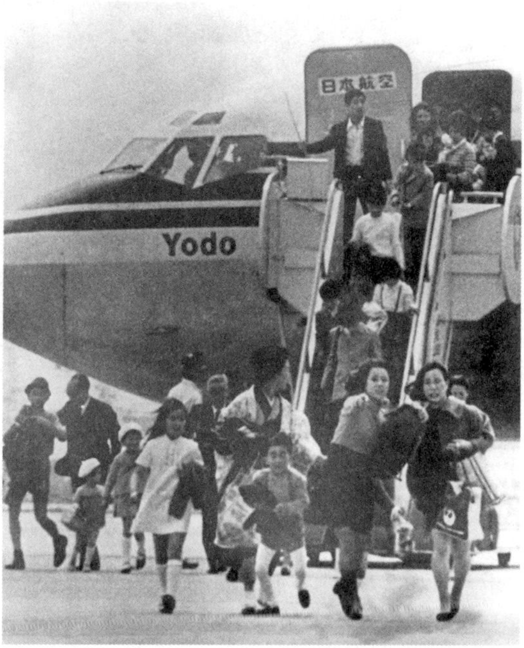

Figure 48 Release of the hostages at Fukuoka airport in Japan on 31 March 1970.

with a samurai sword (Figure 48). However, the public did not see the remaining hostages, and they also missed the most curious part of the hijacking somewhat later: because the hostage-takers had demanded that they be allowed to continue their flight to Communist North Korea, the Japanese authorities disguised Seoul airport in South Korea as North Korean and re-routed the plane there.[68] 'Only a few minutes after landing did the kidnappers realise that they were in South Korea,' writes Vowinckel, 'supposedly because they noticed the lack of larger-than-life images of the dictator Kim Il Sung, none of which could be obtained in South Korea, as their possession was a punishable offence.'[69] In contrast to the PFLP plane hijackings, there was no specially organised

press conference when the hijackers finally landed in North Korea, so that images remained scarce and the kidnappers' identities were reduced to a series of mugshots.

Similarly, most images of the hijacking of the Lufthansa plane 'Landshut' in October 1977 by the Palestinian martyr Halimeh Commando – an event reported in great detail by the West German media and hence deeply embedded in German memory – were initially only taken from a distance. The plane, which was supposed to fly holidaymakers from Palma de Mallorca to Frankfurt, was hijacked on 13 October by two men and two women belonging to the PFLP. The hijackers hoped not only to draw attention to the plight of the Palestinian people, but also to lend support, as was mentioned before, to the RAF's hostage-taking of Hanns Martin Schleyer, where success seemed increasingly unlikely.

At the first stopover in Rome, the only opportunity to photograph the plane on the ground was once again through a wire-mesh fence (Figure 49). 'In the foreground of a photo distributed through AP, there are several cars and individuals who could be onlookers or journalists', Annette Vowinckel speculates.[70] Images of the next stop in Dubai, where the plane was parked in the blazing sun for three days, were even less informative (Figure 50). Several photographs showed no more than the distant aeroplane standing in the shimmering heat of the desert landscape. Only when the air conditioning failed were the crew finally permitted to open the doors, and thus two images of this stop, which subsequently became famous, showed scenes normally hidden from view. In one of these, the hijackers' leader appears in the open door, wearing a red Che Guevara T-shirt, and in the other, the pilot Jürgen Schumann can be seen, dressed in the white shirt of his uniform (Figure 51).[71]

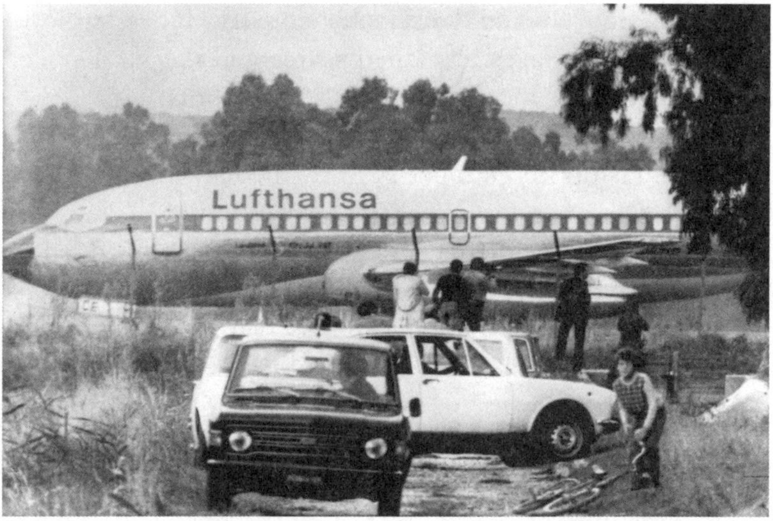

Figure 49 The hijacked Lufthansa plane 'Landshut' during a stopover at Rome airport on 13 October 1977.

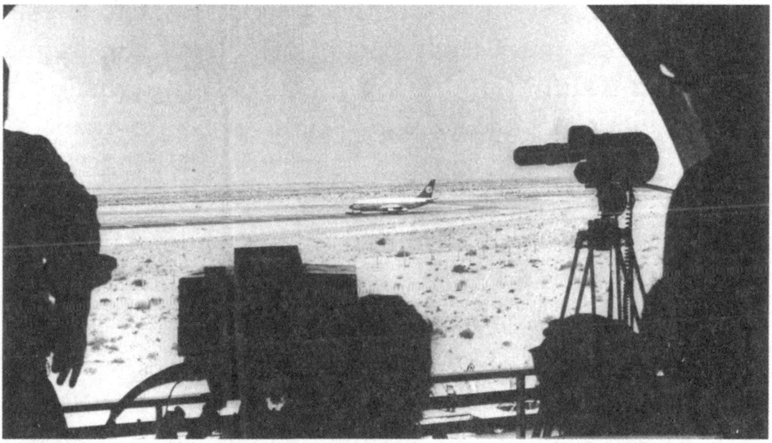

Figure 50 The hijacked Lufthansa plane 'Landshut' during a stopover at Dubai airport on 14 October 1977 (detail).

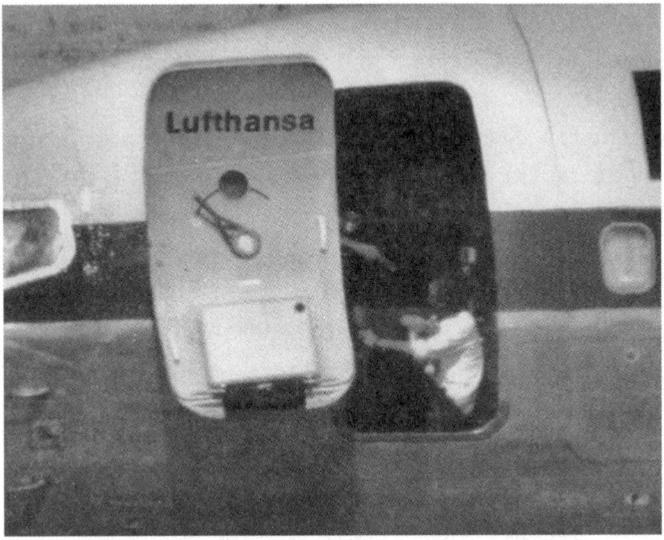

Figure 51 Captain Jürgen Schumann in the open cabin door of the hijacked Lufthansa plane 'Landshut' on 15 October 1977 (detail).

By the last stopover in Aden, a short time later, Schumann was already dead – shot by the hijackers' leader for passing information about the hostages on to the authorities. His body was released down a slide at the rear of the plane the following day.

If this hijacking had gone wrong and the Commando had made real its threats to blow up the aeroplane, the only shots besides these few images would have been of the wreckage – such as those circulating in 1988 after a Pan Am plane was blown up in the air above Lockerbie in Scotland.[72] However, on 18 October 1977 in Mogadishu – the last destination for the 'Landshut' – the German elite unit GSG9 stormed the plane, shot dead three of the four kidnappers and freed all of the hostages. GSG9 had been trained specifically for this purpose and no one had been aware of the unit before the

event. One year previously, the Israeli air force had freed the hostages from a hijacked Air France plane in Entebbe, Uganda, in a controversial operation that led to a complaint before the UN Security Council. Operation Entebbe and the liberation of the 'Landshut' hostages brought the chapter of Palestinian plane hijackings to an end. Instead of a press conference organised by the PFLP, they were followed by the usual images of successfully freed hostages being met at the aeroplane by politicians and then falling, relieved, into their relatives' arms (Figure 52). In Mogadishu, the West German press had been alerted and were present, and

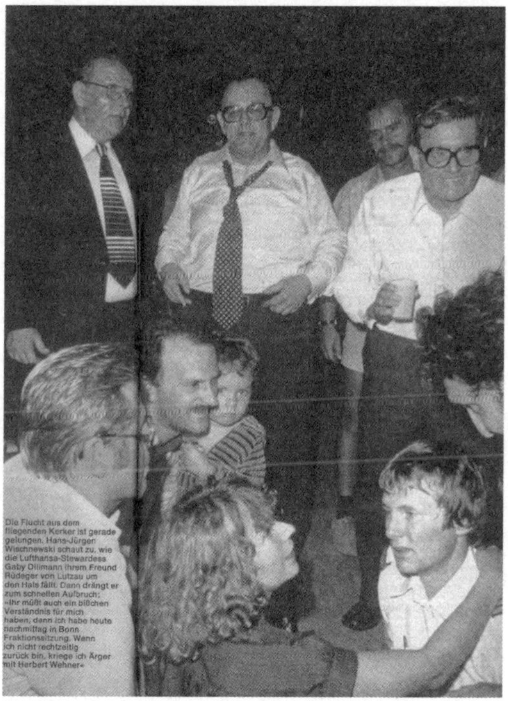

Figure 52 Released hostages on the airfield in Mogadishu on 18 October 1977.

thus the journalists were able to take pictures of the dead Commando members on the runway at the same time as photographing the rescued hostages. The images were published in several journals and newspapers, including *Stern* in its first issue after the events. Readers saw the only surviving hijacker lying on a stretcher, heavily injured but still raising her hand to make the victory sign (Figure 53). Above all, they saw the group's dead leader, outstretched and half naked, on the front cover of the magazine (Figure 54). The images are notable for both their pitiless exposure and their

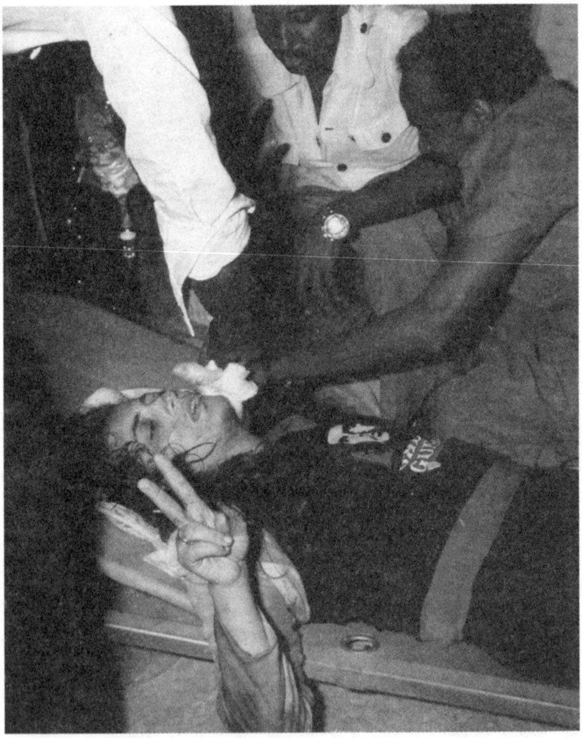

Figure 53 Surviving hijacker after the storming of the Lufthansa plane 'Landshut' in Mogadishu on 18 October 1977.

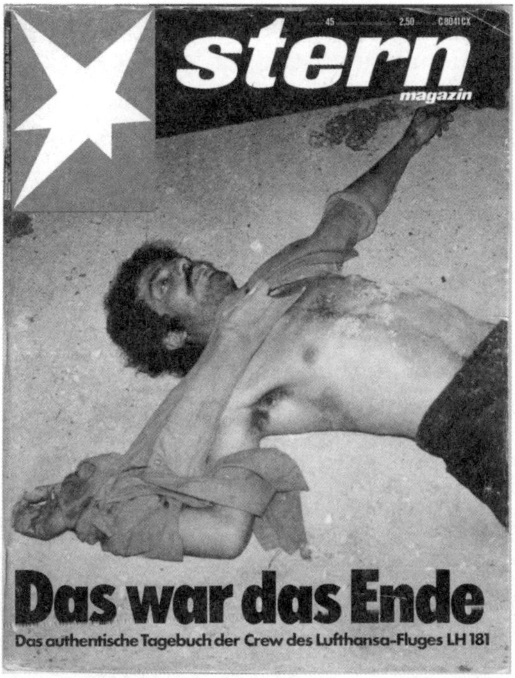

Figure 54 The dead leader of the group on the airfield in Mogadishu on 18 October 1977.

striking aestheticism. The cover picture almost amounts to a retrospective defamatory image, transforming the assassin's corpse into a formal echo of the journal's logo, a blazing white star on a red ground triumphing over the hijacker's blue and grey lifelessness.

Between fact and fiction

When the Belgian artist Johan Grimonprez presented his video installation *Dial-H-I-S-T-O-R-Y* at the documenta X in Kassel in 1997, sensational aircraft hijackings seemed to be a thing of the past. Strict airport security had made

them far more difficult to carry out, and after the end of the Cold War international terror had lost the hinterland that until then had offered a safe place of retreat for planning attacks. At the time of the release nobody could foresee that planes themselves would one day be employed as bombs, and Grimonprez could blithely combine documentary footage of hijackings with scenes from science fiction and disaster movies. He trivialised all of this by adding harmless or surreal shots, such as a deer on a bed in front of flowery wallpaper, a bride and groom underwater and cartoon characters. Accompanied by David Shea's dramatic music and quotes from novels by Don DeLillo, the video suggests that fact and fiction are impossible to distinguish, and that the media are simply offering entertainment when hijackings occur – no more, no less. The video concludes with DeLillo: 'News of disaster is the only narrative people need. The darker the news, the grander the narrative.'[73]

In light of the threats that have arisen in the twenty-first century, this conclusion now seems somewhat disconcerting. However, the void resulting from the lack of news and images during a hostage-taking or hijacking is quickly filled by a host of narratives and media adaptations, creating a wealth of facts and fictions that soon become indistinguishable from one another. Unlike attacks, kidnappings offer the possibility of a happy ending, and afterwards often lend themselves to dramatisations in which the heroes and villains are quickly identified. The course of events itself provides a narrative structure with a clear beginning, dramatic climax and final conclusion. Autobiographies by rescued hostages offer insights into their suffering and resistance,[74] and soon after a hijacking has come to an end, all the details of the drama unfolding in the cabin can usually be experienced on the big or small screen. The Entebbe kidnapping

and rescue were reconstructed in three documentary dramas within a few months.[75] Similarly, the occupation of the American embassy in Tehran has been made into a film twice,[76] as has the hijacking and storming of the 'Landshut' in Mogadishu.[77] The scenes that took place on United Airlines flight 93 before it crashed in Pennsylvania on 11 September 2001 have also already been retold (with varying degrees of accuracy) in five films.[78]

Occasionally, the documentary film versions use original footage that was not published during the events themselves. The leader of the Commando that hijacked the 'Landshut', for example, borrowed a passenger's camera and photographed the pilot Jürgen Schumann (who was later murdered), the co-pilot Jürgen Vietor and two stewardesses, telling them to 'keep smiling'. Heinrich Breloer tracked down these images for his 1997 film reconstruction of events, and thus we are suddenly able to see faces that still reflect all of the situation's tension and uncertainty, many years after the rescue of Mogadishu.[79]

We can assume that in the future photos such as these will become public during and not after kidnappings, as nowadays nearly every mobile phone is also a recording device with internet access. In the case of the United Airlines plane that crashed in Pennsylvania on 11 September 2001, there were live recordings of announcements and phone conversations, which formed the basis for later documentaries and docudramas.[80] In the films the ordeal and suffering of the hostages have been visualised so extensively that the events, which originally seemed distant, have been transformed into close experiences that make it difficult to distinguish between fact and fiction. There has always been a gulf between our quest for truth and our ignorance of the facts, a gap that is quickly and easily filled with projections.

How much they dominate the imagery of terror is particularly obvious in the stereotypical depictions of the enemy that circulate during and immediately after an assault and in the self-presentations of the perpetrators – the subject of the next chapter.

Chapter 3

Images of perpetrators: from wanted posters to propaganda videos

In the autumn of 2011, posters appeared in the streets of Berlin advertising an exhibition entitled *The Uncanny Familiar: Images of Terror* at the C/O Berlin gallery.[1] They showed a black-clad man standing on a balcony, wearing a balaclava, looking menacing yet strangely familiar (Figure 55). There was something deeply unsettling about him. Some images of terror are, to borrow the ambivalent title of the exhibition, 'uncannily familiar' and, as the previous chapters have shown, the repertoire of such images is surprisingly limited. Only a few are still remembered years later, discussed in academic research or even turned into artworks. The image of the man on the balcony is one of them.

The Berlin poster was based on a photograph from 2001, for which the Austrian group of artists G.R.A.M. had re-enacted a famous image from the attack on the Israeli delegation during the 1972 Olympic Games in Munich. The original photo of a man wearing a balaclava had been taken by Kurt Strumpf on 5 September and subsequently sent to the photo agency AP (Figure 56). As the re-enacted G.R.A.M. photo and the Berlin exhibition poster show, to this day Strumpf's image seems to epitomise

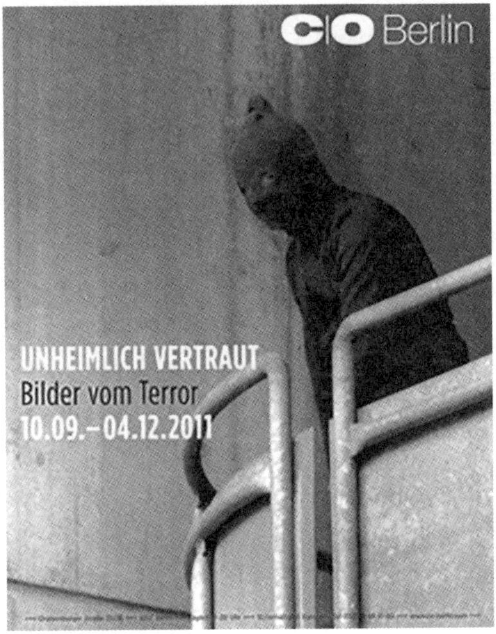

Figure 55 Exhibition poster, C/O Berlin 2011.

the vague feeling of threat and anxiety that accompanies terror attacks.

In the early hours of 5 September 1972, eight members of a Palestinian terror group entered the lodgings of the Israeli Olympic team, shot dead two athletes and took nine hostages. The Olympic Games in Munich was the first major international sports event to be broadcast live on television, and there were numerous press photographers and journalists on the scene, as well as several thousand TV reporters and camera people.[2] By midday, the attackers had issued several ultimatums. Israel was not prepared to meet the kidnappers' demands to release Palestinians jailed in Israeli prisons, so negotiations were difficult. Most of the action took place at the entrance to the Olympic Village. The leader of

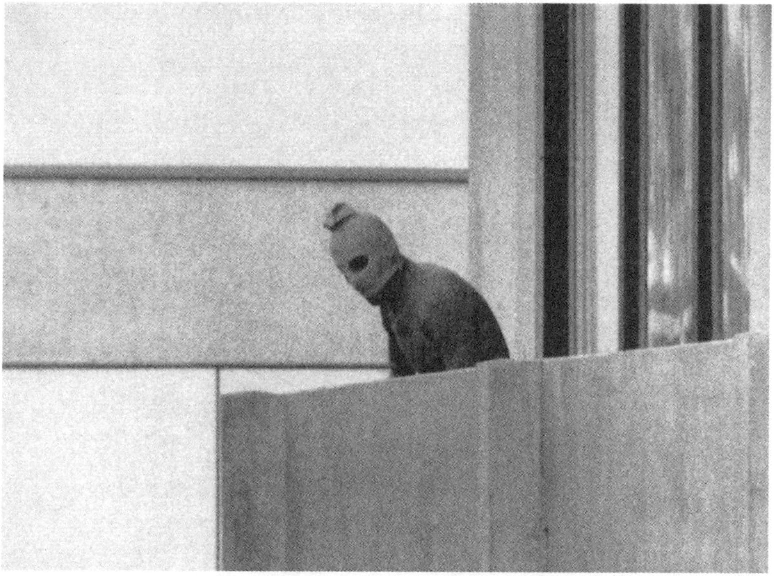

Figure 56 A masked hostage-taker on the balcony of the Israeli apartments in the Olympic Village in Munich on 5 September 1972. Kurt Strumpf.

the group, known by his code name Issa, posed confidently for the cameras each time he came to the door. 'His face is ... blackened', *Stern* magazine reported soon after:

> He wears sunglasses and a white hat. In the chest pockets of his safari suit are two clearly visible hand grenades. The safety levers hang over the edges of the shirt pockets. In his right hand, he holds a third grenade, ready to pull the pin. In fluent German he says to the policeman: 'Stay where you are. You can see what I have here.'[3]

For most of the time, however, there was little happening and the assembled press and a growing number of onlookers stood waiting at the perimeter fence of the Olympic village. It was only in the late afternoon that things suddenly started moving again. With a naivety that seems

astonishing in hindsight, a police unit took up position on the roof of the adjoining building to prepare an assault, seemingly ignorant of the fact that not only people on the scene but also the public and thus the kidnappers could see them on their TV screens.[4] When the kidnappers then threatened to kill their victims, the planned assault had to be stopped at around 6 p.m. The photo of the masked man on the balcony was taken soon after, and it came to symbolise the dark, mindless menace of terror, all the more so since another attempt to free the athletes that same night also failed dramatically. The kidnappers and their victims were killed in a German police operation on the nearby Fürstenfeldbruck airfield.

As the media scholars Klaus Forster and Thomas Knieper noted, Strumpf 'was not the only one who pressed the shutter release at this moment but only he was far enough from the balcony … to capture the masked head exactly between the two horizontal lines traced by the roof of the neighbouring house'.[5] Over the following days, the photo appeared in the international press, and in Germany it made it onto the front pages of the *Frankfurter Allgemeine Zeitung* of 7 September 1972 and *Die Zeit* of 8 September 1972. The G.R.A.M. re-enactment on the C/O Berlin poster lacks the original's perfect architectural framing. The lines plunge more steeply, sinuous architectural features typical of the 1970s have been added, the face mask has become black, and instead of blank, dark eye sockets there are now eyes gazing at the viewer. The message is clear: terror is anonymous, and even years after an event it remains incomprehensible and frightening and can be repeated anywhere and anytime. Thus the artists' re-enactment reinforces the vague fear that unknown perpetrators appearing out of nowhere might suddenly strike.

It is an abstraction that lacks depth and detail, particularly since it has been stripped of history. What is obliterated, for example, is that the Munich massacre was a result of political developments in the early 1970s, and that at the time the perpetrators and their aims were very far from being unknown. Newspapers reported that Fatah had trained the underground terror group Black September, who committed the attack in Munich in revenge for the expulsion and murder of Palestinians in Jordan after the aircraft hijackings of 1970. A prime motive was to draw attention to all those people who had become stateless in the process.[6] The members of Black September did not act on impulse, driven to despair by Israel's treatment of the Palestinians, but were experienced secret service agents of a well-known Palestinian political organisation pursuing a clear strategy which was hardly a secret.

An effective stereotype creates an abstraction of the enemy that is detached from historical and social reality, and although these stereotypical images are fed by concrete experiences, their emotional power draws on known patterns that only need updating. As Sybil Wagener explains, the stereotype, contrary to an actually existing enemy, is 'part of a "virtual" conception made up of words and ideas. It is initially nothing more than a projection, a collective phantasm.'[7] The personal characteristics and motivations of a real adversary must be pushed aside and made obscure, so that the evil that is thus identified remains vague and mysteriously threatening, and may justify security measures and restrictions of civil rights and liberties that would not have been enforceable under normal circumstances.

After the 9/11 attacks, for example, it became obvious that not all available images of the enemy were suited for this purpose. The then most wanted person in the US,

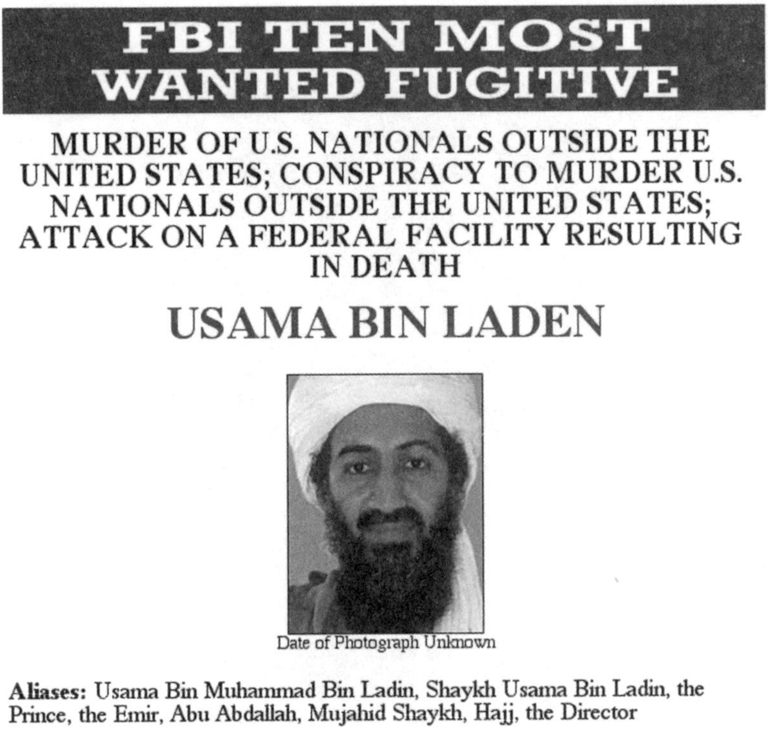

Figure 57 Osama bin Laden on an FBI wanted poster from 1999.

Osama bin Laden, had already featured on an FBI poster in 1999. He appeared as a man with a turban and beard, facing the camera with a steady gaze and a serene smile (Figure 57). At this time bin Laden was wanted for attacks on US embassies in Tanzania and Kenya in August 1998 during which 200 people were killed. After 9/11 similarly benign pictures of him continued to appear in Western media and on wanted posters. They were mostly stills taken from video messages in which the leader of Al-Qaida addressed his followers and the *ummah*, the worldwide community of Muslims.[8] Since none of these was suitable as a stereotype, the image

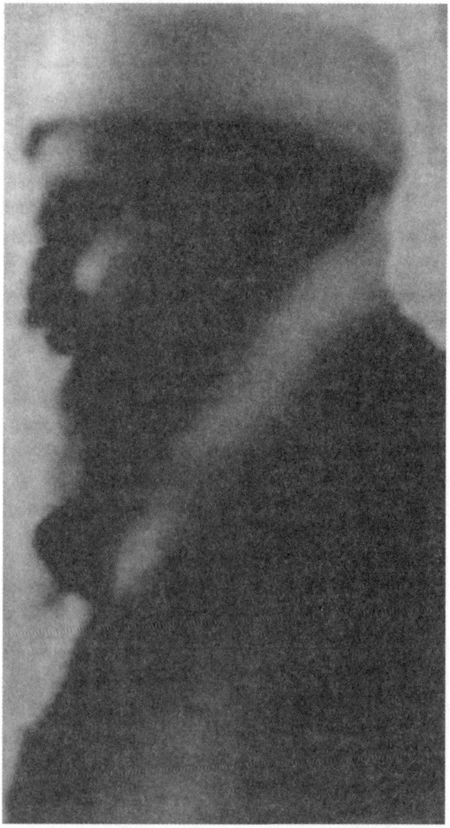

Figure 58 Osama bin Laden in the *New York Times* of 16 December 2001.

published by the *New York Times* on 16 December 2001 and a little later by the German tabloid *Bild* and other newspapers reduced him to a dark, threatening and shadowlike being, an abstract template of evil (Figure 58).[9]

Stereotyping the enemy initially fulfils two contradictory functions: it makes adversaries seem disproportionately powerful and at the same time it diminishes them. According to Sybil Wagener, this is 'part of the conditioning

for the attack in so far as it morally exonerates [us]', for it affirms that the enemy is 'worse than us'.[10] In the case of Osama bin Laden, this helped to legitimise a major military intervention in Afghanistan. It took no more than two months to defeat the Taliban regime,[11] but the Al-Qaida leader would remain the most wanted man for another ten years, until on 2 May 2011 he was tracked down and shot dead by the US special operations force Navy SEALs in his house in Abbottabad in Pakistan.

With his death, the disproportionate power of his image disappeared. Instead, abasement and humiliation came to the fore, and the urge for revenge and retaliation was given free rein. Just a few days after the news that bin Laden was dead, a clamour of voices in the media demanded to see the photo of his body (see Introduction). But even if the US government had released such an image – and there were good reasons for not doing so, as we will see at the end of this chapter – the picture would, contrary to the claims, certainly not have shown the true face of the murderer either.[12] A photograph of the dead body of bin Laden would not have revealed any more or any less than what remains of a human being shortly after the moment of a violent death.

Yet, just how great the need is to abase and humiliate the perpetrators after an attack was revealed by images that circulated in the media following the November 2015 attacks in Paris. The attacks themselves had produced scarcely any iconic images. There was very little to be seen apart from the rescue work at the five locations that had come under fire. Over the following days, strikingly symbolic images that visualised grief and resistance began to appear, such as the Eiffel Tower illuminated in the French national colours. Other images also became well known, among them a drawing of the peace symbol with the Eiffel Tower in its

centre that had gone viral on social media, and photos of red and white roses that people had placed in bullet holes. Some of the attackers were still on the run and the situation remained tense. After five days, the alleged mastermind of the group, Abdelhamid Abaaoud, was tracked down in the Paris suburb of Saint-Denis, but since he was killed during the raid and no photo was taken, there were no significant images of him that could be circulated. This gap was filled by a photo that appeared in the international media the next day. It showed the naked buttocks of a suspected supporter who had been arrested soon after the raid, surrounded by heavily armed security forces who had stripped him to check his body for explosives (Figure 59).[13] Although

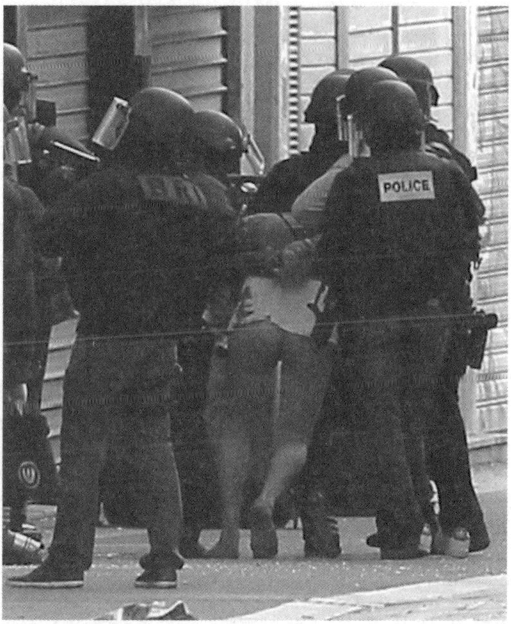

Figure 59 An arrest in the Paris suburb of Saint-Denis on 18 November 2015.

it lacks the distortions that rendered the face of bin Laden so diabolical, this image, too, is a stereotype. It presents the alleged adversary in an ignominious and above all anonymous way, without any new or important information. Its release merely served to satisfy pent-up feelings of revenge.

Images of this kind are clearly of very little help in the fight against terror. As early as the 1970s, Walter Laqueur, the pioneer of terrorism research, had noted that a large majority of those who carry out terror attacks are not motivated by mindless hatred. Most of them come from educated backgrounds, and their actions are usually based on a calculated, strategic choice.[14] This is also true for radical Salafi organisations such as Al-Qaida and Islamic State (IS). The journalist Christoph Reuter has shown that most of the strategic leaders of IS in Iraq and Syria were well-trained former secret service functionaries of Saddam Hussein whose actions were based on power calculations rather than religious convictions.[15] What is striking, however, is that within IS there are far fewer graduates among those trained for combat and sent to the West than in any previous terror group, including Al-Qaida. A recent study found that a relatively high proportion of IS perpetrators came from a petty criminal milieu and precarious living conditions. Religiosity seems to be a consequence of choosing violence rather than its cause.[16]

A decade earlier, the political scientist Tore Bjørgo concluded, on the basis of a significant number of studies concerning the personality profiles of politically motivated perpetrators, that the actions of terror recruits are mostly rational and intentional, and that they are motivated by political goals developed in interaction with different ideologies and groups.[17] Upon close examination of their backgrounds, their motives appear comprehensible even if the

actions themselves cannot be justified. As more recent research has repeatedly shown, the idea that anonymous terror is driven by meaningless hatred and ideological delusion and that attacks are carried out for similarly incomprehensible reasons ultimately only feeds an economy of fear that makes it more difficult to find a political solution for conflicts.[18]

As the cultural theorist Sara Ahmed has argued, emotions such as hatred, fear and contempt are not a private matter when it comes to stereotypes. Societies cultivate, channel and perpetuate these emotions independently of the personal experiences which originally fed into them.[19] It is all the more remarkable, then, that the negative stereotypes discussed so far, which ultimately only serve to regulate collective affects, are not the only images of perpetrators which circulate after terror attacks. They are not even the most dominant ones, but merely constitute one of three variants, which I will discuss in more detail in what follows. Most of the early images on various wanted posters do not project a clear stereotype but are much more ambivalent. After all, the media quite often publish photos taken by the attackers themselves, such as those of the hostage-takings in Tehran or the ones staged by members of the PLPF during aircraft hijackings in the 1970s (see previous chapter). And more often than not, the images contain inherent traces of normality, which persist even if the people shown are perceived as a threat.

Ambivalent images: from wanted posters to surveillance camera footage

Directly after an attack, the affected societies initially have a rational interest in investigating all the details of the

crime. Security forces hunting the perpetrators and trying to understand their motives and backgrounds do not only use forensics, but also try to compile detailed profiles of the attackers and circulate information and wanted photos. The aim is to recruit the populace to help with intelligence-gathering and searching. During the anarchist attacks in the late nineteenth century, police stations in various European countries kept collections of photos of criminals, so-called rogues' galleries.[20] Before this, authorities often used lists of names, descriptive texts and images in various documents, since even in pre-modern times identifying people was important, especially – but not only – if they were criminals.[21] However, it was not until the scientific and technological revolutions of the nineteenth century (and then the twentieth and twenty-first) that new opportunities opened up to meet the challenge of reliable identification.[22]

Although the French criminologist Alphonse Bertillon had already tried to standardise police identification systems at the end of the nineteenth century,[23] showing the perpetrators in two photographs – one frontal, one in profile – and recording physical measurements and later also fingerprints, rogues' galleries and wanted posters of various kinds, assembled largely from private sources, continued to be used.[24] To this day there is no single international standard for communicating descriptions of persons wanted by the police. The photos on wanted posters are only very rarely taken during arrests. Most of them come from commercial photographic studios and were taken before the person depicted had embarked on a criminal career. Some are even private snapshots. After the introduction of passport photos (the first British ones date from 1915), they were also occasionally gleaned from official sources.[25] Since the beginning of the twenty-first century, surveillance camera footage

or images which the wanted individuals have previously posted on social media have also been used.

The variation in imagery on wanted posters is thus simply a result of practical considerations and availability. For the population who are asked to help with the investigations they are, however, a challenge: what people see are ordinary, everyday faces that mostly lack any particularly unusual characteristics. The apparent normality of alleged criminals can be confusing and is at odds with the general public's urge to deduce deviations from the images. The clues needed to identify wanted individuals become particularly blurred when several heads are presented next to each other on the same poster, as was the case during the biggest and most comprehensive manhunt in German history, the search for members of the Red Army Faction (RAF) in the 1970s.

The first document to be circulated in that search was a wanted poster for Ulrike Meinhof (Figure 60). What was unusual about it was the long text stating well-known facts, such as her involvement in the recent escape of Andreas Baader, as well as a detailed – and somewhat superfluous – description of her physique below the photo of her face. At the time, Meinhof was very far from being unknown. As the media and communications scholar Susanne Regener noted, 'there were innumerable public images – but the one that was chosen represents the wanted woman as someone who is herself troubled by her situation'.[26] The choice of this picture mirrored widespread public bewilderment about Meinhof's path from renowned journalist, wife and mother, to a terror activist who in 1970 had just been accused of attempted murder.

Two years later, the Federal Criminal Police Office released a poster showing nineteen suspects, entitled

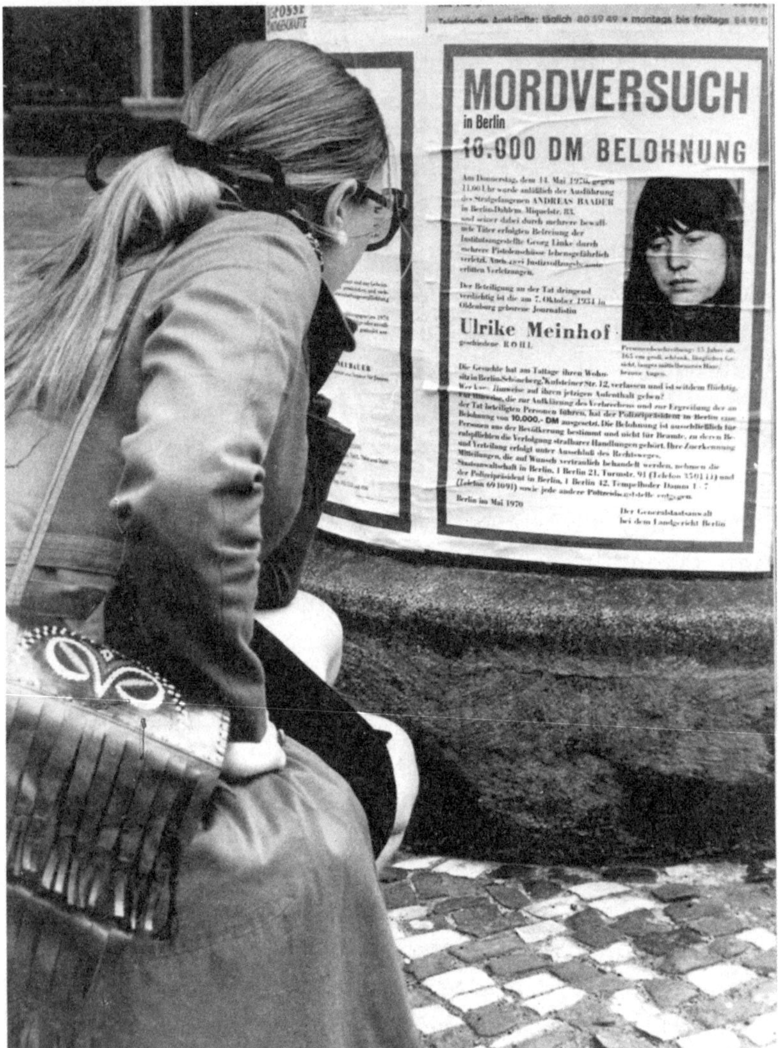

Figure 60 Wanted poster of Ulrike Meinhof on an advertising column in Berlin in the summer of 1970.

Anarchistische Gewalttäter – Baader/Meinhof-Bande (Anarchist criminals – Baader/Meinhof gang; Figure 61). There was very little text, as the space under each photo was just sufficient for the name and date of birth of each wanted individual. The images showed a variety of different portrait types. Some were informal photos, like those of Ulrike Meinhof, Siegfried Hausner, and Andreas Baader. Others were passport photographs from photo booths with or without background curtains – for example, of Bernhard Braun – or professional photo studio images, which showed those depicted, among others Jan-Carl Raspe, with high-contrast lighting and in three-quarter view. This suggests that the Federal Criminal Police Office used very different sources to compile this poster.[27] Only a few images were taken from registered official documents like identity cards or driving licences; others must have come into the possession of the police via friends or family of the wanted individuals.

None of these photos conjured up the image of a dangerous adversary. Since all the photographs had been taken before the individuals portrayed had gone underground, they conveyed an attitude to life that was not marked by fundamental hostility. According to Regener, many of the then 18–25 year-olds had 'long hair and a middle parting … or a fringe like Ulrike Meinhof and Gudrun Ensslin … The young men sported "unkempt, straggly" mid-length hair and often had a beard, like Klaus Jünschke and, on a later wanted photo, Jan-Carl Raspe.'[28] The wanted individuals were not called terrorists but anarchist criminals, so that the terror remained, initially at least, nameless. Only later were posters and handbills headed 'urgently wanted terrorists', but even then the police rarely had their own photos at their disposal.

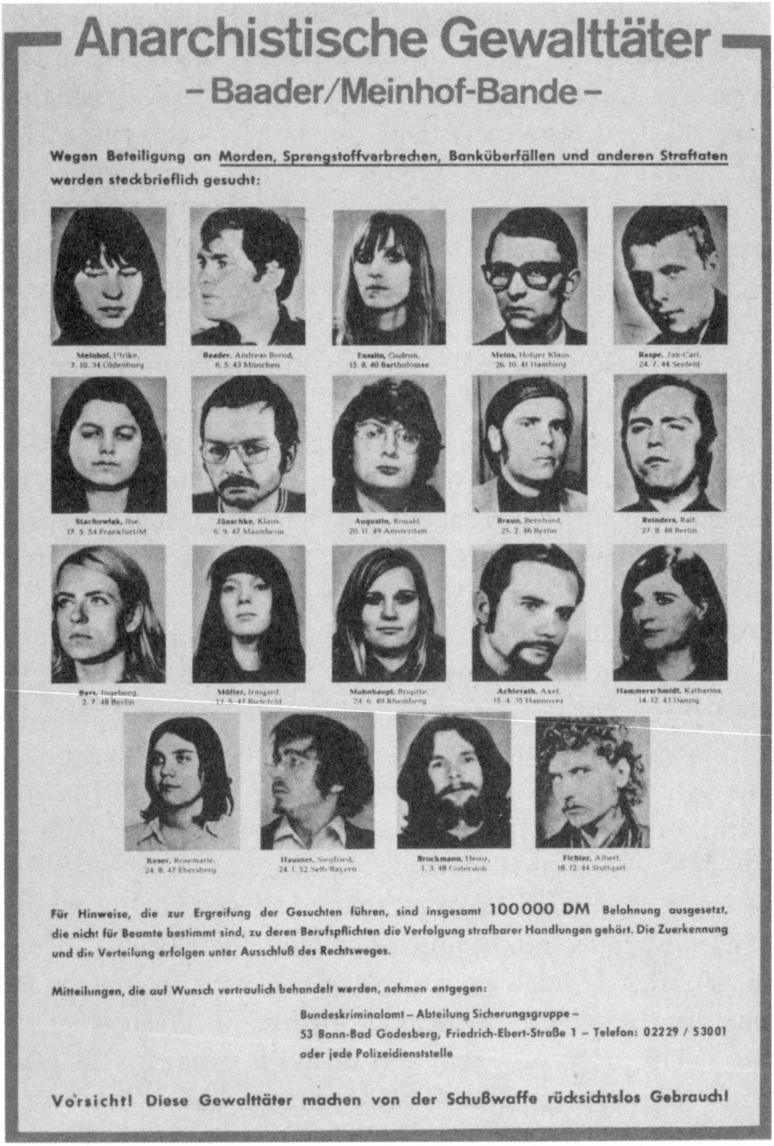

Figure 61 Members of the RAF on a Federal Criminal Police Office wanted poster from 1972.

To this day, the sources from which police obtain photographs for inclusion on wanted posters or release to the press are similarly varied. Sometimes there is only a single image. Often, however, there are more, accompanied by additional information about physical characteristics. In 2009, for example, the Federal Criminal Police Office used three images and a description of the wanted jihadist Houssain Al Malla (Figure 62) that trace his trajectory from a Westernised youth in 2005 to a religious radical in 2007. Yet it is unclear whether the pictures helped to identify him, for the difference between the central one and the two others is so great that it is difficult to find any similarities at all. What this poster did more than anything else was to issue a general warning about the radicalisation of a section of the population. The fact that the three photographs made the wanted person look different each time undermined rather than served the request to the public for help.

During the 1970s manhunts in the Federal Republic of Germany, many young men with long hair and women without blow-dry hairstyles were suspected of being activists or at least sympathisers of the RAF. Pious Muslims with beards and Islamic dress, on the other hand, such as the Lebanese-born Houssain al-Malla, who along with the German-born Salafi Eric Breininger had appeared in propaganda videos for the Islamic Jihad Union and been arrested in 2011 by Turkish police in Izmir,[29] tend to look more intrinsically alien to most non-Muslims in Western societies.[30] The problem is that this makes it easier for the general public to perceive a threat in images that show wanted offenders with religious attributes than in the faces of young people on the RAF wanted posters of the 1970s.

Just how dangerous it can be to deal in rash generalisations and stereotypes in this context was shockingly

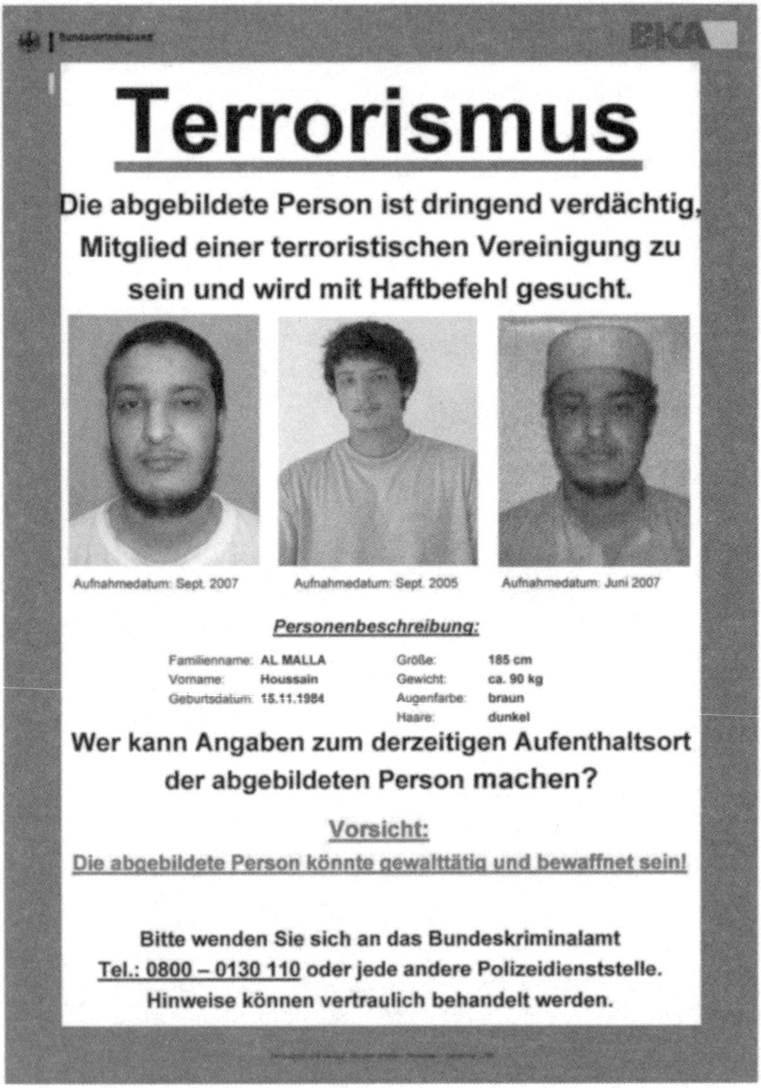

Figure 62 Houssain Al Malla on a Federal Criminal Police Office wanted poster in the autumn of 2009.

demonstrated very soon after the second attempted suicide bombings, allegedly carried out by Al-Qaida, on the London Underground on 21 July 2005. Since the attackers were still on the run and it was feared that they might strike again, the police released surveillance camera footage only a day later, showing the men just before or after the attempted attack (Figure 63). None of that footage was of a

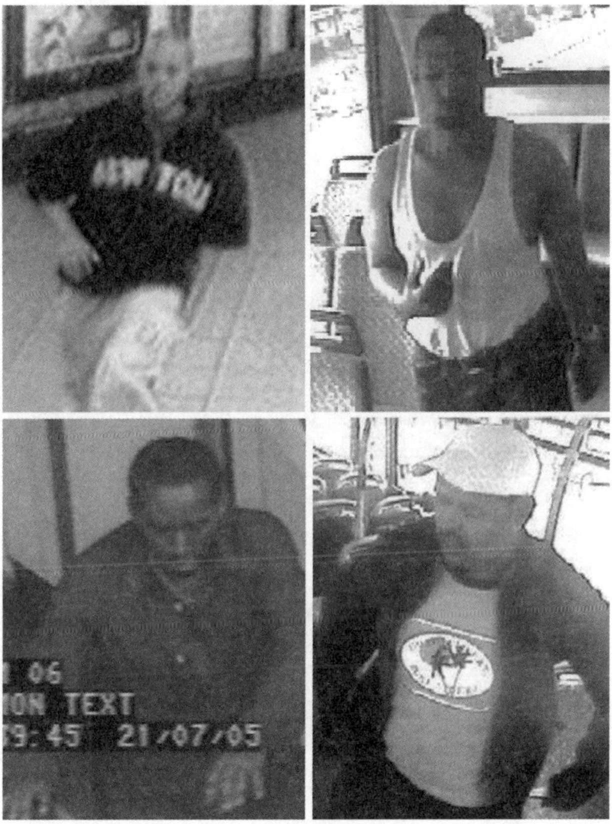

Figure 63 Surveillance camera footage of the perpetrators just before or after their failed suicide bombing attacks in London on 21 July 2005.

brutal man with a fiendish gaze that revealed an intention to kill. Instead, there were images like the one on the top left here, showing a young man with cleanly shaved head and face wearing a black hoodie with lettering and light-coloured baggy trousers, running along the corridors of Oval Underground station. The image next to it shows another attacker in a white vest and dark trousers on a bus. It was one of the many taken by London surveillance cameras, which cover just about every corner of the city.

On the basis of the videos, police were able to reconstruct events almost minute by minute, but when they raided the flat of this suspect, an undocumented migrant in south London, they failed to catch anybody. The image on the bottom right shows one of the attackers wearing a white baseball cap. Shortly after this photo was taken, he detonated a bomb on a double-decker bus in London. The explosion was very small and nobody was injured. He was the first to be identified and hence the CCTV image was soon replaced by an official passport photo. The man in the blue jacket shown on the bottom left has his arm outstretched to his right as if he wanted to jump over a barrier, and his face is blurred by the high-angle shot. Unlike in other images of these men circulated at the same time, there is no visible black rucksack, the best-known common attribute of the perpetrators at the time. During the attacks two weeks earlier, the suicide bombers had transported their bombs in black rucksacks, and the panic and fear of another attack were subsequently so great and the pressure on the police to find the culprits so intense that the next day, an innocent Brazilian, Jean Charles de Menezes, was shot dead at Stockwell tube station by the Anti-Terrorist Branch of the Metropolitan Police. He had the misfortune to be dark-skinned and to be carrying a black rucksack

while running across the platform in his haste to catch a train.[31]

The publication of wanted photos treads a fine line. On the one hand it allows the authorities to show that the state and its security services have not lost control and possess at least a certain amount of information about the perpetrators. On the other, it confronts the public with images of people who are not significantly different from any others in society. As Roland Barthes noted in 1980, the 'portrait-photograph is a closed field of forces':

> Four image-repertoires intersect here, oppose and distort each other. In front of the lens, I am at the same time: the one I think I am, the one the photographer thinks I am, and the one he makes use of to exhibit his art.[32]

The effect of a photographic portrait is thus strongly determined by the context of its creation, which for photographs of wanted persons is rarely hostile, unless they are taken from police sources and show the perpetrator during or soon after an arrest. Even the CCTV footage of the London attackers from shortly before or after the attempted bombings is very similar to much of what is recorded every day. There is thus always the danger that the subject depicted will resemble a significant number of people in the general population, who might then be stigmatised or become suspects. After a terror attack, photos of wanted criminals can give a face to the horror and try to dispel the uncanny feeling of threat. As images suitable for stereotyping the enemy, however, they are useless. What can be seen is mostly very ordinary people from mainstream society, and thus the act of terror either becomes normalised or appears even more mysterious. This ambivalence is then often countered by humiliating images of arrested perpetrators of such overdetermined clarity that

the subjects depicted now seem to be completely deprived of agency, so that their acts become even harder to understand.

Humiliating images: 'A naked terrorist is no longer a threat'

By the late nineteenth century, images of arrested criminals had become part of the standard repertoire of illustrated newspapers. If possible, papers printed images of the arrest and sometimes also the execution which awaited violent anarchists in Russia, France and elsewhere at the end of their trials. As has been argued in the first chapter, they served as confirmation that the state's monopoly of power, shaken by the acts of terror, remained unbroken. But at the same time they also satisfied another, much more irrational desire – the need for humiliation and thus retribution for the suffering that had been experienced.

Until around 1900, images of executions still marked the conclusion of severe political acts of violence. Yet even after the abolition of the death penalty in most Western states in the twentieth century, photographs of defeated assassins have not disappeared from the media. Indeed, some of them are even more extreme in their depiction of humiliation than earlier representations. While the Russian anarchists who assassinated Tsar Alexander II in 1881, sketched in the moment of the last rites, still seemed defiant and thus retained a personal integrity demonstrated by strength of will (see Chapter 1, Figure 7), later images often do not show a similar respect for the integrity of the accused. In contrast to the defiance and dignity demonstrated in images from the end of the nineteenth century, corresponding shots of RAF members from the second half of the twentieth century focus solely on debasement. The French anarchist

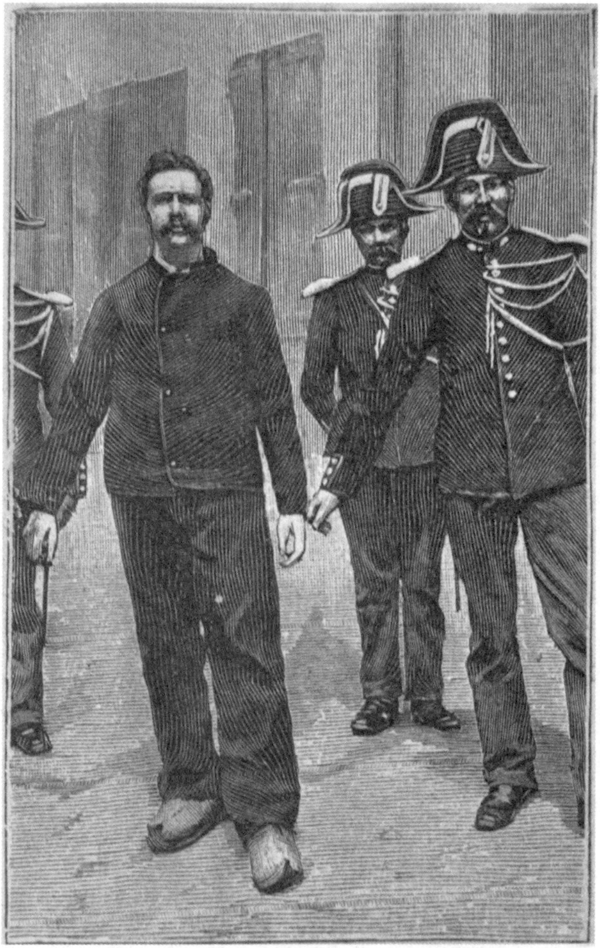

Figure 64 Ravachol in Montbrison prison, July 1892.

Ravachol, for example, looked proud and purposeful in a print based on a photograph that appeared in the press after his arrest (Figure 64).[33] The pictures of the arrests of the leading members of the RAF, on the other hand, testify to a boundless need to humiliate, which today, five decades on, is rather difficult to comprehend.

It remains unclear why the media were present when Andreas Baader, Holger Meins, and Jan-Carl Raspe were arrested in a garage in Frankfurt in the early hours of 1 June 1972.[34] The following day, *Bild* published a photograph of the naked Baader, his genitals skilfully concealed by the chosen frame. The caption read: 'A naked terrorist is no longer a threat' (Figure 65). Meins was shown being led away, also naked and emaciated, his face distorted in a scream. 'After fear of "intelligent but dangerous criminals" had been fomented for months,' writes Andreas Elter,

> the readers were now shown the image of shattered and disoriented terrorists. Meins wears only shoes, socks and underpants in the photos, since the police had ordered him to undress in case he had hidden a weapon or explosives. Baader, who had been shot by a police marksman, had his clothes removed to have his wounds treated. So in these two cases it cannot be implied that the police were trying to humiliate the terrorists in this way since there were practical reasons for stripping them of their clothes.[35]

The images on the front page of *Bild*, however, showed something else and the captions and text, accordingly, fulfilled a different purpose.

Throughout the 1970s, the German media published similarly pitiless images of politically motivated offenders being overpowered by the police. In the previous chapter, the image of the dead hijackers published in *Stern* magazine after the storming of the Lufthansa aircraft 'Landshut' in Mogadishu in autumn 1977 was discussed. Three years later, the same magazine released the now famous police photos of the dead RAF prisoners in Stammheim prison in Stuttgart. We still do not know how they came to be made public.[36] They included an image of Irmgard Möller, who had survived knife wounds to the chest during the deadly

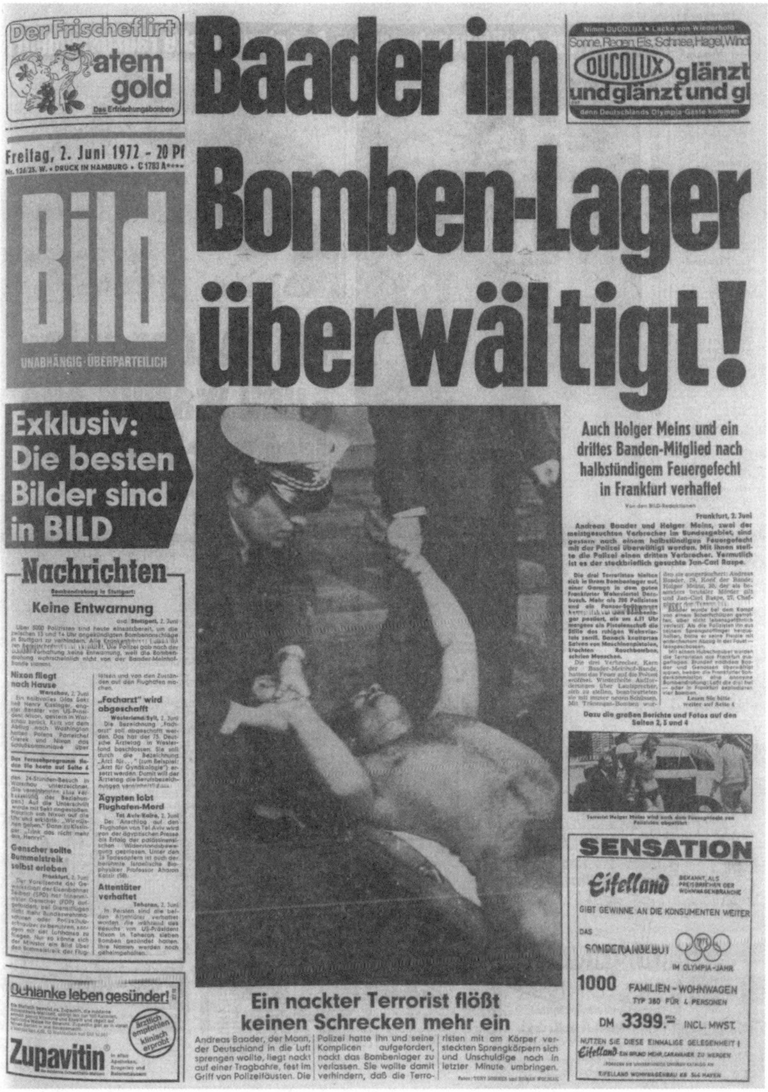

Der Frischeflirt atem gold Das Erfrischungsbonbon

Baader im Bomben-Lager überwältigt!

Freitag, 2. Juni 1972 – 20 Pf

Nr. 126/23. W. • DRUCK IN HAMBURG • C 1783 A

Bild

UNABHÄNGIG · ÜBERPARTEILICH

Nimm DUCOLUX • Lacke von Wiederhold

Sonne, Regen, Eis, Schnee, Hagel, Wind

DUCOLUX glänzt und glänzt und gl

denn Deutschlands Olympia-Gäste kommen

Exklusiv: Die besten Bilder sind in BILD

Auch Holger Meins und ein drittes Banden-Mitglied nach halbstündigem Feuergefecht in Frankfurt verhaftet

Von den BILD-Redaktionen

Frankfurt, 2. Juni

Andreas Baader und Holger Meins, zwei der meistgesuchten Verbrecher im Bundesgebiet, sind gestern nach einem halbstündigen Feuergefecht mit der Polizei überwältigt worden. Mit ihnen stellte die Polizei einen dritten Verbrecher. Vermutlich ist es der steckbrieflich gesuchte Jan-Carl Raspe.

Die drei Terroristen hielten sich in ihrem Bombenlager auf, einer Garage in dem guten Frankfurter Wohnviertel Dornbusch. Mehr als 200 Polizisten und ein Panzer-Schützenwagen [illegible] Bombenlager postiert, als um 6.11 Uhr morgens ein Pistolenschuß die Stille des ruhigen Wohnviertels zerriß. Danach knatterten Salven von Maschinenpistolen, krachten Rauchbomben, schrien Menschen.

Die drei Verbrecher, Kern der Baader-Meinhof-Bande, hatten das Feuer auf die Polizei eröffnet. Wiederholte Aufforderungen über Lautsprecher, sich zu stellen, beantworteten sie mit immer neuen Schüssen. Mit Tränengas-Bomben wurden sie ausgeräuchert: Andreas Baader, 29, Kopf der Bande; Holger Meins, 30, der als besonders brutaler Mörder gilt und Jan-Carl Raspe, 27, Chefplaner der Truppe.

Baader wurde bei dem Kampf von einem Scharfschützen getroffen, aber nicht lebensgefährlich verletzt. Als die Polizisten ihn aus seinem Sprengstofflager herausholten, hatte er seine Pistole mit entsichertem Abzug in der Faust — [illegible]

Mit einem Hubschrauber wurden die Terroristen aus Frankfurt ausgeflogen. Stunden nachdem Baader und Genossen überwältigt waren, bekam die Frankfurter Sonderkommission eine anonyme Bombendrohung: Laßt die drei frei — oder in Frankfurt explodieren vier Bomben.

Lesen Sie bitte weiter auf Seite 4

Dazu die großen Berichte und Fotos auf den Seiten 2, 3 und 4

Ein nackter Terrorist flößt keinen Schrecken mehr ein

Andreas Baader, der Mann, der Deutschland in die Luft sprengen wollte, liegt nackt auf einer Tragbahre, fest im Griff von Polizeifäusten. Die Polizei hatte ihn und seine Komplicen aufgefordert, nackt das Bombenlager zu verlassen. Sie wollte damit verhindern, daß die Terroristen mit am Körper versteckten Sprengkörpern sich und Unschuldige noch in letzter Minute umbringen.

Nachrichten

Bombendrohung in Stuttgart:

Keine Entwarnung

Nixon fliegt nach Hause

„Facharzt" wird abgeschafft

Ägypten lobt Flughafen-Mord

Genscher sollte Bummelstreik selbst erleben

Attentäter verhaftet

Schlanke leben gesünder!

Zupavitin

ärztlich empfohlen klinisch erprobt

SENSATION

Eifelland

GIBT GEWINNE AN DIE KONSUMENTEN WEITER

DAS SONDERANGEBOT IM OLYMPIA-JAHR

1000 FAMILIEN-WOHNWAGEN TYP 380 FÜR 4 PERSONEN

DM 3399.– INCL. MWST.

Figure 65 The shot and wounded Andreas Baader on a stretcher on 1 June 1972. *Bild-Zeitung*, 2 June 1972.

night in Stammheim, showing her naked breasts from a low-angle shot on a hospital bed. The photo appears to have been taken while she was still unconscious.

Although images of humiliation like these have been circulated after various terror attacks – the photographs of the naked suspect after the Paris attacks of November 2015, mentioned earlier, is a comparable recent example – it is notable that they are particularly extreme in the case of female attackers. Violent women are a clear minority in ordinary crime statistics, yet not exceptional in political terrorism. 'From [the Russian anarchist] Vera Zasulich in the late nineteenth century … to Waffa al-Edress, the first female Arab "suicide bomber" in Israel in January 2002, women have been front-line actors and, consequently, pioneer recasters of gender roles', summarises the historian Charles Townshend.[37] It is noticeable that the media always followed female terrorists more closely than their male comrades in arms. They were either stylised as stars, like the 25 year-old Palestinian Leila Khaled, who was compared to Audrey Hepburn by the press and turned into a pin-up of terror in 1969 after she forced a TWA flight to land in Damascus,[38] or they appeared as sexualised corpses, like Hind Alameh, one of the four hijackers of the 'Landshut'. After being shot dead during the police assault in Mogadishu, she was photographed on the runway with fresh blood running from her mouth and nose. Her body, lying on its side, is turned towards the viewer, her red-and-white Che Guevara sweatshirt is pushed up to reveal a naked abdomen, and her trousers are open (Figure 66). Whereas Zohair Youssif Akache, the dead leader of the Commando, was seen with outstretched arms as a defeated hero (see Figure 54), the image of Hind Alameh focused on her femininity in a powerless state. The other female hijacker, Souhaila Andrawes,

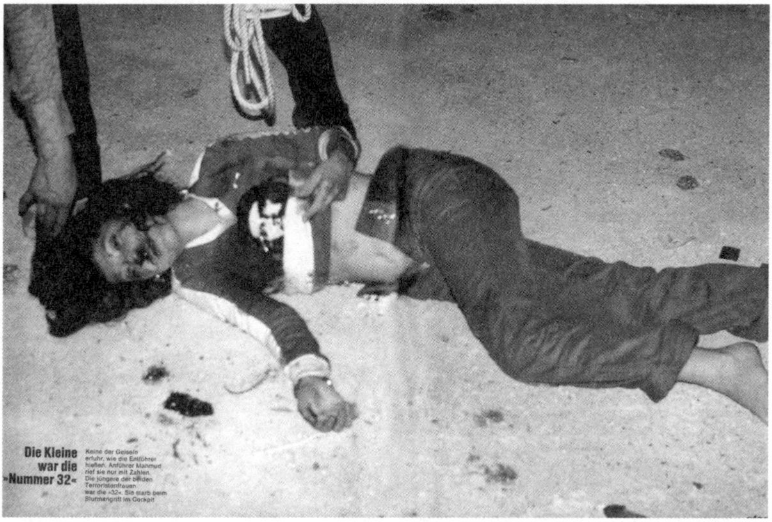

Figure 66 Dead body of an attacker on the runway in Mogadishu on 18 October 1977.

who showed her defiance as she lay injured on a stretcher by lifting her arm to make a victory sign, was described as particularly cruel and above all corpulent, and thus not really female at all.[39]

A few years earlier, the press had dealt in a very similar manner with the first RAF fatality, Petra Schelm, who was killed in 1971 during a large-scale manhunt in northern Germany. Schelm, who had received military training in Jordan the previous year, crashed through a police road block in Hamburg with her companion Werner Hoppe. The police gave chase; Schelm's car was stopped and a policeman shot her as she fled on foot. She was killed by a bullet that struck her below the left eye.[40] A few months later, an image of her dead body was published in *Stern* (without any reference to the source) as part of the magazine's coverage of bomb attacks on the US V Corps barracks in Frankfurt

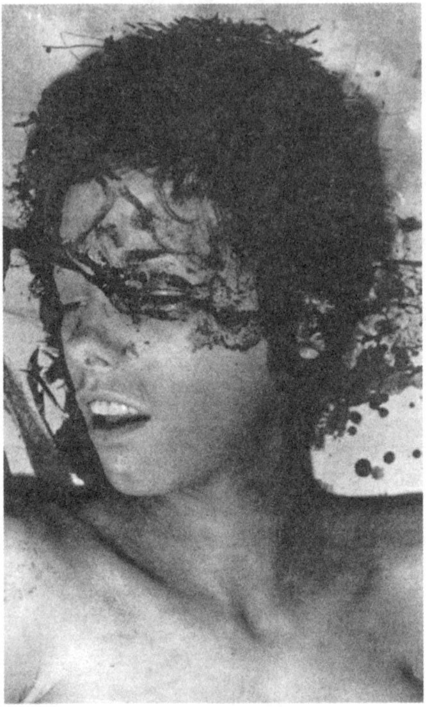

Figure 67 Dead body of RAF member Petra Schelm.

and the Springer Press headquarters in Hamburg (Figure 67). The photo shows the top of her head spattered with blood; her eyes are half closed, her mouth open and her upper body exposed. The caption intensified the almost ecstatic, sensual impression the picture conveyed. Readers were told that Schelm had been 'in love with a member of the Baader-Meinhof group', had seized her pistol while attempting to escape and was subsequently shot – that was all.[41] This was in a magazine that wooed potential buyers with a cover featuring a sexualised image of a naked woman on a beach in half rear view and advertising topics like 'The Trip' (young Germans travelling around the world), and 'weather and

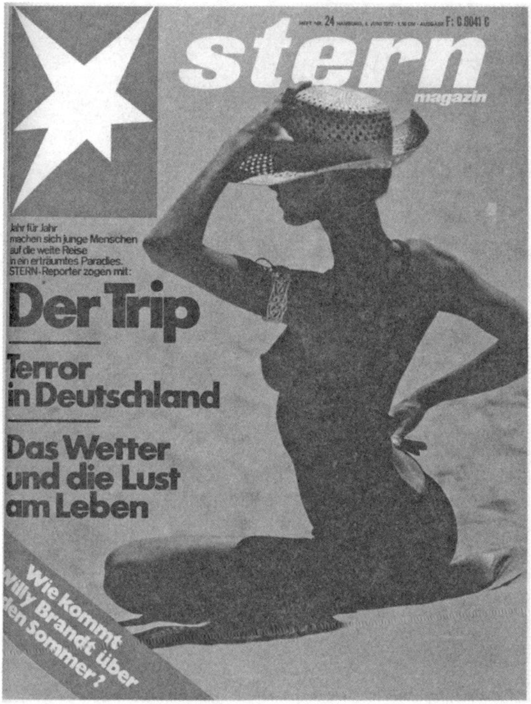

Figure 68 Front page of *Stern*, 24, 1972.

the lust for life' in the same breath as 'terror in Germany' (Figure 68).[42]

According to the journalist Eileen MacDonald, women are 'the protectors and givers of life, rather than the destroyers'.[43] Thus, the part they play in violent terror apparently requires a particular form of revenge.[44] Depicting their deaths seems not to be enough to atone for the twofold transgression that women commit when they fight. The fact that female attackers both use violence and challenge the traditional image of women has brought about a particular form of denigration at the moment of their violent deaths. Even in death they are eroticised, yet only to be denied the status of

an active subject twice over. As a beautiful corpse, a woman is more than just a naked enemy who 'is no longer a threat', as *Bild* commented on the images of Baader's capture in 1972. She also becomes a creation of the desiring gaze – a creation that can thus be controlled.

If they are captured rather than shot dead immediately, women accordingly often react with non-compliance as a way to defend themselves against this kind of humiliation. When Meinhof was photographed by the police in a Hanover flat two weeks after the arrest of Baader, Meins and Raspe, she tried to make her face unrecognisable (Figure 69). This photo, too, found its way into the press and was subsequently published on the cover of *Quick* magazine on 28 June 1972 as well as in other papers.[45] Here, however, Meinhof's grimace did not connote non-compliance, but rather confirmed her hostile disposition.[46] In circumstances like these,

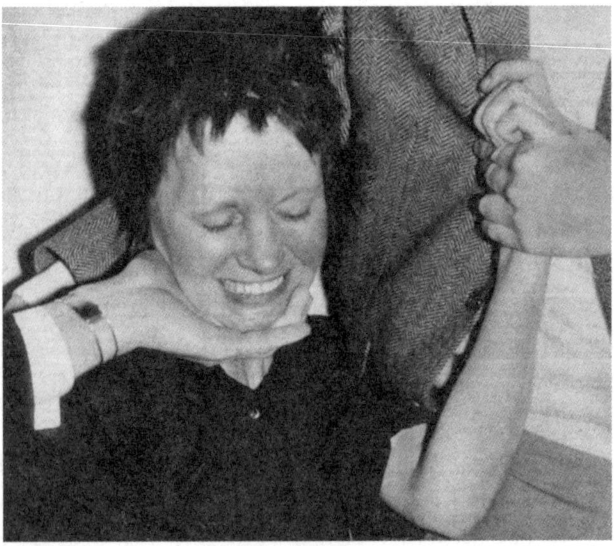

Figure 69 Arrest of Ulrike Meinhof on 15 June 1972.

nobody ever questions the ethics of the images' circulation and asks how they reached the public. The acts committed by the subjects photographed exclude any criticism of the authorities who produced them. In every case, however, the pictures' release would not have been possible without the active collaboration of state employees.

Self-styling: from courtroom to propaganda video

The perpetrators themselves, nevertheless, are not mere silent executors of gruesome crimes, whose only defence against their declared enemies' humiliating strategies is non-compliance. They too use every available forum – from the courtroom to the internet – to inform others about their allegedly just goals. Because terror attacks are essentially politically motivated, those who commit them always try to convince as large an audience as possible that their acts are legitimate. Since their intention is to destabilise or even topple governments and claim mass support, their violence always has a purpose and forms part of a political strategy that relies significantly on media amplification. This is why nearly all underground groups have used manifestos and propaganda texts to garner support for their cause. The members of Narodnaya Volya in the nineteenth century already produced declarations of this kind, and the first generation of the RAF initially depended mainly on printed texts to communicate with their sympathisers among the population.[47] But once a group had gone underground, there were usually no more opportunities for effective visual self-representation beyond the acts of terror themselves as presented in the media. In most cases, this changed abruptly once members were captured. The far-left groups of the 1970s, particularly the RAF, were very well aware that their

imprisonment and trials gave them new opportunities to assert themselves and advertise their cause.

Already in the late nineteenth century, the courtroom was turned into the perpetrators' last grand stage. Ravachol, for example, only achieved the fame that would make him the founding father of French anarchism through a fiery speech he gave at his trial. 'Ravachol succeeded in presenting himself as a noble avenger', writes the historian Jörg Requate:

> 'Nous travaillons pour le bonheur du peuple', he declared in the courtroom, showing that he considered himself not as a lone perpetrator, but as part of a movement that was making the world a better place.[48]

Émile Henry, who was responsible for the attacks on the police station in rue des Bons-Enfants and the Café Terminus, similarly used the courtroom to present his political motives in a powerful speech. As in the Ravachol trial, the press reported Henry's statements and demeanour in great detail. A court sketch, for example, showed him calm, relaxed and composed at the moment his death sentence was pronounced (Figure 70). Precisely because he had previously been regarded as a quiet loner, someone from a poor background who had not achieved much in life, his eloquence and cool resolve in the courtroom were registered with surprise and even admiration.[49]

Shortly before the RAF was officially founded, its first generation put on an equally impressive performance in court. On 14 October 1968, Andreas Baader, Gudrun Ensslin, Thorwart Proll and Horst Söhnlein appeared in the dock for the first time at a regional court in Frankfurt am Main. They were accused of carrying out firebomb attacks on two Frankfurt department stores on the night of 2–3 April of

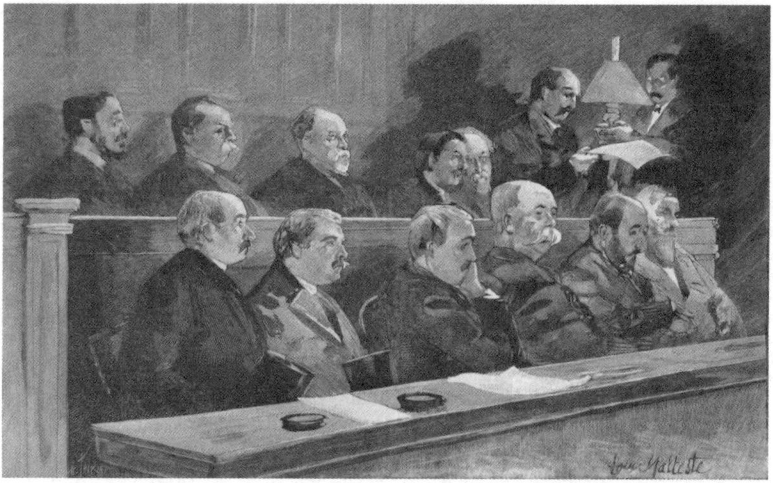

Figure 70 Émile Henry during the proclamation of his sentence.

that year. The defendants denied that their act had been criminal, declaring that both the arson and their trial were nothing less than a performance, or, in the language of the time, a political happening.[50] Hence, the trial repeatedly threatened to descend into farce. For example, when asked his name, Proll claimed to be Baader, and Baader gave 1789 as the year of his birth. The photographs taken in the courtroom on the first days of the proceedings, which were circulated widely in the press, showed Baader and Ensslin as a couple – he looking casual in scuffed jeans, she wearing a red leather jacket – and the two co-defendants cheerfully lighting up Cuban cigars in the courtroom (Figure 71).[51] It was easy to romanticise these pictures, since they appeared as counter-images to the much duller media representations of everyday life in West Germany.[52] Yet the RAF's increasingly brutal terror that overshadowed the 1970s prevented their avant-garde self-styling from entering pop culture at the time.

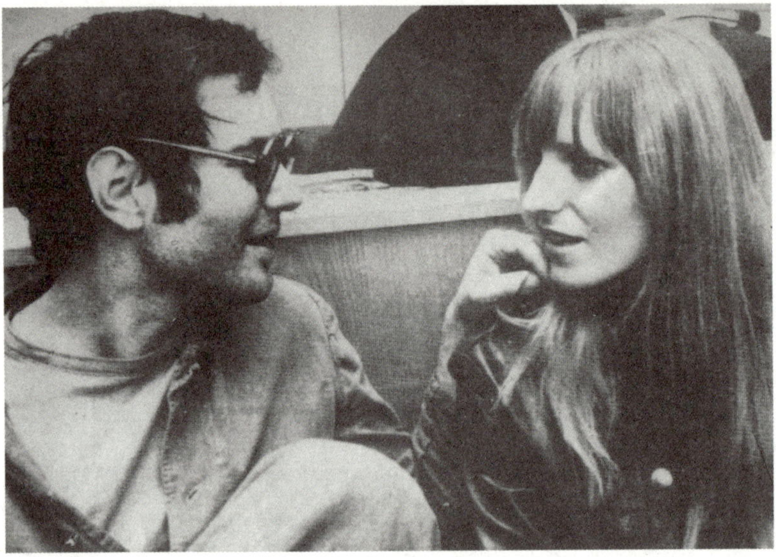

Figure 71 Gudrun Ensslin and Andreas Baader in the dock during their trial for the arson attack in Frankfurt in the autumn of 1968.

After the trial, photos continued to appear that showed the underground existence of the group in Paris in the early 1970s, mainly featuring Baader and Ensslin looking cool and trendy.[53] Even so, the *joie de vivre* expressed in these images was difficult to sell to the broader public after Baader's violent rescue in 1970 and the first casualties. It was only much later, towards the end of the twentieth century when the group no longer posed a threat, that a different perception set in. A volume of photographs entitled *Hans und Grete*, published by the former RAF member Astrid Proll in 1998 and showing hitherto unknown images of their time in Paris, played a key role in this shift.[54] When the rock band Rammstein advertised their album *Made in Germany* in 2012, using an only slightly modified photo from the arson trial, it no longer caused a public outcry.

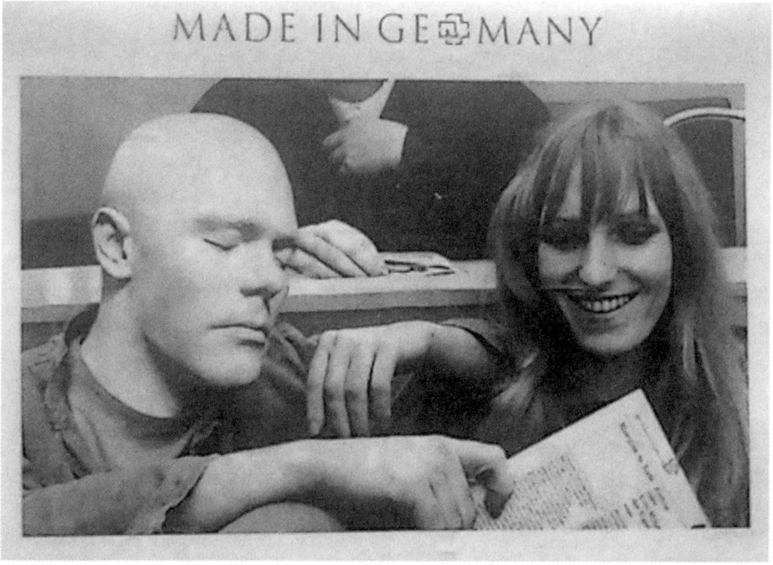

Figure 72 Advertising campaign for the album *Made in Germany* by the heavy metal band Rammstein on a wall poster in Berlin in 2012.

One of their promotional posters showed the mask-like face of a band member, with his eyes closed and his arm around Ensslin, who is sitting next to him in the dock and smiling (Figure 72). For Niels Werber, this appropriation of the RAF by contemporary pop culture, of which the Rammstein album promotion is only one example, is a sign that the historical dimension of far-left terror has been forgotten:

> Once the essence has been removed, all that remains is a thesaurus of easily quoted superficial elements ... Without any need for originality, everyone draws on the same repositories of knowledge, whose elements only need to be chosen and arranged.[55]

A similar public appropriation of the group's self-styling as youthful rebels would have been unthinkable in the

1970s. However, the images of the arson trial and of their underground life in Paris were the last self-presentations of leading RAF members to reach the public before their imprisonment. The ban on photographs, video and audio recordings, which had been in force since 1964 for public trials in West Germany, meant that their lengthy trial from 21 May 1975 to 28 April 1977 resulted in fewer opportunities for self-representation than the accused might have hoped for.[56] The only images of the defendants themselves that appeared at the time were courtroom sketches and photographs showing them en route from their cells to a specially constructed high-security building in the grounds of Stammheim prison.[57] Today, too, authorities usually try hard to deprive politically motivated perpetrators of a media platform. In August 2012, for example, the court in Oslo restricted public access to the proceedings against the far-right mass murderer Anders Breivik for this very reason, prohibiting photography, sound and video recordings during his defence speech.[58]

'We never really tried to use the power of images', Proll wrote in her later description of the RAF's strategy during the 1970s.[59] This is, however, not entirely true. It would be an exaggeration to claim that the leaders of the group launched an elaborate image campaign: after Baader and his comrades went underground and founded the organisation, they initially only wrote texts and polished the design of the RAF's emblem.[60] But by the time they were in prison, using hunger strikes to try to generate public support, a different strategy had come to the fore. From then on, photographs played a significant role in their struggle. The huge success of images showing the corpse of Meins, who had died in autumn 1974 while on hunger strike, had demonstrated that photographs taken in prison could be

an effective propaganda tool. With the agreement of his family they were supplied by his lawyers to the magazine *Stern*.[61] They showed his laid-out emaciated body and inevitably invited comparisons with images of the dead Jesus or Che Guevara.[62] Hans-Joachim Klein, who joined the Revolutionary Cells shortly after Meins's death, stated that he carried one of the images with him 'so [his] hatred would not diminish'.[63] Stefan Wisniewski, who allegedly was involved in the Hanns Martin Schleyer kidnapping, was so appalled by the photo that he later declared that going underground was an easy step for him.[64] We will probably never know whether the release of a photograph taken of Meinhof one year previously in the JVA Ossendorf prison in Cologne pursued a similar aim. It showed the prisoner, her hands interlaced on top of her head, with short, tousled hair and wearing a prison uniform, in a pose reminiscent of depictions of the martyrdom of St Sebastian (Figure 73). The photo was published the following year in *Stern* and *Spiegel* as well as other magazines, and a cropped version focusing on Meinhof's face only also appeared in an RAF publication a few years later.[65]

The collection of images and texts published under an innocuous title by the Swedish house Bo Cavefors in October 1977 shows particularly well that the RAF's leadership was still banking on the power of images at that time.[66] In autumn 1976, when it was clear that their trial would end in life sentences, Baader, Raspe and Ensslin photographed themselves with a Minox camera that had been smuggled into the prison.[67] The pictures did not show desperate prisoners, but fairly relaxed individuals talking and making plans (Figure 74). The publication of these images obviously aimed to signal to RAF supporters and sympathisers that Baader, Ensslin and Raspe were far from renouncing their

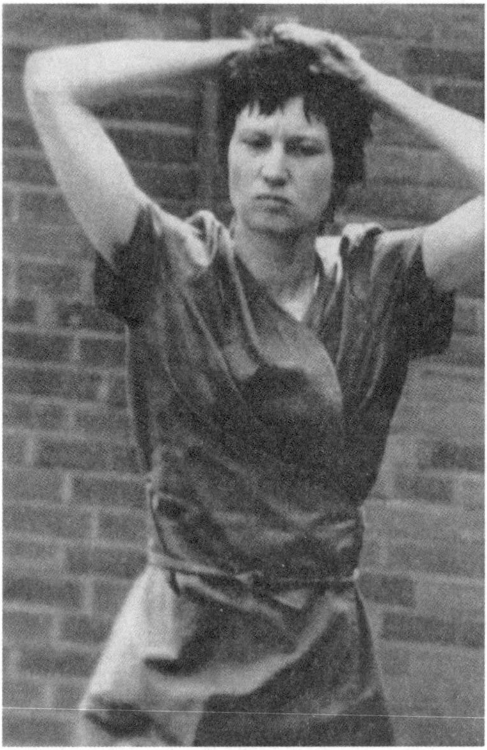

Figure 73 Ulrike Meinhof in the exercise yard of Ossendorf prison in Cologne (detail).

claim to strategic leadership, despite their imprisonment. However, when after Schleyer's abduction the last attempt to free them failed (with the storming of the 'Landshut' in Mogadishu), the prisoners must have realised that they no longer had any way out. They committed suicide on the night of 18–19 October 1977 in Stammheim prison.

Compared to the founders of the RAF, whose final attempts at self-representation seem almost desperate in retrospect, perpetrators of terror who enjoy major popular – and possibly even state – support have always had it easier.

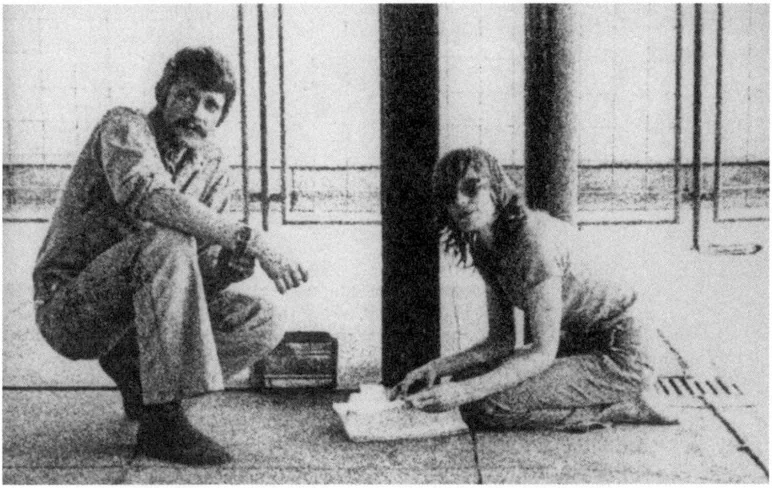

Figure 74 Gudrun Ensslin and Jan-Carl Raspe, photographed by Andreas Baader in Stammheim prison in Stuttgart.

The celebration of heroes on murals in Ireland and on posters in Palestine and Hezbollah-dominated southern Lebanon has been well documented.[68] Bin Laden, too, knew from an early date how to exploit favourable political conditions in countries such as Afghanistan in order to effectively control his image in the media. In May 1998, he organised a press conference with the aim of publicising his fatwa against the United States and its allies to a group of selected international journalists. After darkness had fallen, the media-savvy bin Laden made his appearance in a remote mountaintop camp in Afghanistan, surrounded by heavily armed mujahedeen who fired rounds of ammunition and rocket flares into the sky.[69] According to the journalist Peter L. Bergen, who was present at this conference, bin Laden's main goal was to attract international attention to himself and his organisation.[70] But after the events of 9/11, he no longer needed to make the effort. From then on every audio

and video recording he circulated met with widespread response in the Western media.[71]

On 7 October 2001, for example, only a few hours after the US airstrikes on Afghanistan, the Arab news channel Al Jazeera broadcast a perfectly timed video in which bin Laden declared for the first time that the New York attackers had died as martyrs for the course. Two months later, after he had escaped once more during the battle of Tora Bora in northern Afghanistan, Al Jazeera broadcast another video message that showed bin Laden in combat mode, carrying a Kalashnikov and wearing military camouflage as he knelt on the ground in front of a rock face (Figure 75).[72] Images showing the Al-Qaida leader in the pose of a classic mujahedeen warrior riding a horse were subsequently shown all over the world. These images were followed by videos and photographs that, according

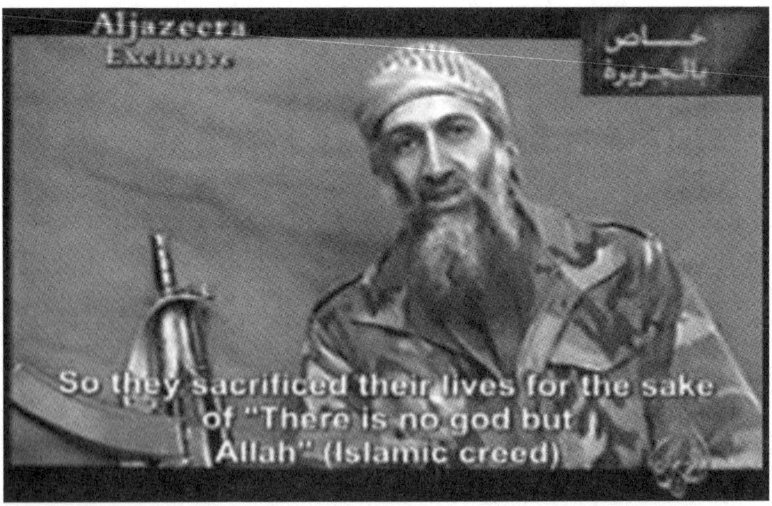

Figure 75 Still from a video message by Osama bin Laden broadcast by Al Jazeera on 27 December 2001.

to Thomas Riegler, increasingly emphasised bin Laden's status as a religious authority:

> The Palestinian keffiyeh establishes a link to the Al Aqsa Mosque, an important Islamic site. When being filmed or photographed, Bin Laden also liked to wear a white turban, indicating a clerical status (he was never seen in a black turban, which would have identified him as a descendant of the family of the Prophet). A knife typical of the Arab Peninsula, which is usually reserved for authorities claiming historic legitimacy, was often seen hanging from his belt. Each time Bin Laden made an important statement – for example, when calling for a jihad against America (in 1998 and again after 9/11) – he wore a ring with a black stone set in silver, symbolising his connection to Mecca's holy sites, which he aimed to liberate from the rule of the Saudi royal family and its infidel allies.[73]

In one of his last video messages, just before the US presidential elections in November 2004, bin Laden once again appeared in a golden robe and white turban. This time, however, he spoke not as a revolutionary, seated on the ground with an automatic rifle slung over his shoulder, but from a lectern like an elected politician. 'During this 13-minute speech,' Riegler writes,

> Bin Laden for the first time avoided quoting from the Quran or the 'Hadith' (the 'sayings of the Prophet') and made no attempt to underpin his arguments with theology. His statement was clearly political: terrorism was the logical response to U.S. aggression and was by no means caused by a hatred of freedom.[74]

The last video before his death, which was published in 2007, likewise showed him not as the militant leader of a terror group, but in the role of the wise statesman. In his shift from warlike jihadi leader to political statesman, Osama bin Laden pursued a strategy of self-presentation

that aimed to legitimate him not just within the community of Muslim believers, but in the eyes of the whole world. By now, however, he was no longer able to convey this new role convincingly. After 9/11 his evil stereotype was so firmly established in the Western media that his change of speech and habitus went unnoticed. Because the manner of his political message was radically new, it failed to reach or to convince Western audiences.

Al-Qaida was the first terror organisation whose messages were characterised by 'excellent quality and … masterful timing', as the political analyst Bruce Hoffman writes. Besides weapons, their fight also employed

> the Minicam and videotape; editing suite and attendant production facilities; professionally produced and mass-marketed CD-ROMs and DVDs; and, most critically, the laptop and desktop computers, CD burners and e-mail accounts, and Internet and World Wide Web access that have defined the information revolution today.[75]

Although videos in which (mainly suicide) attackers took responsibility for acts and talked about their goals and motivations had existed since the 1980s and were broadcast on Lebanese, Syrian or Palestinian television channels, they rarely made it into the international media. The mostly blurry film clips taken first by secular left-wing Palestinian groups, then by radical Shi'a organisations in Lebanon and from the 1990s onwards by radical Sunni groups, conveyed a certain authenticity, but were usually not produced in a manner particularly appropriate for the media.[76] Only after Al-Qaida's attacks on Western cities in the early twenty-first century did the Western media take greater notice of such videos, which were now uploaded to the internet in high resolution and mostly broadcast by Al Jazeera. Although their iconography never followed a unified pattern – the

responsible organisation's emblem was sometimes visible in the background, sometimes not – their content was more or less similar: the uncanny performance of a murderer who was by then already dead, calmly and clearly presenting his motives.[77]

To an even greater extent than Al-Qaida, IS almost completely controlled the image of itself and its actors that appeared in the Western media. While perpetrators of past acts of terror were rather unsuccessful when they tried to mediatise themselves beyond the images generated by their deeds, the tables have now turned. Media coverage of IS, for example, depended almost entirely on the visual material circulated by the organisation itself. A five-part film broadcast by the internet news channel Vice News in August 2014 showed how far the media were prepared to go. Taking up an invitation by IS, the filmmaker Medyan Dairieh spent three weeks travelling through areas in Syria and Iraq then occupied by the organisation. His aim was to convey the first glimpse of life on the ground there.[78] However, IS controlled everything he saw, heard and filmed, so that the Vice News film eventually only showed images of staunch fighters, grateful citizens and penitent prisoners. A short time later, while the series was still being broadcast, the US journalist James Foley died at the hands of IS, showing how dangerous independent coverage had become.

It is not easy to defuse images like those that IS circulate on the internet, showing fighters on top of jeeps with waving flags, beaming children and benevolent preachers, as well as brutally punished enemies and confused-looking opponents. How difficult this is became clear during an initiative that the US government launched in the summer of 2014. The Center for Strategic Counterterrorism Communications

(CSCC), set up by the US government, published a video on YouTube entitled 'Welcome to ISIS Land', which at first sight looked like an IS propaganda film. It featured decapitated heads, hanged corpses and brutal shootings of prisoners in various locations in Syria. Only the subtitles revealed that the victims were not murdered 'infidels', but people living under the IS regime. The pictures were in fact intended as counter-images to IS's self-glorifying promotional videos, in which the organisation promised its potential supporters a life in Syria full of luxurious villas, fast cars and sexual gratification.[79]

IS immediately responded with a further counter-video entitled 'Run Do Not Walk to the US Terrorist State', and at the same time critics in the US and elsewhere vigorously questioned the goal and purpose of the CSCC's propaganda video. Whether 'Welcome to ISIS Land' ever had any deterrent effect is uncertain, since the brutality shown merely reflected the fascination that made IS attractive to so many people in the first place. There was criticism from inside the government, too. Richard Stengel, former editor-in-chief of *Time Magazine* and later director of public diplomacy in the US Department of State, brought up what is known as the 'backfire attempt', which occurs first and foremost when dealing with thoroughly ideologised believers.

In the end, the CSCC's director was fired and a new campaign launched, for which Stengel – as WikiLeaks revealed in April 2014 – asked Hollywood and in particular Sony Pictures for support.[80] It is not known which direction this support has taken, but we can assume that any such initiative met with as little success as its various predecessors, including some that tried to engage in counter-propaganda using cartoon drawings.[81] In retrospect, the most successful

antidote to the recruitment efforts of IS was presumably the experience of the brutal and corrupt life in the areas occupied by the organisation. This is at least what is suggested by a study by the American psychologist Anne Speckhard and the Turkish sociologist Ahmet S. Yayla, who interviewed thirteen Syrian IS defectors. Although all of them remained radical 'true believers', it was not any counter-image that had driven them into exile in the southern Turkish border town of Şanlıurfa, but the murderous and unprincipled character of the IS regime itself.[82]

The migration of images: from enemy to martyr

The previous chapters have shown that images and counter-images are used strategically by both sides to influence the course of events following acts of violence. Yet how little is gained by these means is demonstrated by the self-representations of the perpetrators and the images circulated by their opponents. Nothing and nobody can guarantee that an image which for one side clearly represents an enemy will not become the means for hero worship on the other side, and vice versa. The police photograph of Ravachol did not just offer proof that a dangerous criminal had been apprehended, but also provided anarchists and sympathisers with a model image of a martyr. What was a sign of the prisoner's intransigence in one context, became a symbol of resistance in the other. A print that was circulated among anarchists after Ravachol's execution, for example, was an adaptation of precisely the police photo that appeared after his imprisonment in the French press. Although he now stands under the guillotine, his chest is proudly bare and a golden sun rises behind him, symbolising the new age that he has inaugurated (Figure 76).

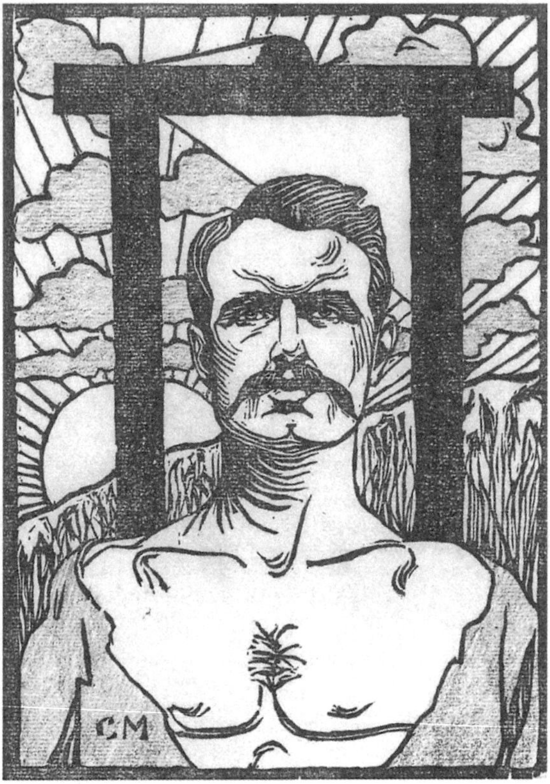

Figure 76 Charles Maurin, *Ravachol as Martyr*, 1893.

Even the police photo of the dead Petra Schelm was later used on a flyer produced by sympathisers of the RAF in an attempt to mobilise the public during the trial of the policeman who had fired the fatal shot.[83] Similarly, the driving licence photo of Mohammed Atta, the alleged leader of the 9/11 attacks, which was published by the FBI and printed in the *New York Post* two days later as the 'face of utter hatred', has since appeared in various Al-Qaida martyr images. They, too, use backgrounds that help to glorify the purported martyrs' cause of death as

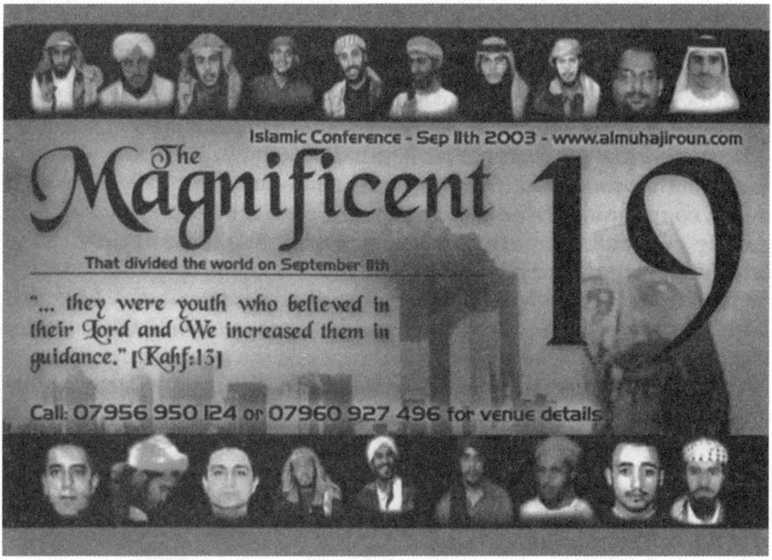

Figure 77 Images of 19 Al-Qaida martyrs, including Mohammed Atta's driving licence photo (third from left, bottom row).

a heroic deed, much like the anarchist pictures before them (Figure 77).[84] Conversely, the image of bin Laden that appeared on FBI wanted posters was taken from a video message in which he was primarily advertising his cause to his own supporters. And after the Paris attacks of November 2015, the media published images of the alleged leader Abdelhamid Abaaoud that had previously appeared in IS's online propaganda magazine.[85] He was shown as a friendly young man, smiling confidently, who – while wearing combat gear and carrying a machine gun – gave an impression of innocence that betrayed nothing of the strategic operations that he conveyed in the IS publication of February 2015. In the interview accompanying the picture, he prides himself on his ingenuity that helped him to escape from Belgian security services during a raid that

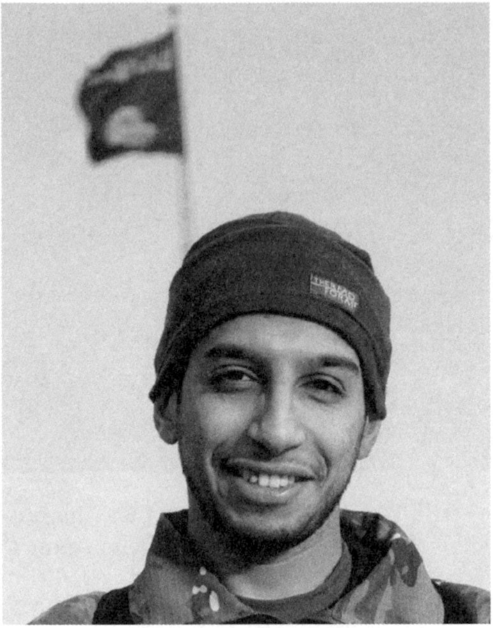

Figure 78 IS propaganda photo of Abdelhamid Abaaoud.

had taken place shortly beforehand (Figure 78).[86] Even the bloody face of the dead Al-Zarqawi that the US government presented as a trophy in its fight against Al-Qaida, mentioned in the Introduction, went straight into the fund of martyr images circulated by that organisation.[87]

The US government's decision not to publish an image of the dead Osama bin Laden following his shooting in 2011 presented a welcome break to this pattern. As the president stated two days later, they neither wanted to display the dead man as a trophy, nor encourage a martyr cult.[88] Unfortunately, the US government did not keep to these words, and it did not take long before an extremely humiliating image of bin Laden appeared in the media. It is unlikely that this photograph would have been released by

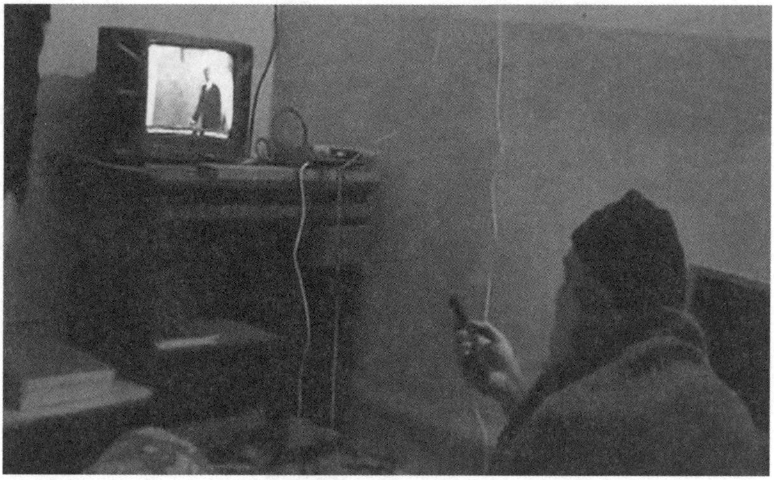

Figure 79 Still from a private video of Osama bin Laden, circulated by the US Department of Defense on 13 May 2011.

the Pentagon without White House authorisation. Taken from a 'home video' that the Navy SEALs had found during their invasion of bin Laden's complex in Abbottabad, it showed an old man slumped in a brown dressing gown and cap, sitting in front of a television and watching recordings of his former glorious self (Figure 79). Thus, an image became public that showed the arch-enemy as a grey shell of himself who had nothing left at the end of his life apart from narcissistic self-reflection.

Unlike real weapons, pictures are unable to defeat or destroy an enemy. On the contrary: as the photograph of the dead body of Holger Meins shows, images are able to radicalise, but can seldom pacify when constructed in the mode of image and counter-image. No counter-image can deny the reality of a previous representation; with depictions, this kind of negation is not possible. Yet precisely this is what enemy images usually aim to achieve, and therefore they

often – as in the case of bin Laden – obstruct rather than contribute to clarification. As Louise Richardson writes:

> If the US does not even know what its enemies are fighting for, it cannot hope to counter them effectively. It has come to believe its own rhetoric that they are driven by uncontrolled evil and limitless ambition to harm it. Americans have tended to imagine all the terrible things terrorists could do to them and then to attempt the impossible task of defending against all of them. Instead, the US needs to figure out, on the basis of sound intelligence, the things they have (or might soon have) both the motive and the capability to do to it, and defend itself accordingly. It also needs to figure out how it can most effectively weaken them.[89]

Of course, images are necessary to gain an idea of the severity of an act and its consequences, and to gather information about the perpetrators. But as this and the preceding chapters have shown, no photograph ever provides neutral information about an event. In the context of terror in particular, many images are responses to previous insults and injuries, and often follow the logic of image and counter-image determined by the perpetrators. Since boundaries are swiftly crossed and fundamental principles easily violated, a responsible handling of images is all the more important. The foundation for this is the respect for human dignity, a principle that is anchored not only in German Basic Law, but also in the 1945 Charter of the United Nations. However, to be able to judge when and under what conditions terror images violate this principle, their function needs to be understood first. On the basis of this, the last chapter will now attempt to define the parameters that should govern a responsible usage of images in the context of terror.

Chapter 4
Image ethics

Images of terror come as a shock, each time anew. The closer they approach our own lives, the more we are involved and the more we are reminded of other, comparable attacks. Media and communication research on the psychological impact of news images has shown that visuals produce a stronger sense of involvement than texts and carry a more powerful emotional charge.[1] Although we all know that photographs and film or video footage only show part of what could be seen and might sometimes even be manipulated, we do not realise this when we look at them.[2] As Roland Barthes noted,

> A specific photograph, in effect, is never distinguished from its referent (from what it represents), or at least it is not *immediately* or *generally* distinguished from its referent (as is the case for every other image – encumbered from the start, and because of its status – by the way in which the object is simulated).[3]

But where the representation and what is represented become indistinguishable, we are also quick to make moral judgements. This happens more readily with photographs than with other kinds of images, although we are well aware that they too can reveal only a particular, very

limited truth. What is more, images produced and viewed without a second thought in one context may suddenly become objectionable in another. The photos of US soldiers in Abu Ghraib prison in Iraq are a notorious case in point.[4] The extent to which moral judgements depend on and are influenced by the place of creation and publication of an image never became clearer than in this case.

The previous chapters have explored the patterns and limitations of terror coverage in the Western media. If I now return to this discussion in a more general manner, it is because it forms the basis for the ethical considerations that are the subject of this final chapter. In order to define the grounds and go beyond a purely situational verdict, we have to look closely at the conditions that determine the use and function of images in this context.

Image and reality: patterns and structures

Every image, no matter whether it was taken with a camera or produced by other means, shows something that is different from itself and that becomes visible only in and through that image. While this process of mediation is taken for granted in the reception of paintings, drawings, prints and art photography, we rarely pay attention to it in news images. Although they too 'turn the physical fact of a material surface into the field of an articulated attention',[5] this mediation goes largely unnoticed. Hence we have to deduce from the context what we do not see in the mediated representation itself. In fact, the stronger a picture's relation to reality, and the closer it moves towards a situational perception of everyday life, the greater our need for commentaries and further images.[6] If we ignore this aspect of embeddedness and seriality and focus merely on individual

photographs, on their effect and reception, we risk generalising what are in fact very specific cases. In this case it is only images with strong situational cues and aesthetic contrasts, or with constellations of figures that draw on earlier iconographic models, like those discussed in Robert Hariman and John Louis Lucaites' book *No Caption Needed*, that are considered.[7] In the first case the emotional power of the image is normally explained aesthetically, in the second it is through associative comparisons.[8]

Yet these photographs have become media icons precisely because they were unusual. The majority of images that appear in the wake of a terror attack work according to a different logic. Conscious or unconscious use of pre-existing motifs, as in Thomas E. Franklin's photograph of three firefighters on 11 September 2001 or in that of the charitable helper at the Edgware Road tube station on 7 July 2005 in London, is rather rare (see Figures 25 and 28). And photographs with strong formal contrasts, such as Stephen Platt's burning towers of the World Trade Center in front of a bright blue sky or Karl Strumpf's hostage-taker on the balcony of the Olympic village in Munich, became media icons because they were exceptional (see Figures 21 and 56). They managed to condense aesthetically a seemingly inexplicable situation so that it became at least visually comprehensible. Most of the images discussed in the previous chapters, however, do not employ iconographic or aesthetic condensations of this kind. They derive their meaning solely from the context of other images and statements, which in turn follow a pattern which goes back to the late nineteenth century. The pattern provides the basic structure in which the images acquire their place and meaning. At first there is a need to get as close as possible to the location of the incident. These images are, however, quickly

followed by others that focus above all on the functioning of society, so that the shock that is initially conveyed is quickly attenuated.

Images of hostages also acquire their meaning within a series rather than as individual shots. A single image may well attract a wave of sympathy, but it is only the whole set of released images that can reveal whether the hostage-takers felt compelled by circumstances to change their strategy, as happened during the abduction of Hanns Martin Schleyer by the RAF in the autumn of 1977, or whether they were not really interested in resolving the conflict, as was the case during the numerous kidnappings in Lebanon during the 1980s. The execution pictures by IS from 2014 are exceptional in this respect, since the lives of the hostages never served as a means of extortion. Their death was in fact the precondition for the calculated effect that the images were expected to generate. In this case the images solely served as a demonstration of power and cruelty, for which IS drew on various models, including Hollywood films. Portraits of perpetrators in turn, circulated during and after an incident, like those discussed in Chapter 3, are strangely normal outside the context of their circulation. They too gain their meaning only within this context and within previously established patterns of stereotypes that denote them as depictions of enemies. Long before it is taken and published, therefore, each image of terror is thus part of a horizon of meaning that has been tried, updated and modified many times before.[9]

The power of images: empiricism and hermeneutics

In previous chapters I have sometimes referred to the impact of images. How to assess their effectiveness has been a question that media and communication scholars have tried to

answer by examining people's reactions in relation to different news formats.[10] So far, however, only a few researchers have gone beyond single case studies. And even where the scope is wider, as in Nicole Haußecker's study of the German television coverage of terrorism, which examined different emotions and their intensity between 2007 and 2009,[11] the results tend to be rather disappointing. In the first part of her book, Haußecker broadly confirms the findings and assumptions of earlier scholars about the framing of news in the media. As early as 1993, the political scientist Robert Entman had noted a recurring pattern: identification of the problem was followed by reports analysing causes, and finally suggestions for possible remedies.[12] In this sense images of terror fit the description well, even though it is difficult to assign them clearly to one or the other category. Images of attacks and of victims might initially serve to visualise the problem, while those of perpetrators seem to help to illuminate the causes. However, photographs of the work of rescue and security services may sometimes be essential for defining the problem, yet they can also be seen as a remedy. They may even, as happened after 9/11, contribute to finding a possible mode of action – in this case the preparation for military retaliation. Images of perpetrators too show overlaps between assessment and solution. And as we have seen in the previous chapter, representations of arrests often oscillate between humiliation and redemption.

Haußecker acknowledges that different categories of images may interfere with each other. It is therefore all the more disappointing that the second part of her study, which analyses empirical data, offers few new insights or surprises. Summing up her research, she writes that 'depictions of blood, injured children, corpses, extreme injuries and weapons' elicit the 'most strongly negative' responses

and that women show 'stronger emotional reactions than men'.[13] While there are some striking individual results, especially those that relate to the emotional impact of images highlighting the 'terror risk of religious perpetrators',[14] the shortcomings of empirical studies are all too obvious: they may confirm certain assumptions about the content and meaning of images, but they only rarely deliver new insights into the way they operate.

One of the underlying problems is the intercultural mobility and inherent ambivalence of images. As the examples in the previous chapter have shown, nobody can guarantee that something perceived as fear-inducing in one context will not be admired in another. Researchers who have studied the reactions of multilingual and multiethnic groups have therefore come to less clear-cut conclusions than Haußecker. The political scientist Ben O'Loughlin, for example, who conducted an empirical intercultural reception study over three years, concluded that media images never achieve their desired effect *per se*. Their impact always depends on very specific contexts of pre-existing ideas and attitudes.[15] Yet how these different horizons of interpretation develop in the first place and which images and media are decisive within them appear to be questions that so far have eluded empirical research.

A hermeneutic study such as this cannot claim to offer an explanation either. It cannot deliver empirical evidence for the impact that it ascribes to the images within the contexts of their publication and circulation. The strength of a historical perspective lies elsewhere: it shows that images of terror never operate in a historical vacuum of the present, but follow patterns that often go back a long way. Moreover, it can show, as I have done here, how patterns can differ depending on whether the images show attacks, hostages

or perpetrators. What these comparisons reveal are shifts in meaning that necessarily elude empirical reception studies. While all the images of attacks discussed in Chapter 1, for example, share the same general framework of reporting, each event shows a slightly different horizon of meaning that is shaped by the very specific political dynamic prevalent in each state at the moment of the act of terror. And only comparisons of series of hostage images, like those discussed in Chapter 2, expose the differences that allow us to determine the function of images within the various contexts of their reception. Images of perpetrators, finally, are so over- and underdetermined at the same time that we can only see in hindsight, once the threat has disappeared, which hopes and fears have been associated with them. Only then can we begin to understand their role as temporary regulators of emotions instead of seeing them as vehicles for the resolution of conflicts.

A historical study of images of terror is therefore first and foremost an attempt to situate the depictions within the specific contexts of conflict in which they appear and to determine the pattern that forms the foil for their meaning. Despite this, there have been instances in the previous chapters where a moral judgement seemed to suggest itself; for example, in the case of the execution videos of IS in Chapter 2 and the humiliating images of perpetrators in the West German media in the 1970s in Chapter 3.

If, however, we want to establish a more systematic basis for such judgements, we first need to understand the interests and justifications of those institutions and organisations that normally regulate the circulation of images of terror. Governments have occasionally legislated to prohibit certain publications, while press and media watchdogs have developed frameworks for their dissemination.

Human rights organisations, on the other hand, have occasionally ignored both in order to draw attention to the blatant injustices at the heart of these conflicts and the shortcomings of the media that represent them. It should go without saying that an investigation of the motivations for judgements can neither be a plea for banning such images altogether nor for its opposite, their indiscriminate dissemination. Just as it is impossible to categorically distinguish between morally good and bad weapons, images relating to acts of terror always have to be considered in the context of their use. In what follows I will therefore focus on a few controversial cases in order to consider questions of responsibility in the light of fundamental human rights.

Debating these issues is of far-reaching importance in an age where the dissemination of images of terror has ceased to be the preserve of established institutions and organisations. One consequence of the expansion of the media landscape in recent years has been that many images reach the public via non-traditional channels – a development that the sociologist Andrew Hoskins and the political scientist Ben O'Loughlin have described with the term 'new media ecology'.[16] The range of those who produce and circulate images has expanded enormously and potentially now includes anyone who carries a mobile phone with a camera and has access to the internet.[17] Consequently, more people than ever before have to grapple with ethical questions about image use.

Controlling images: State, media and human rights organisations

As we have seen in earlier chapters, there is no doubt that images of terror serve above all the interests of the attackers.

Hence they present a particular moral dilemma for the societies concerned, which have no choice but to share the news of an attack, since the event is usually of a scale that challenges peaceful everyday existence. Caught between empathy with the plight of the victims and refusal to give in to extortion, governments have occasionally taken steps to limit the circulation of images. In order to allay public alarm and gain room for manoeuvre, they have often justified these measures by emphasising the danger to national security and the special need to protect the victims. A rather extreme case was the measures taken against the Tupamaros by the Uruguayan government between 1967 and 1973, which banned any reports of their acts of terror and even prohibited mentioning their name in the press. This led to the permanent closure of eight newspapers and one television station, and to thirty-six further temporary closures.[18] The British government also strictly regulated reporting on Irish terror organisations during the 1970s. After a number of controversial television broadcasts, it prohibited direct interviews with activists in 1988, with the absurd consequence that even statements from Sinn Féin, the legal political arm of the Irish independence movement, had to be dubbed.[19]

In hindsight, even the initiative of the US government, which after the attacks of 9/11 urged the media not to give a platform to Osama bin Laden's news and video messages, has been considered counter-productive for understanding the threat.[20] Equally controversial was the imposition of a so-called news blackout, which the West German government agreed with the press during the abduction of Schleyer.[21] The consequences of the government's action in autumn 1977, and the fact that it was not in the interest of the victim, have already been discussed in Chapter 2.

As in the US after 2001, the government hoped that the media would exercise some form of voluntary self-control. Nevertheless, the German Press Council subsequently took exception to this kind of state intervention.[22] Although images of kidnap victims document the unlawful detention of a person, which is a serious criminal offence, and may violate the dignity of the person who is portrayed, they may also be a source of hope for hostages in situations where their lives are used as bargaining chips by the kidnappers.[23] In every single instance where media bans were enforced or negotiated by governments, they touched on the right to freedom of expression and have thus always been problematic and controversial in Western democracies.

In the aftermath of terror attacks, members of the public nevertheless sometimes call for the state to pass laws that regulate the release of images or even ban them altogether. It is questionable whether those who make such demands are aware of the consequences. The extent to which civil liberties might be restricted through such actions is rarely considered. Laws of this kind could in fact easily be seen as a success for the attackers in their attempt to undermine the societies that they target. Moreover, governments themselves are often not particularly scrupulous over the means they use in the battle of images, so that it cannot automatically be assumed that a sense of proportion and judgement prevails. It is worth remembering in this context that most Western countries have equivalents of the German Press Council or the British Independent Press Standards Organisation (IPSO), bodies that can compel the media to adhere to ethical standards and that in the case of violations can publicly reprimand offenders. Their principles are based on internationally recognised human rights and constitutional regulations – above all the preservation

of human dignity and the personality rights deriving from it. They also stipulate that journalists have to uphold certain principles of truth and due diligence.[24] The public can report violations, on which the complaints committee of the Press Councils adjudicate and which they may punish with sanctions. But since this can only ever happen after the event, this procedure is as blunt an instrument as civil action based on personality rights when it comes to regulating images in this context. Images of terror gain their power to influence the course of events precisely at the moment when they are first released, and their impact diminishes later on.

The rulings are nonetheless revealing, since they give us an insight into how the media that circulate such images see themselves. In an exemplary analysis of rulings after 9/11, the journalist Stefan Leifert has shown that the German Press Council tends to value the media's duty to inform more highly than the protection of personality rights. According to him, the point at which the right to protection of a photographed individual takes precedence over the public's right to information is 'where the reporting complements identifying photos of individuals with their names and details. The border is thus not automatically crossed if the image alone makes a person recognisable.'[25] As plausible and ethically sound as this principle may seem at first, its handling in practice is questionable. An example may demonstrate this.

Among the many images circulating after the terror attack on the World Trade Center in New York on 11 September 2001, one in particular caused a public outcry. It was a photograph sent to Associated Press showing a person who in his despair threw himself from the towers. *Falling Man* by Richard Drew showed the body of a man in free fall.

He was one of hundreds who jumped out of the windows of the burning towers – probably in the desperate hope of escaping their certain fate. But since the news tended to cover the destruction and the rescue of the victims rather than the people dying, this tragedy was almost invisible in the media, even though it was documented by many camera teams and photographers. As already mentioned in Chapter 1, Drew's photo was the exception. It appeared in numerous newspapers, including the *New York Times* on 12 September 2001, and a day later in Germany in the *Süddeutsche Zeitung* and *Die Welt*.[26] The photo was met with outrage, such that it initially disappeared from public view. Yet those who had seen it could not forget it. It was later evoked in literary treatments of the attacks, became the subject of a documentary film and was discussed in numerous academic publications, making it one of the best-known photographs of 9/11 today.[27]

The photo was one of many that Drew took with a motor drive camera at the moment of the fall. But only this particular image showed the figure in an astonishing, almost monumental state of calm. The body of the man can be seen at the bottom edge of the upper third of the picture, roughly at the image's golden ratio point, his arms were still clinging to his chest, and his right leg angled as if in the pose of a dancer. Only the horizontal row of windows showed that he was in free fall, following an optical line running down towards the bottom right. Neither a beginning nor an end was in sight. The division between the black and white halves and the position of the man in the place where they converge turned the image into a graphic visualisation of despair, and thus an analogy for the limbo between life and death. By metaphorically condensing and at the same time arresting the hopelessness in a succinct aesthetic contrast,

the photo fulfilled all the conditions for a media icon. It is therefore not surprising that photo editors all over the world picked precisely this image from the databases of the picture agencies and approved its publication on the very day of the attack.

To see the suffering of a human being who was still alive but already condemned to death, frozen in this image forever, was hard to bear for many readers. The German Press Council received complaints from a number of people, who claimed the image was irreverent, sensationalist and disrespectful to all those who had lost a loved one in this tragedy.[28] The complaints committee rejected all of them, arguing that publication was justified by the image's documentary value, and since the person could not be identified, this did not constitute a violation of the right of personality.[29] It is worth noting that the aesthetic quality of the image, on which its pathos is founded, was not mentioned in this response.

There are formal and iconographic parallels between Richard Drew's photo and Théodore Géricault's famous painting *The Raft of the Medusa* of 1819. The latter was also inspired by a real event with political consequences, a shipwreck off the northwest coast of Africa nearly 200 years before 9/11. Here, too, the image is dominated by contradictory diagonals and documents a painful moment between hope and death. Géricault did meticulous research, made preliminary studies in the morgue and portrayed a surviving victim,[30] and although art historians such as Godehard Janzig have emphasised that Drew's *Falling Man* is the result of 'decades of experienced and tireless attention' by a professional journalist 'as well as his technical equipment' that 'led to a result that would never have been perceivable with the naked eye',[31] the reality effect in the news image is

infinitely more dominant than in the painting. The knowledge of the temporal co-existence of the camera and the captured scene produces a sense of being an eyewitness that is absent in the reception of Géricault's *Raft of the Medusa*. It subsequently led to attempts to trace the identity of the man in the photo. The family of the person eventually named were deeply distressed, partly because they were Catholics and the implication of suicide was irreconcilable with their faith. It later turned out that this was a misidentification, and before long another name was circulated, though this too has never been confirmed with certainty.[32]

What we have already seen at the beginning of this chapter was also true here: because of its documentary character, *Falling Man* was never perceived as an individual image, but its meaning was sought within a situational context and with reference to other images, such as portraits of the victims taken before their death. As we will see, this is what made the photograph ethically controversial at the time. In the image itself the person is not identifiable, so that we have to agree with the German Press Council that there is no violation of any personality rights. Nevertheless, this answers only a portion of the complaints. The charge of irreverence, sensationalism and lack of respect for the victims probably did not primarily relate to the person portrayed and his family, but to the sensitivity and emotions of whoever might look at the image. Yet given the historical importance of the tragedy, ethical considerations of this kind cannot provide sufficient justification for curtailing the duty to inform. We must therefore agree once more with the German Press Council's judgement. According to Susan Sontag – and I will come back to this in more detail later – there is even an ethical obligation to engage with such images:

> No one after a certain age has the right to this kind of innocence, of superficiality, to this degree of ignorance, or amnesia. There now exists a vast repository of images that make it harder to maintain this kind of moral defectiveness.[33]

However, as we have just seen, the need to name the person in the picture was so strong and the media so relentless that several different identifications have been projected onto this photograph.

It is one of the fundamental tenets of the German Press Council that the identity of victims has to be given special protection. According to the press code, 'knowledge about the victim's identity is generally irrelevant for understanding an accident occurrence, the circumstances of a disaster or crime. Publication of the name and photograph of the victim is permissible if the victim, the relatives or other authorised persons have given their consent or if the victim is a public figure.'[34] Yet under the intense competition that media outlets face today this special protection is often ignored, as can be seen in the reception of *Falling Man*. When *Bild* printed a photo spread a year after 9/11, showing portraits of people who had jumped from the towers in despair,[35] the complaints committee of the German Press Council decided once again that this was justified, since the families themselves had released these images or had made them public on memorial sites.[36] What was overlooked here was that the portraits may well have come from the families, but the images of the dead bodies, which *Bild* also reprinted, did not.

If I merely describe *Falling Man* here instead of showing it, this is not because I think the image itself is in any sense morally objectionable. On the contrary, it might well be a particularly successful representation of suffering of a kind that is rarely found in news reports on terror.[37] But as long

as media outlets continue to handle images in a way that leads to significant violations of personality rights, a gesture of not showing might be the only adequate response, at least for as long as these events are still in the news. The same applies to depictions of corpses and body parts, which after 9/11 and the Madrid commuter train bombings on 11 March 2004 were spread via dubious websites, as mentioned in Chapter 1. There may come a time when photographs like Richard Drew's and the reality that they represent are less indistinguishable and their political functionalisation has become a matter of the past. Only then will it be possible to consider them in a different framework and under a different light and perhaps reproduce them again. It is hard to predict when this time might come. Often many years have to pass before a reassessment within a less emotionally charged context is possible in the public sphere. In Germany in 2004, an art exhibition about the RAF in the 1970s still caused an outcry from the press, politicians and members of the public.[38] The violence of terror leaves deep wounds, both individual and social, which sometimes take decades to heal.[39]

As we have seen with *Falling Man*, the media are often more concerned with newsworthiness than with the personality rights of victims and their families. The popular press and private broadcasters only respect the guidelines for the protection of victims in the most blatant cases of violation. In response to the IS execution video of James Foley, for example, most Western media showed it almost entirely pixelated and only as a still. Yet when it comes to images of perpetrators, personality rights tend to be ignored altogether. Press codes frequently include a passage like the one in the guidelines of the German Press Council, which states that where serious crimes have been

committed the public has a right to know the identity of the suspects or perpetrators, and it is therefore permissible to circulate names, photos and other information.[40] This effectively authorises the dissemination not just of wanted photographs, but also of degrading images of individuals, without any differentiation between the two. The blurring of the lines is problematic, however, because it ignores the fact that personality rights derive from the foundational principle of respect for human dignity, to which even somebody who has committed a serious and brutal crime is entitled – otherwise prisons could turn into dungeons and the punished would have to endure inhumane treatment. In her thought-provoking book on the consequences of terror attacks, the journalist Carolin Emcke, whose godfather was murdered by the RAF, wrote: 'If we do not just smugly invoke human dignity, but truly respect it, then we have to grant it to everyone, even to those who would not grant it to others.'[41] The failure of, for example, the German Press Code to draw a distinction between wanted photographs and degrading images is thus inadequate and ethically unjustifiable.

There are, however, instances in which images have to be shown while the battle against terror is still ongoing, even if they violate the human dignity of those represented. The most appropriate place for these would of course be the courtroom, since they document violations of human rights by organs of the state, but in many cases it is only after the media have disseminated them that there is any chance of legal proceedings.[42] In the past, Amnesty International led targeted campaigns to circulate graphic images of victims of torture without any attempt to conceal the victims' identities.[43] Today, NGOs pursuing human rights issues often use the internet to persuade governments to take

action, a strategy that would hardly have any chance of success without such images. In contrast to their previous approach, Amnesty International and Human Rights Watch, as well as newer organisations such as WITNESS, now use verified images from eyewitnesses and publish them on YouTube, sometimes pixelated to safeguard the anonymity of those shown.[44] Others, like the Israeli human rights organisation B'Tselem, give video cameras to those concerned – in this case selected Palestinians in the West Bank – to document violations of human rights by Israeli security forces.

The apparent evidentiary status of these images is not without problems, however. Sam Gregory, an activist working for the human rights organisation WITNESS, has shown how certain photos of human rights violations circulating online can re-emerge in quite unanticipated contexts,[45] and those who produce image material for B'Tselem are both victims and co-opted members of an Israeli organisation which gives them special protection. Nevertheless, the rapid distribution of these images via the internet shows a trend already mentioned in the discussion about self-presentations of perpetrators in the previous chapter: mainstream media are no longer the only platform for disseminating powerful images within the context of terror. Today, the internet has assumed a leading and often far less predictable role.

In early 2016, for example, B'Tselem published a video on its website and on YouTube which showed Israeli soldiers executing a Palestinian attacker who was lying injured on the ground.[46] The video confirmed allegations that witnesses had repeatedly made since the start of the knife attacks by Palestinians against Israelis in October 2015: the brutal violence with which Israeli security forces countered the

terror. But it showed more than this. While the paramedic attended to the victim of the attack, whose condition was not critical, the knife attacker, whose name is mentioned by B'Tselem, appeared to be gravely injured, yet neither the Israeli security forces nor the paramedics were seen to be offering help. His face is clearly visible in the video and his head is still moving from left to right. Then a soldier, who is far less discernible in the picture, fires a shot. That the head of the shot Palestinian is shown pixelated from then on probably owes more to respect for public sensitivities than to any ethical considerations about the dignity of the murdered person. After the event, none of the people present seemed to be particularly upset, and the removal of the dead and injured continued without any sign of disturbance.

At first the international press reported this execution without images. However, after the video quickly spread online and stills appeared in the media all over the world,[47] pressure on the Israeli government increased. But when the gunman was arrested in Israel it caused an outcry of indignation, which led to threats against the video producer. Nine months later a military court in Tel Aviv found Elor Azaria, the soldier who fired the shot, guilty. The sentence of eighteen months in prison again produced a wave of public protest and the Israeli prime minister Benjamin Netanyahu and other leading politicians demanded an immediate pardon.[48] It is very unlikely that this chain of events would have happened without the video circulating on the internet.

There is thus no doubt that the release of this video was necessary to increase international pressure on the Israeli judiciary to punish state security forces for violations of human rights. Yet, the video raises numerous ethical questions. Was it important to name the video producer and expose him to threats? Was it imperative to show the

attacker's face initially without pixelating it, just to make it clear that he was still alive before he was shot? And what about the many soldiers and ambulance crews who might be accused of having failed to render assistance? Disregarding this fundamental principle of human care has penal consequences in Israel, just as in most other states.[49] Is such public exposure ethically justifiable, one might ask, if the details are ultimately only relevant for the prosecution and in court? And why did nobody press charges here? These are questions that need to be asked, though they do not discredit in any way the important and courageous work that B'Tselem is doing. We can presume that even a slightly pixelated video without names would have had the same public impact. The video as it was shown not only violated the personality rights of several people, it also encouraged uncontrolled revenge in a political situation that was already extremely tense.

Legal and ethical dilemmas like these pose a challenge even if images are circulated with the best intentions. They also show that human rights organisations, just like governments and the media, pursue their own objectives in the fight against terror. In doing so, none of them is a natural guardian of fundamental ethical and legal standards. The numerous non-professionals whose films now play an important role in the coverage of acts of terror are even less likely to consider such issues.[50] The attacks on the London underground on 7 July 2005 marked a historical turning point. As already mentioned in Chapter 1, this was the first time that a photo taken on a mobile phone appeared on the BBC website and then in the international press. There have been very few terror attacks since then during which decisive moments were not filmed by non-professional eyewitnesses and disseminated online or via print media or television.[51] The

quality of the images is often irrelevant. What counts is their apparent authenticity. One such example is a video of an explosion on Sultanahmet Square in Istanbul on 12 January 2016, a suicide attack during which twelve people, almost all Germans, were killed. A tourist had filmed the explosion by chance. In the centre of a still taken from the video, we can see the lower part of the obelisk on the square next to which the group was standing when the suicide bomber detonated his bomb (Figure 80). On the right, a group of dark figures appear that are blurred by the flare of the explosion. In the context in which it was published, the image was evidence of an act of terror. Yet it did not really show anything. Nonetheless, several papers, including *Süddeutsche Zeitung* and *Tagesspiegel*, printed it the next day.[52]

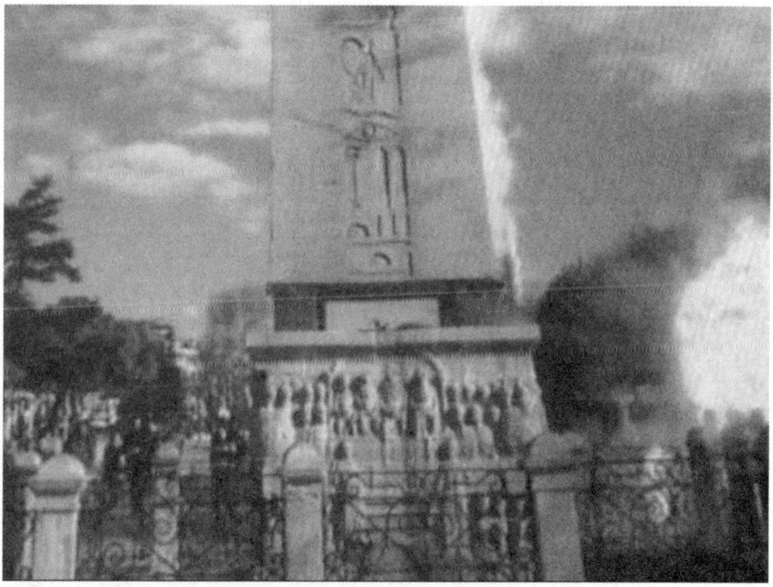

Figure 80 Still from a film of the suicide attack on Sultanahmet Square in Istanbul on 12 January 2016.

Previous chapters have already discussed the role and function of new ways of mediatising images. The development of the illustrated press in the nineteenth century gave modern terror an effective platform to spread fear to the masses, and the invention of the polaroid and video camera in the 1970s, which enabled kidnappers to circulate instant photographs of hostages quickly and without risky detours via a laboratory, helped them to increase pressure on governments. The internet, finally, gave attackers opportunities for forms of self-presentation that until then would have been impossible to circulate to a wider public. The dissemination of non-professional videos and photographs after an attack is thus merely the most recent development in a long series of technical advances which have helped to make images of terror effective. What is new, however, is that at least some of the responsibility has shifted from the usual agencies to social media users. Instead of merely being recipients of images, they now actively contribute to the production, circulation and consumption of images, and therefore assume a role that has aptly been described as 'prosumers'.[53]

Image usage and responsibility: eyewitnesses and media prosumers

Three examples may suffice to demonstrate this development and its consequences for images of terror.[54]

On 22 May 2013, a radical jihadist who had just killed the British soldier Lee Rigby near the Royal Artillery Barracks in Woolwich, southeast London, demanded to be filmed by an eyewitness. The attacker, with blood-covered hands, brandishing a cleaver and a knife, used this moment to claim that he had committed his deed in the name of God.

In the street behind him lay the victim unattended. Given that the attacker and his accomplice were arrested on the spot, and the video was filmed neither under threat of death nor as a response to the fate of the victim, it ultimately only had one aim: it gave the murderer the opportunity to publicly stage his claim of responsibility. Since the video was later broadcast as an exclusive on ITV News, we may even assume that money changed hands for it. The *Sun* also obtained visual material, and numerous news channels and press agencies showed either selections or stills from the video. That its publication served above all the interest of the attackers did not seem to bother any of the news editors. The Press Complaints Commission did receive objections, but since these merely criticised the brutality on display, the only recommendation was to issue a warning for sensitive viewers when showing emotionally disturbing material like this in the future. The logic of the material itself was ignored. No consideration was given to the fact that the producer of the video had unwittingly become the henchman of a brutal murderer and that the material was afterwards publicly disseminated. To put oneself in the service of an attacker in this way is not only highly problematic in the situation, but also ethically and strategically profoundly questionable.

Even graver consequences followed the decision of an eyewitness who filmed the aftermath of an attack on the French satirical magazine *Charlie Hebdo* in Paris on 7 January 2015 and immediately uploaded his video on Facebook. Fifteen minutes later it could be seen on YouTube, and an hour later on French television. After hearing gunshots from outside his flat, the man had hurried to the window with his camera to capture what was happening in the street below. The police officer who had tried to prevent the two gunmen

from fleeing, Ahmed Merabet, lay on the ground critically injured. The video shows how the attackers return to execute Merabat, who is pleading for his life, with a shot in the head.[55]

The filmmaker later apologised to the family and expressed regret for his actions. After considerable public pressure, Facebook and YouTube blocked the material, and the French broadcasting watchdog Conseil Supérieur de l'Audiovisuel later reprimanded the television channel which had broadcast it. But once the film was online, it could no longer be removed. For the attackers and their sympathisers the pictures are trophies; for the victim's friends and family they document an abyss of suffering. Whereas professional press photographers are usually aware of their responsibility, the same is clearly not always the case for ordinary citizens with digital cameras and access to the internet. Instead of handing over the footage to the police, they often publish it on social media platforms without thinking. Images uploaded on the internet, however, spread fast. In their efforts to find newsworthy images, mainstream media readily turn to footage produced by amateur eyewitnesses, since professional photographers are seldom on the scene quickly enough to capture what happens directly after an attack. Yet what is rarely considered is the personality rights of the victims, who are filmed or photographed in situations where almost nobody would want to be exposed to the anonymous gaze of the public. If any thought is given to them at all, it is only after the sensation value of the images has boosted the ratings of TV news programmes and the circulation of newspapers. For all these reasons, it is important that non-professional image producers also begin to reflect on the consequences of their actions before they circulate their material online.

But there are other, more accidental, images of acts of terror – and this is the third and final example – which fulfil a completely different and indeed constructive function. Since they do not fit neatly into a particular pattern of media reporting of the kind described in previous chapters, they do not normally attract the same amount of attention. One such video was allegedly taken by a resident of a West London housing estate on 29 July 2005 and handed over to the police. It showed the arrest of two of the attackers who had been on the run after the failed underground bombing eight days earlier. The footage was shown briefly on television and stills were published in the papers.[56] It then quickly disappeared from the news and only resurfaced two years later, after a still from it was shown in the trial of the attackers, to be subsequently released by the police (Figure 81).[57]

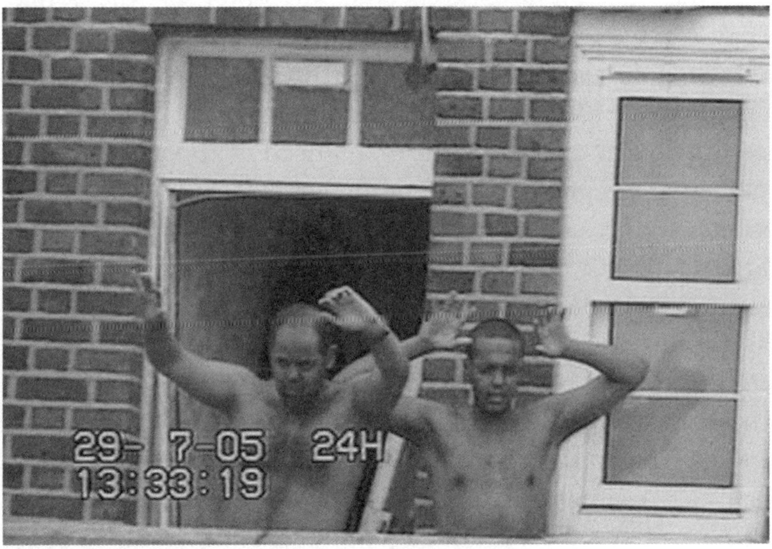

Figure 81 Still from a film showing the arrest of two attackers in London on 29 July 2005.

The video did not feature wild-eyed fanatics, but two young and very anxious-looking men with their arms up, standing on the balcony of the flat they had used as a hide-out. The area had been quietly evacuated, a large number of special units were present, and sharpshooters were in position on the roofs. The police had assumed that the two suspects would trigger explosives if arrested and thus kill not only themselves but also residents and security forces. Instead, the attackers had willingly followed police orders, removed their clothes and gone onto the balcony as instructed. This is where they were filmed from some distance. The footage shows that they were completely unprepared for this moment. The younger of the two, seen on the right, shouts 'I have rights, I have rights'. Although just a week earlier he had directly challenged the state's monopoly of force and its duty to safeguard its citizens, he now surprisingly invoked its protection for himself.

No one used the photograph to stereotype the attackers, and no one treated the two men as heroes or martyrs. Their unexpected cooperativeness during their arrest led to an image that departed significantly from the pattern of perpetrator depictions discussed in the previous chapter. The photograph has none of the qualities essential for media icons, so it is perhaps not surprising that it has almost been forgotten. Yet it has lost none of its power. Directing attention to the fragile human condition of those who are determined to kill in the name of God, it contradicts the idea of the perpetrators as monsters. Moreover, by departing from it so radically it demands considerable tolerance of ambiguity from the viewers.[58] Images like these make it infinitely more difficult to justify our own need for revenge by the supposed inhumanity of others, and for this reason they are all the more important.

Soon after 9/11, Susan Sontag, still following the premise that viewers are merely consumers of images, demanded: 'Let the atrocious images haunt us … The images say: This is what human beings are capable of doing.'[59] What Sontag does not explain is which images are supposed to haunt us in this way and which should not. Which ones are 'an invitation to pay attention, to reflect, to learn', and which ones glorify the acts of terror or prolong the humiliation of the people they portray?[60] Images of acts of violence are clearly not all the same, and it is important to understand the differences, as the non-professional productions discussed here have shown.

In an essay about the images from Abu Ghraib prison, Judith Butler responded to some of Susan Sontag's reflections:

> So the photograph is linked through its 'tense' to the grievability of life, anticipating and performing that grievability. In this way, we can be haunted in advance by the suffering or deaths of others. Or we can be haunted afterwards, when the check against grief becomes undone … This is an initial moment of cognition, an apprehension, but also a potential judgment, and it requires that we conceive of grievability as the precondition of life, one that is discovered retrospectively through the temporality instituted by the photograph itself.[61]

It is unfortunate that the filmmaker in Paris had not previously been haunted by the suffering or death of others before he released his footage on the internet. It is after all not impossible within the context of terror to produce and circulate images that convey the suffering inflicted on humans by other humans without degrading another person. Richard Drew's *Falling Man* is one example. The image falls outside the known patterns because it shows neither clearly recognisable victims, nor cruel perpetrators,

nor functioning civil societies. In fact, it constitutes, to use Susan Sontag's words again, an 'invitation to pay attention, to reflect, to learn'.[62] One day, perhaps, the protective wall against grief will fall, the wall which prevents us from comprehending the value of life cruelly brought to an end. Only then will it become possible for *Falling Man* to convey the fragility of human life without the need to assign the pain to an identifiable individual.

Not all images of violence, however, document merely the fate of the victims, and not all violations of personality rights automatically contravene the first paragraph of the German Basic Law ('Human dignity is inviolable') and its equivalent in the UN Universal Declaration of Human Rights of 1948. Secretly taking a photo of a well-known figure and publishing it might violate their personality rights, but only very rarely would it count as degradation. 'One should not fall prey to the fatal autosuggestion that the solution to detailed … cases, just as to urgent problems of the future, has been provided simply through the correct understanding of the inalienable Article 1, Paragraph 2 of Basic Law', writes the legal philosopher Horst Dreier.[63] The sentence is too weighty for this, its historical genesis too protean and its interpretation too varied.[64]

Yet the examples discussed here show that images can directly or indirectly violate this fundamental right. A direct violation takes place if, as in the execution videos of Al-Qaida and IS, human beings have to die so that images can be circulated. An indirect violation happens if degrading images of perpetrators are published solely for this purpose and photographs of the fatal or non-fatal suffering of recognisable victims are disseminated without the victims' knowledge or consent. Dreier also concedes that we do not necessarily have to base our judgement on a particular and

always controversial, positive definition of human dignity in order to note its violation in a concrete situation. According to him, non-definitions are sufficient

> for particularly grave cases (torture, degradation, ostracism, etc.); moreover, this emphasises the fundamental function of human dignity, which is independent of particular ethical, political or ideological positions.[65]

In the context of terror, it is of course highly unlikely that anybody, least of all the perpetrators, will take legal action on the grounds that their personality rights have been violated. Prison sentences are hardly a deterrent here and the damage done cannot be undone through court cases. Each attack strikes new victims, and once their images are circulated they remain in the public domain. But even if there are no plaintiffs, the fundamental ethical agreements anchored in national and international constitutions are no less binding.

One example discussed in this chapter, however, the photograph of the murderer of Lee Rigby, neither violates the dignity of a person nor any concomitant personality rights. Here, the problem lies elsewhere. It was not just the passer-by shooting the film but also the media that published the image who put themselves in the service of the attacker. To inadvertently become the tool of an attacker may not be a punishable offence, but from an ethical point of view it is nonetheless extremely problematic. Since images of terror attacks are always in the interest of the perpetrators, it is vital to consider the thin line between the need for information and the desire for sensation. In this case the situation was unambiguous: the duty to inform the public does not in any way justify aiding and abetting the propaganda sought by the murderer. Perhaps it will one day be

acceptable to show this video. But at the moment of the attack, the video's primary role was to aid in the perpetrator's self-glorification, a major motive for the murder. Its publication shortly after the murder was therefore scarcely justifiable. As the conflict still continues, I too have for now refrained from illustrating it in this book.

As all of these examples show, spontaneous reactions are rarely adequate responses to acts of terror. Whoever produces images and circulates them publicly needs to take a step back and reflect. Only once the public know about the pattern of news reporting in which such images appear, as well as the interests they might serve, and have understood their responsibility for the victims and their families, can we anticipate what suffering and damage we might inflict by our own actions. We might then finally be able to determine which images help us to comprehend grievability as a precondition of life and which ones impede or obstruct it. Only then will responsible engagement with images of terror be possible and voluntary self-regulation of media prosumers imaginable. In a battle that only knows losers, this reflection may prove vital.

Notes

Introduction

1 Hans Magnus Enzensberger, 'Ausblicke auf den Bürgerkrieg', *Der Spiegel*, 25 (1993), p. 174.
2 See Jens Eder and Charlotte Klonk, 'Introduction', in Jens Eder and Charlotte Klonk (eds), *Image Operations: Visual Media and Political Conflict* (Manchester: Manchester University Press, 2017), pp. 1–22.
3 Herfried Münkler, *The New Wars*, trans. Patrick Camiller (London: Polity, 2004), p. 111.
4 For works written after 9/11, see the sociologist and advisor to Congress Audrey Kurth Cronin and the historian and government advisor James M. Ludes (eds), *Attacking Terrorism: Elements of a Grand Strategy* (Washington, DC: Georgetown University Press, 2004); the terrorism expert and strategy consultant Bruce Hoffman, *Inside Terrorism*, 2nd edn (New York: Columbia University Press, 2006); and the political scientist and vice-chancellor of Oxford University Louise Richardson, *What Terrorists Want: Understanding the Terrorist Threat* (London: John Murray, 2006).
5 Judith Butler, 'Torture and the ethics of photography: Thinking with Sontag', in Judith Butler, *Frames of War: When is Life Grievable* (London and New York: Verso, 2010), pp. 63–100, here p. 64.
6 *Ibid.*, p. 74.
7 See among others Robert M. Entman, 'Framing: Toward clarification of a fractured paradigm', *Journal of Communication*, 4 (1993), 51–8; Joseph N. Cappella and Kathleen H. Jamieson, 'News frames, political cynicism, and media cynicism', *Annals*

of the American Academy of Political and Social Science, 546 (1996), 71–84; Bertram Scheufele, *Frames – Framing – Framing-Effekte. Theoretische und methodische Grundlegung sowie empirische Befunde zur Nachrichtenreproduktion* (Wiesbaden: Westdeutscher Verlag, 2003).

8 Aby Warburg, 'Dürer and Italian antiquity', in Aby Warburg, *The Renewal of Pagan Antiquity*, ed. Kurt W. Forster, trans. David Britt (Los Angeles, CA: Getty Publications, 1999), pp. 553–8.

9 Thomas Riegler's historically and geographically comprehensive overview, especially its thematic structure, has provided an important foundation for the present study: Thomas Riegler, *Terrorismus. Akteure, Strukturen, Entwicklungslinien* (Innsbruck: StudienVerlag, 2009).

10 On the term 'media event', see Daniel Dayan and Elihu Katz, 'Medienereignisse', in Ralf Adelmann, Jan O. Hesse, Judith Keilbach *et al.* (eds), *Grundlagentexte zur Fernsehwissenschaft. Theorie – Geschichte – Analyse* (Konstanz: UTB, 2002), pp. 413–53.

11 Gerhard Paul, *BilderMacht. Studien zur Visual History des 20. und 21. Jahrhunderts* (Göttingen: Wallstein, 2013), p. 9.

12 See, for example, Chitra Nagarajan, '#Bringbackourgirls hasn't brought back Chibok's girls, but it has changed Nigeria's politics', *Guardian* (14 April 2015), www.theguardian.com/commentisfree/2015/apr/14/nigeria-women-activists-boko-haram (accessed 8 December 2018).

13 Hoffman, *Inside Terrorism*, pp. 1–41.

14 Gerd van den Heuvel, 'Terreur, Terroriste, Terrorisme', in Hans Ulrich Gumbrecht, Rolf Reichardt and Gerd van den Heuvel (eds), *Handbuch politisch-sozialer Grundbegriffe in Frankreich 1680–1820*, vol. 3 (Munich: De Gruyter, 1985), pp. 89–132.

15 Edmund Burke, *Reflections on the Revolution in France* (London: Dodsley, 1790).

16 Henner Hess, 'Die neue Herausforderung. Von der RAF zu Al Qaida', in Wolfgang Kraushaar (ed.), *Die RAF und der linke Terrorismus*, vol. 1 (Hamburg: Hamburger Edition, 2006), p. 104.

17 Jörg Baberowski, *Der rote Terror. Die Geschichte des Stalinismus* (Munich: DVA, 2003).

18 Walter Laqueur, *The New Terrorism: Fanaticism and the Arms of Mass Destruction* (New York: Oxford University Press, 1999).

19 Henner Hess, 'Terrorismus und Terrorismus-Diskurs', in Henner Hess, Martin Moerings and Dieter Paas (eds), *Angriff auf das Herz des Staates. Soziale Entwicklung und Terrorismus*, vol. 1 (Frankfurt am Main: Suhrkamp, 1988), pp. 55–74, here p. 55.

20 Kai Ambos, 'What international law says about the killing of Bin Laden', *Der Spiegel* (13 May 2011), www.spiegel.de/international/world/terrorists-have-rights-too-what-international-law-says-about-the-killing-of-bin-laden-a-762417.html (accessed 8 December 2018).

21 Münkler, *The New Wars*, pp. 99–116. On the debate, see Matthias Dahlke, *Demokratischer Staat und transnationaler Terrorismus. Drei Wege zur Unnachgiebigkeit in Westeuropa 1972–1975* (Munich: Oldenbourg, 2011), pp. 26–7.

22 Dahlke, *Demokratischer Staat*, p. 27.

23 For a critical evaluation of this distinction, see among others Jan Philipp Reemtsma, 'Terroristische Gewalt. Was klärt die Frage nach den Motiven?', in Michael Beuthner, Joachim Buttler, Sandra Fröhlich *et al.* (eds), *Bilder des Terrors – Terror der Bilder. Krisenberichterstattung am und nach dem 11. September* (Cologne: Herbert von Halem Verlag, 2003), pp. 330–49, here p. 334; and Talal Asad, *On Suicide Bombing* (New York: Columbia University Press, 2007), p. 94.

24 First and foremost David Rapoport, *Assassination and Terrorism* (Toronto: CBC, 1971); Brian Jenkins, *International Terrorism: A New Kind of Warfare* (Santa Monica, CA: Rand, 1974); Yonah Alexander, *International Terrorism: National, Regional, and Global Perspectives* (New York: Praeger, 1976); Walter Laqueur, *A History of Terrorism*, expanded edn (New Brunswick: Transaction, 2016).

25 See Claire Sterling, *The Terror Network: The Secret War of International Terrorism* (New York: Holt, Rinehart, and Winston, 1981); Edward S. Herman, *The Real Terror Network: Terrorism in Fact and Propaganda* (Boston, MA: South End Press, 1982). Sterling emphasised the role played by the Eastern Bloc states in supporting global terror, while Herman made the USA the focal point of his study.

26 In particular, Mark Juergensmeyer's groundbreaking studies *The New Cold War? Religious Nationalism Confronts the Secular State* (Berkeley, CA: University of California Press, 1993) and *Terror in the Mind of God: The Global Rise of Religious Violence* (Berkeley, CA: University of California Press, 2000).

27 David Rapoport, 'The four waves of modern terrorism', in Cronin and Ludes, *Attacking Terrorism*, pp. 46–73.

28 Rapoport, 'Four waves', p. 49.

29 *Ibid.*, p. 57.

30 Alexander Demandt (ed.), *Das Attentat in der Geschichte* (Cologne: Böhlau, 1996).

31 Jenkins, *International Terrorism*, p. 4.
32 See among others Peter Waldmann, *Terrorismus. Provokation der Macht* (Munich: Gerling Akademie, 1998); Hoffmann, *Inside Terrorism*; Münkler, *The New Wars*. A good overview of the state of research informed by this perspective on 1970s terror in West Germany can be found in Klaus Weinhauer, 'Terrorismus und Kommunikation. Forschungsstand und -perspektiven zum bundesdeutschen Linksterrorismus der 1970er Jahre', in Nicole Colin, Beatrice de Graaf, Jacco Pekelder *et al.* (eds), *Der 'Deutsche Herbst' und die RAF in Politik, Medien und Kunst. Nationale und internationale Perspektiven* (Bielefeld: Transcript, 2008), pp. 109–23.
33 Dahlke, *Demokratischer Staat*, pp. 29–30.
34 Thus, for example, Anthony D. Buckley, *Symbols in Northern Ireland* (Liverpool: Institute of Irish Studies, 1998); Mahmoud Abu Hashhash, 'On the visual representation of martyrdom in Palestine', *Third Text*, 3–4 (2006), pp. 391–403; Laleh Khalili, *Heroes and Martyrs of Palestine: The Politics of Commemoration* (Cambridge: Cambridge University Press, 2007); Zeina Maasri, *Off the Wall: Political Posters of the Lebanese Civil War* (London: I.B. Tauris, 2009); Maximilian Rapp, *Murals in Nordirland. Symbol der ethno-kulturellen Identität und Spiegel des politischen Wandels* (Baden-Baden: Nomos, 2014).
35 The radical left-wing so-called urban guerrillas of the 1970s mark an exception to this list since they were very much concerned with producing startling shock effects in their own country. Yet they enjoyed relatively little support from the population and had no hinterland that they controlled and to which they could withdraw.
36 Martin H. W. Möllers and Robert Chr. van Ooyen, *NSU-Terrorismus. Ergebnisse der parlamentarischen Untersuchungsausschüsse und Empfehlungen für die Sicherheitsbehörden* (Frankfurt: Verlag für Polizeiwissenschaft, 2015), pp. 216–18.
37 Bart Schuurman, 'Topics in terrorism research: Reviewing trends and gaps, 2007–2016', *Critical Studies on Terrorism* (2019), DOI: 10.1080/17539153.2019.1579777.
38 Hoffman, *Inside Terrorism*, p. 183. Despite its title, Philip Jenkins's *Images of Terror: What We Can and Can't Know about Terrorism* (New York, de Gruyter, 2003) contains not a single image. In this book, 'images' refers to the idea of terror.
39 Münkler, *The New Wars*, pp. 99–116.
40 Gerhard Paul, *Der Bilderkrieg. Inszenierungen, Bilder und Perspektiven der 'Operation Irakische Freiheit'* (Göttingen: Wallstein, 2005), p. 158.

41 Zeynep D. Gürsel, 'Framing Zarqawi: Afterimages, headshots, and body politics in a digital age', in Olga Shevchenko (ed.), *Double Exposure: Memory and Photography* (Piscataway, NJ: Transaction, 2014), pp. 65–90.
42 Mohammed M. Hafez, 'The origins of sectarian terrorism in Iraq', in Bruce Hoffman and Fernando Reinares (eds), *The Evolution of the Global Terrorist Threat: From 9/11 to Osama bin Laden's Death* (New York: Columbia University Press, 2014), pp. 436–60.
43 Richardson, *What Terrorists Want*, pp. 95–132.
44 Ernst H. Gombrich, *The Image and the Eye: Further Studies in the Psychology of Pictorial Representation* (London: Phaidon, 1994); and E. H. Gombrich, 'The evidence of images: The variability of vision', in C. S. Singleton (ed.), *Interpretation: Theory and Practice* (Baltimore, MD: Johns Hopkins University Press, 1969), pp. 35–68. For a critical discussion of different image theories of pictorial evidence, see Ludger Schwarte, *Pikturale Evidenz. Zur Wahrheitsfähigkeit der Bilder* (Paderborn: Wilhelm Fink, 2015).
45 On these examples in a different context, see Charlotte Klonk, 'Image terror', in Sue Malvern and Gabriel Koureas (eds), *Terrorist Transgressions: Gender and the Visual Culture of the Terrorist* (London: I.B. Tauris, 2014), pp. 15–37.
46 On the controversy, see Rajiv Chandrasekaran, 'Sole informant guided decision on Afghan strike', *Washington Post* (6 September 2009), front page and p. A12; Ulrike Demmer, Markus Feldenkirchen, Ullrich Fichtner *et al.*, 'Ein deutsches Verbrechen', *Der Spiegel* (5, 2010), pp. 34–57.
47 *Frankfurter Allgemeine Zeitung* (3 May 2001), front page.
48 Paul Farhi, 'How to show bin Laden is dead', *Washington Post* (4 May 2011), p. C10.
49 Eugene Robinson, 'Why I would've released the bin Laden photos', *Washington Post* (4 May 2011), www.washingtonpost.com/blogs/post-partisan/post/why_i_wouldve_released_the_bin_laden_photos/2011/03/04/AFztulpF_blog.html?wprss=post-partisan (accessed 11 December 2018).

Chapter 1

1 Quoted by Louise Richardson, *What Terrorists Want: Understanding the Terrorist Threat*, London, John Murray, 2006, p. 207.
2 See the extensive bibliography 'Deutsch- und englischsprachige Monographien, Sammelbände und Themenhefte zum 11.

September 2001', compiled by Jonas Brendebach as at 15 August 2011, *Zeithistorische Forschungen/Studies in Contemporary History*, 8 (2011), 463–74, www.zeithistorische-forschungen.de/sites/default/files/medien/material/Bibliographie_11_09_2001.pdf (accessed 26 February 2019).

3 For the context of Karlheinz Stockhausen's remark, see Klaus H. Grabowski, 'Die Stimmen der Intellektuellen und ihr Echo', in Felicitas von Aretin and Bernd Wannenmacher (eds), *Weltlage. Der 11. September, die Politik und die Kulturen* (Opladen: Leske und Budrich, 2002), pp. 195–208; Otto Karl Werckmeister, 'Ästhetik der Apokalypse', in Bazon Brock and Gerlinde Koschik (eds), *Krieg und Kunst* (Munich: Wilhelm Fink, 2002), pp. 195–207.

4 Richardson, *What Terrorists Want*, p. 207. 'The 3,000 casualties inflicted by al-Qaeda, while enormous, pale in comparison to the 30,000 suicides and 16,000 homicides in the US in the same year, or even the 15,000 Americans who died in falls in 2001' (*ibid.*, p. 183).

5 The following discussion is based on an earlier essay on images of terror and their history in Charlotte Klonk, 'Macht der Bilder – Attentate als Medienereignisse', *Aus Politik und Zeitgeschichte* 45–46 (2013), 30–9.

6 *Illustrated London News* (19 March 1881), p. 266.

7 See the 1879 programme of the executive committee of Narodnaya Volya (quoted in Rudolf Walther, 'Terror, Terrorismus', in Otto Brunner, Werner Conze and Reinhart Koselleck (eds), *Geschichtliche Grundbegriffe. Historisches Lexikon zur politisch-sozialen Sprache in Deutschland*, vol. 6 (Stuttgart: Klett-Cotta, 1990), pp. 323–444, here p. 389.

8 Walther, 'Terror, Terrorismus', pp. 388–90.

9 Hans-Joachim Torke, 'Die Narodniki und Zar Alexander II (1881). Ein Vorspiel zur Revolution', in Alexander Demandt (ed.), *Das Attentat in der Geschichte* (Frankfurt am Main: Suhrkamp, 1999), pp. 298–316, here p. 308.

10 Quoted from the English translation in George Woodcock (ed.), *The Anarchist Reader* (Glasgow: Fontana, 1977), pp. 43–4.

11 *Illustrated London News* (19 March 1881), p. 266.

12 Deborah Hardy, *Land and Freedom: The Origins of Russian Terrorism* (New York: Greenwood Press, 1887); Torke, 'Die Narodniki', pp. 298–316.

13 For the history of the *Illustrated London News* and the kind of photo journalism it established, see Peter W. Sinnema, *Dynamics of the Pictured Page: Representing the Nation in The Illustrated London News* (Aldershot: Ashgate, 1998).

14 Leipzig *Illustrirte Zeitung* (2 April–23 April 1881), pp. 262, 263, 289, 292, 293, 337; *L'Illustration* (26 March–30 April 1881), pp. 200–1, 273, 288.
15 David Reed, *The Popular Magazine in Britain and the United States 1880–1960* (London: British Library, 1997).
16 Patrick Quinlivan and Paul Rose, *The Fenians in England, 1865–1872* (London: John Calder, 1982).
17 What caused a particular stir was a failed attempt to liberate one of their members from Clerkenwell Prison, during which six local residents died in a dynamite explosion (Quinlivan and Rose, *Fenians in England*, pp. 95–6).
18 Kenneth R. M. Short, *The Dynamite War* (Dublin: Gill and Macmillan, 1979), p. 50.
19 Lindsay Clutterbuck, 'The progenitors of terrorism. Russian revolutionaries or extreme Irish Republicans?', *Terrorism and Political Violence*, 1 (2004), 154–81, here pp. 165–6.
20 *Illustrated London News* (14 April 1883), p. 354.
21 *Illustrated London News* (24 April 1883), p. 376.
22 *Illustrated London News* (3 November 1883), p. 426.
23 *Illustrated London News* (19 April 1884), front page.
24 *Illustrated London News* (7 June 1884), pp. 543–6.
25 See *Illustrated London News* (31 January 1885 and 2 May 1885).
26 Clutterbuck, 'Progenitors of terrorism', p. 176.
27 Richardson, *What Terrorists Want*, p. 23.
28 John Merriman, *The Dynamite Club: How Bombing in Fin-de-Siècle Paris Ignited the Age of Modern Terror* (London: JR Books, 2009), pp. 69–87.
29 See *L'Illustration* (10 February 1894), pp. 112–13.
30 For a detailed description of the attacks and their aftermath, see Jean Maitron, *Ravachol et les anarchistes* (Paris: Gallimard, 1992).
31 Henrie Varennes, *De Ravachol à Caserio, notes d'audience* (Paris: Farnier frères, 1895), p. 217.
32 James Joll, *The Anarchists* (London: Methuen, 1964); Alex Butterworth, *The World That Never Was: A True Story of Dreamers, Schemers, Anarchists, and Secret Agents* (New York: Vintage, 2010).
33 Richard Bach Jensen, *The Battle against Anarchist Terrorism: An International History, 1878–1934* (Cambridge: Cambridge University Press, 2014).
34 Hoffman, *Inside Terrorism*, pp. 20–1.
35 Joseph Conrad has described the cosmopolitan London anarchist scene around 1900 in his novel *The Secret Agent* (1907).

36 This was a rule which was tactitly adopted from war reporting: Bodo von Dewitz, 'Zur Geschichte der Kriegsphotographie des Ersten Weltkrieges', in Rainer Rother (ed.), *Die letzten Tage der Menschheit. Bilder des Ersten Weltkrieges* (Berlin: Ars Nicolai, 1994), pp. 163–76, here p. 170.
37 See among others David Nye, *American Technological Sublime* (Cambridge, MA: MIT Press, 1994); Lynda Nead, *Victorian Babylon: People, Streets, and Images in Nineteenth-Century London* (New Haven, CT: Yale University Press, 2000); Paul Fyfe, 'Illustrating the accident: Railways and the catastrophic picturesque in The Illustrated London News', *Victorian Periodicals Review*, 1 (2013), 61–91. The discussion of early illustrated war reporting has also concentrated on individual images and their pictorial conventions for confining terror, see e.g. Ulrich Keller, *The Ultimate Spectacle; A Visual History of the Crimean War* (New York: Routledge, 2001) and Bernd Hüppauf, *Fotografie im Krieg* (Munich: Fink, 2015).
38 For the technical development, see Reed, *The Popular Magazine*. The supposed claim to objectivity of photomechanical illustration has long been a subject of critical debate. See, for example, Estelle Jussim, *Visual Communication and the Graphic Arts: Photographic Technologies in the Nineteenth-Century* (New York: Bowker, 1974); Joel Snyder and Neil W. Allen, 'Photography, vision, and representation', *Critical Inquiry*, 2 (1975), 143–69; Neil Harris, 'Iconography and intellectual history: The halftone effect', in John Higham and Paul K. Conkin (eds), *New Directions in American Intellectual History* (Baltimore, MD: John Hopkins University Press, 1979), pp. 196–211.
39 Quoted by Richardson, *What Terrorists Want*, p. 121.
40 Jens Eder, 'Affective image operations', in Jens Eder and Charlotte Klonk (eds), *Image Operations: Visual Media and Political Conflict* (Manchester: Manchester University Press, 2017), pp. 63–78.
41 Alexander Kluge, 'Die Macht der Bewußtseinsindustrie und das Schicksal unserer Öffentlichkeit', in Klaus von Bismarck, Günter Gaus, Alexander Kluge *et al.* (eds), *Industrialisierung des Bewußtseins. Eine kritische Auseinandersetzung mit den 'neuen' Medien* (Munich: Piper, 1985), pp. 51–129, here p. 99.
42 Georg Seeßlen and Markus Metz, *Krieg der Bilder – Bilder des Krieges. Abhandlung über die Katastrophe und mediale Wirklichkeit* (Berlin: Edition Tiamat, 2002); Joachim Buttler, 'Ästhetik des Terrors – Die Bilder des 11. September 2001', in Michael Beuthner, Joachim Buttler, Sandra Fröhlich *et al.* (eds),

Bilder des Terrors – Terror der Bilder? Krisenberichterstattung am und nach dem 11. September (Cologne: Herbert von Halem Verlag, 2003), pp. 26–41.

43 Seeßlen und Metz, *Krieg der Bilder*, p. 69.

44 Gerhard Paul, *Bilder des Krieges – Krieg der Bilder. Die Visualisierung des modernen Krieges* (Paderborn: Schöningh, 2004), p. 446.

45 See among others Magnum Photographers (eds), *New York, September 11, September* (New York: powerHouse Books, 2001). On the use of the CNN material, see Brian A. Monahan, *The Shock of the News: Media Coverage and the Making of 9/11* (New York: New York University Press, 2010).

46 Susan Sontag, *Regarding the Pain of Others* (London: Hamish Hamilton, 2004), pp. 24–5.

47 The *New York Times*, for example, published a photo of the damage at the Pentagon on its front and inside pages, but none of the plane crash near Shanksville in Pennsylvania (12 September 2001, front page and p. A5). However, later some photos did become known (albeit to a lesser extent), especially a photo taken by a local Shanksville woman that showed a cloud of smoke rising behind a green field and houses after the crash: Sean D. Hamill, 'A Sept. 11 photo brings out the conspiracy theorists', *New York Times* (11 September 2007), p. A20.

48 See among others Anne Marie Hacht (ed.), *Gale Encyclopedia of U.S. History*, vol. 2 (Detroit, MI: Gale, 2008), p. 621; Hermann Kinder and Werner Hilgemann (eds), *Von der Französischen Revolution bis zur Gegenwart* (Munich: DTV, 2009), cover; Philip Parker, *Kompakt und Visuell. Geschichte* (Munich: Dorling Kindersley, 2010), p. 411; Bernd Störer, *United States of America. Geschichte und Kultur* (Munich: C.H. Beck, 2012), p. 626.

49 Clément Chéroux, *Diplopie: L'image photographique à l'ère des médias globalisés: essai sur le 11 septembre 2001* (Paris: Le Point du Jour, 2009).

50 Sontag, *Regarding the Pain of Others*, p. 76.

51 Iconic in the sense of Reinhold Viehoff and Kathrin Fahlenbrach's definition: 'Media culture icons … are "key images" … of the global media sphere. Media culture icons not only reflect media culture as external, reproducible and easily visible forms that attune viewers' emotions and are spread *en masse*, but also always constitute this culture's internal, integrative, and unique content, establishing its identity'; Reinhold Viehoff and Kathrin Fahlenbrach, 'Ikonen der Medienkultur. Über die (verschwindende) Differenz

von Authentizität und Inszenierung der Bilder in der Geschichte', in Beuthner *et al.*, *Bilder des Terrors*, pp. 42–59, here p. 44.

52 William S. Cohen, 'Preparing for a grave new world', *Washington Post* (26 July 1999), p. A19; also see Richard Cohen, 'The terrorism story – and how we blew it', *Washington Post* (4 October 2001), p. A31.

53 A comparative analysis by the US transnational *International Herald Tribune* and the Arabic transnational *Al-Hayat* has shown that both newspapers printed similar or identical images of the events of 9/11 on their front pages. These images were sourced via the world's three largest picture agencies (AP, AFP and Reuters). See Shahira Fahmy, *Filling out the Frame; Transnational Visual Coverage and News Practitioners' Attitudes. Towards the Reporting of War and Terrorism* (Saarbrücken: VDM Verlag, 2007), p. 48.

54 Brooke Barnett and Amy Reynolds, *Terrorism and the Press: An Uneasy Relationship* (New York: Peter Lang, 2009), p. 92.

55 *Ibid.*, p. 81.

56 *New York Times* (12 September 2001), p. A7.

57 Barnett and Reynolds, *Terrorism and the Press*, p. 81.

58 Paul, *Bilder des Krieges*, pp. 433–50.

59 Quoted in Benjamin Runkle, *Wanted Dead or Alive* (New York: Palgrave, 2011), p. 2.

60 Susanne Regener, 'Facial Politics – Bilder des Bösen nach dem 11. September', in Petra Löffler and Leander Scholz (eds), *Das Gesicht ist eine starke Organisation* (Cologne: DuMont, 2004), pp. 203–24.

61 Nadia Khomami, 'Marcy Borders, 9/11's "dust lady", dies of stomach cancer', *Guardian* (26 August 2015), www.theguardian.com/us-news/2015/aug/26/911s-dust-lady-marcy-borders-dies-of-stomach-cancer (accessed 26 February 2019).

62 See among others Viehoff and Fahlenbarch, 'Ikonen', p. 55–7; Paul, *Bilder des Krieges*, p. 448; Robert Hariman and John Louis Lucaites, *No Caption Needed. Iconic Photographs, Public Culture, and Liberal Democracy* (Chicago, IL: Chicago University Press, 2007), p. 93–136; Clément Chéroux, 'The déja vu of 11 September: An essay on intericonicity', http://eitherand.org/social-medium/deja-vu-september-11-essay-intericonicity/ (accessed 8 February 2019).

63 Chéroux, 'Déja vu'.

64 Hariman and Lucaites, *No Caption Needed*, pp. 93–136.

65 Paul, *Bilder des Krieges*, p. 448.

66 Werckmeister, 'Ästhetik der Apokalypse', pp. 195–207.

67 Aaron Edwards, *The Northern Ireland Troubles: Operation Banner 1969–2007* (Oxford: Osprey Publishing, 2011), pp. 61–2.
68 Michaela Wiegel, 'Ohne Strategie. Die französische Regierung verengt die Terrorismus-Debatte auf Sicherheitspolitik', *Frankfurter Allgemeine Zeitung* (5 April 2016), p. 8.
69 For a comparative analysis of the television coverage of these events (CNN, Al Jazeera, BBC, ARD and RTL), see Jürgen Gerhards, Mike S. Schäfer, Ishtar Al-Jabiri *et al.*, *Terrorismus im Fernsehen. Formate, Inhalte und Emotionen in westlichen und arabischen Sendern* (Wiesbaden: VS Verlag, 2011); for the press coverage, see Antje Glück, *Terror im Kopf. Terrorismusberichterstattung in der deutschen und arabischen Elitepresse* (Berlin: Frank und Timme, 2008).
70 *El Pais* (12 March 2004), front page, and *Guardian* (12 March 2004), front page.
71 Christine Seehaus, 'Terrorismus in Bildern. Die Grenzen des rechtlich Zulässigen', in Sonja Glaab (ed.), *Medien und Terrorismus. Auf den Spuren einer symbiotischen Beziehung* (Berlin: Berliner Wissenschafts-Verlag, 2007), pp. 115–38, here p. 122.
72 See among other sources the witness statements given in court: 'Voices of 7/7: The survivors' testimonies form a searing but inspiring memorial to the 52 victims', http://independent.co.uk/news/uk/home-news/voices-of-77-the-survivors-testimonies-from-a-searing-but-inspiring-memorial-to-the-52-victims-2231571.html (accessed 4 February 2019).
73 *The Times* (8 July 2005), front page; *Daily Telegraph* (8 July 2005), front page; *Sun* (8 July 2005), front page.
74 On the assassins' background, see Bruce Hoffman, 'The 7 July 2005 London bombings', in Bruce Hoffman and Fernando Reinares (eds), *The Evolution of the Global Terrorist Threat: From 9/11 to Osama bin Laden's Death* (New York: Columbia University Press, 2014), pp. 192–223.
75 Joan Kristin Bleicher, 'Lesarten des Wirklichen. Narrative Strukturen der Live-Übertragung vom 11. September 2001', in Beuthner *et al.*, *Bilder des Terrors*, pp. 60–73, here p. 63.
76 Paul, *Bilder des Krieges*, p. 448.
77 Glück, *Terror im Kopf*, p. 162.
78 Aldina Quintana and Rolf Kailuweit, '"De Madrid al cielo". (De) Kontextualisierung des 11-M durch Popmusik und Videoclips im Internet', in Ursula Hennigfeld and Stephan Packard (eds), *Abschied von 9/11? Distanznahmen zur Katastrophe* (Berlin: Frank und Timme, 2013), pp. 213–44, here pp. 213–16.
79 Sontag, *Regarding the Pain of Others*, p. 77.

80 See also *New York Times* (8 July 2005), front page.
81 Stuart Allan, 'Citizen journalism and the rise of "mass self-communication": Reporting the London bombings', *Global Media Journal*, Australian Edition, 1 (2007), 1–20.

Chapter 2

1 Keith Bloomfield, 'Hostage taking and government response', *RUSI Journal*, 4 (2001), 23–7, here p. 24. See also Norman Antokol and Mayer Nudell, *No One a Neutral: Political Hostage-Taking in the Modern World* (Medina: Alpha Publications, 1990), p. 93.
2 Christian F. Buck, *Medien und Geiselnahmen. Fallstudien zum inszenierten Terror* (Wiesbaden: VS Verlag für Sozialwissenschaften, 2007), p. 31.
3 See also the report in *Spiegel*, 46 (1979), p. 142.
4 Massoumeh Ebtekar and Fred Reed, *Takeover in Tehran: The Inside Story of the 1979 U.S. Embassy Capture* (Vancouver: Talonbooks, 2000), p. 170.
5 Buck, *Medien und Geiselnahmen*, p. 68.
6 Brigitte L. Nacos, *Terrorism and the Media: From the Iran Hostage Crisis to the World Trade Center Bombing* (New York: Columbia Press, 1994), pp. 94–112.
7 Hamilton Jordan, *Crisis: The Last Year of the Carter Presidency* (New York: Putnam, 1982), pp. 250–91.
8 The only gain that the regime in Iran – which by then had opened up a new conflict zone through the invasion of Iraq – achieved during the negotiations was the release of Iran's assets, which had been frozen in the US after the occupation. It included the Shah's assets, a guarantee of non-intervention in internal affairs, as well as a waiver of compensation claims by the hostages. Thus little, apart from the transfer of the Shah's assets, was achieved beyond the return to the *status quo ante*.
9 See Buck, *Medien und Geiselnahmen*, pp. 67–77.
10 See also, among others, Clive C. Aston, *A Contemporary Crisis: Political Hostage-Taking and the Experience of Western Europe* (New York: Greenwood Press, 1982); Antokol and Nudell, *No One a Neutral*; Nacos, *Terrorism and the Media*; Russell D. Buhite, *Lives at Risk: Hostages and Victims in American Foreign Policy* (Wilmington, DE: Scholarly Resources, 1995); Buck, *Medien und Geiselnahmen*.

11 An exception on which the present study is also based is the by now quite large body of literature about the RAF in Germany in the 1970s (see Rolf Adelmann and Rolf F. Nohr, '"Man versucht sich zu öffnen". Video und RAF – Eine abgeschlossene Geschichte', *Text und Kritik*, 108 (2000), 77–83; Martin Steinseifer, '"Fotos wie Brandwunden"? Überlegungen zur deontischen Bedeutung von Pressefotografien am Beispiel von Hanns Martin Schleyer als Opfer der Roten Armee Fraktion', in Dietrich Busse, Thomas Niehr and Martin Wengeler (eds), *Brisante Semantik. Neuere Konzepte und Forschungsergebnisse einer kulturwissenschaftlichen Linguistik* (Tübingen: Niemeyer, 2005), pp. 269–90; Petra Terhoeven, 'Opferbilder – Täterbilder. Die Fotografie als Medium linksterroristischer Selbstermächtigung in Deutschland und Italien während der 70er Jahre', *Geschichte und Wissenschaft und Unterricht*, 7–8 (2007), 380–99). See also Annette Vowinckel's cultural history of aircraft hijackings, *Flugzeugentführungen. Eine Kulturgeschichte* (Göttingen: Wallstein, 2011), which also includes a thorough discussion of images.

12 In the past, journalists would usually gain access to hostages when a guerrilla group was able to abduct people into an area that it controlled, as was the case with the Revolutionary Armed Forces of Colombia (FARC) (see Victoria Bruce and Karin Hayes, *Hostage Nation: Columbia's Guerrilla Army and the Failed War on Drugs* (New York: Alfred A. Knopf, 2010), pp. 144–54) – or during the kidnapping of Jolo in the Philippines (Buck, *Medien und Geiselnahmen*, pp. 127–46).

13 David L. Altheide, 'Iran vs. US TV news: The hostage story out of context', in William C. Adams (ed.), *Television Coverage of the Middle East* (Norwood: Ablex Publishing, 1981), pp. 128–57, here p. 154.

14 Walter Benjamin, 'Small history of photography', in Walter Benjamin, *On Photography*, ed. and trans. Esther Leslie (London: Reaktion Books, 2015), pp. 59–94, here p. 83.

15 Benjamin, 'Small history of photography', p. 93.

16 Antokol and Nudell, *No One a Neutral*, p. 36.

17 The following summary of the kidnappings in Latin America is based on *ibid.*, pp. 40–53.

18 Claude Fly, *No Hope But God* (Portland, OR: Hawthorn Books, 1973), p. 60; Geoffrey Jackson, *People's Prison* (London: Faber, 1973), pp. 196–8.

19 The term 'urban guerrilla' was coined by the Brazilian rebel Carlos Marighellas, whose *Minimanual of the Urban Guerrilla*, first published in the US in 1970, appeared later the same year in

German translation as *Minihandbuch des Stadtguerilleros*. The RAF explicitly referred to it a year later in one of its publications: *Konzept Stadtguerilla* (Amsterdam: Niemec, 1971).

20 Richard Wigg, 'Envoy writes from Tupamaros cell', *The Times* (27 March 1971), p. 5.

21 I am drawing here on texts already published in other contexts: Charlotte Klonk, 'Bildterrorismus. Von Meins bis Schleyer', in Inge Stephan and Alexandra Tacke (eds), *NachBilder der RAF* (Cologne: Böhlau, 2008), pp. 197–215; and Charlotte Klonk, 'Die Entführung von Hanns Martin Schleyer oder die Entdeckung des Mediums Gesicht im terroristischen Bilderkampf', *Kritische Berichte*, 2 (2008), 49–58.

22 Lutz Hachmeister, *Schleyer. Eine deutsche Geschichte* (Munich: DTV, 2007), p. 382.

23 Rote Armee Fraktion, *Texte und Materialien zur Geschichte der RAF* (Berlin: ID-Verlag, 1997), p. 271.

24 Hachmeister, *Schleyer*, p. 332.

25 *Ibid.*, pp. 323–4.

26 David Gugerli, *Suchmaschinen. Die Welt als Datenbank* (Frankfurt am Main: Suhrkamp, 2009), pp. 64–9.

27 *Interview mit Helmut Schmidt*, in *Todesspiel Teil 1. Volksgefängnis* (BRD, 1997), dir: Heinrich Breloer.

28 Hachmeister, *Schleyer*, p. 311.

29 Stefan Wisniewski, *Wir waren so unheimlich konsequent. Ein Gespräch zur Geschichte der RAF*, 3rd edn (Berlin: ID-Verlag, 2003), p. 30.

30 Terhoeven, 'Opferbilder', p. 383.

31 *Ibid.*, p. 386.

32 Presse- und Informationsamt der Bundesregierung, *Zu den Ereignissen und Entscheidungen im Zusammenhang mit der Entführung von Hanns Martin Schleyer und der Lufthansa-Maschine 'Landshut'*, 2nd edn (Munich: Goldmann, 1977), p. 16.

33 On this meeting, see Buck, *Medien und Geiselnahmen*, pp. 59–63.

34 *Bild-Zeitung* (10 September 1977), front page; *Der Spiegel*, 38 (1977), p. 17.

35 Buck, *Medien und Geiselnahmen*, pp. 58–63.

36 See Steinseifer, 'Fotos wie Brandwunden', p. 284.

37 Presse- und Informationsamt der Bundesregierung, *Zu den Ereignissen*, p. 28.

38 *Ibid.*, p. 36.

39 *Ibid.*, p. 98.

40 Wisniewski, *Wir waren so unheimlich*, p. 41.

41 Hachmeister, *Schleyer*, p. 395.

42 Magnus Ranstorp, 'Hizbollah's command leadership: Its structure, decision-making, and relationship with Iranian clergy and institutions', in John Horgan and Kurt Braddock (eds), *Terrorism Studies: A Reader* (London: Routledge, 2012), pp. 147–73.
43 Thomas Riegler, *Terrorismus. Akteure, Strukturen, Entwicklungslinien* (Innsbruck: StudienVerlag, 2009), p. 98.
44 *Ibid.*, p. 99.
45 Jonathan C. Randal, 'Hostages to be held until at least 1989, PLO official asserts', *Washington Post* (21 February 1987), p. A13.
46 Peter Harclerode, *Secret Soldiers: Special Forces in the War against Terrorism* (London: Cassell, 2001), p. 470.
47 Terry Anderson, *Den of Lions: Memoirs of Seven Years* (New York: Random House, 1993), plate section.
48 See among others John MacCarthy and Jill Morrell, *Some Other Rainbow* (London: Bantam Press, 1993), pp. 134, 191; Terry Waite, *Taken on Trust* (San Diego, CA: Harcourt Brace, 1993), pp. 81–2; Brian Keenan, *An Evil Cradling* (London: Vintage, 1993), pp. 103–235.
49 Riegler, *Terrorismus*, p. 99.
50 Nacos, *Terrorism and the Media*, p. 86.
51 See Walter Goodmann, 'Of television images and hostage realities', *New York Times* (10 August 1989), p. 18.
52 Anderson, *Den of Lions*, pp. 183–4.
53 Nacos, *Terrorism and the Media*, pp. 126–8.
54 Riegler, *Terrorismus*, p. 100.
55 Anderson, *Den of Lions*, plate section.
56 Riegler, *Terrorismus*, p. 297.
57 Gerhard Paul, *Der Bilderkrieg. Inszenierungen, Bilder und Perspektiven der 'Operation Irakische Freiheit'* (Göttingen: Wallstein, 2005), p. 174.
58 Riegler, *Terrorismus*, p. 298.
59 Paul, *Der Bilderkrieg*, p. 178.
60 Will Dahlgrehn, *Terror Video Reached 83% of British Population*, https://yougov.co.uk/news/2014/08/22/terror-video-reached-83-percent-british-people (accessed 28 March 2019).
61 Clemens J. Seitz, 'Das grelle Herz der Finsternis', *Die Zeit* (25 September 2014), 47–8.
62 Aaron Y. Zelin, 'Picture or it didn't happen: A snapshot of the Islamic State's official media output', *Perspectives on Terrorism*, 9 (2015), 85–97.
63 Carolin Emcke, *Dankrede anlässlich der Verleihung des Johann-Heinrich-Merck-Preises der Deutschen Akademie für Sprache und Dichtung 2014*, http://deutscheakademie.de/de/auszeichnungen/

johann-heinrich-merck-preis/carolin-emcke/dankrede (accessed 26 March 2019).

64 Horst Bredekamp, *Das Beispiel Palmyra* (Cologne: Walther König, 2016).

65 Vowinckel, *Flugzeugentführungen*, p. 59.

66 *Spiegel*, 38 (1970), pp. 110–16.

67 Vowinckel, *Flugzeugentführungen*, p. 60.

68 *Spiegel*, 15 (1970), p. 117.

69 Vowinckel, *Flugzeugentführungen*, p. 28.

70 *Ibid.*, p. 89.

71 *Spiegel*, 44 (1977), pp. 20–7.

72 Nacos, *Terrorism and the Media*, pp. 41–3.

73 Johan Grimonprez, *Dial H-I-S-T-O-R-Y*, DVD (Ostfildern: Hatje Cantz, 2003); Don DeLillo, *Mao II* (New York: Scribner, 1991), p. 42.

74 Bestsellers in this genre include Ingrid Betancourt's account of her time as a FARC hostage (Ingrid Betancourt, *Même le silence a une fin* (Paris: Gallimard, 2010)) and Terry Waite's autobiography about his time as a hostage in Lebanon (*Taken on Trust*).

75 *Victory at Entebbe*, USA, 1976 (dir. Marvin J. Chomsky); *Raid on Entebbe*, USA, 1977 (dir. Irvin Kerschner); *Mivtsa Yonatan*, Israel, 1977 (dir. Menahem Golan).

76 *Iran. Days of Crisis*, USA/GB/F, 1991 (dir. Kevin Connor); *Argo*, USA, 2012 (dir. Ben Affleck).

77 *Todesspiel Teil 2. Entführt die Landshut*, BRD, 1997 (dir. Heinrich Breloer); *Mogadischu*, BRD, 2008 (dir. Roland Suso Richter).

78 *Let's Roll – The Story of Flight 93*, GB, 2002 (dir. Chris Oxley); *The Flight That Fought Back*, USA, 2005 (dir. Bruce Goodison); *Flight 93*, USA, 2006 (dir. Peter Markle); *The Heroes of Flight 93*, USA, 2006 (dir. David Priest); *United 93*, USA/GB/F, 2006 (dir. Peter Greengrass).

79 *Todesspiel Teil 2.*

80 For a critical discussion of these recordings in the context of American defence strategy, see Elaine Scarry, 'Who defended the country?', in Daniel J. Sherman and Terry Nardin (eds), *Terror, Culture, Politics. Rethinking 9/11* (Bloomington, IN: Indiana University Press, 2006), pp. 184–205.

Chapter 3

1 Felix Hoffmann (ed.), *Unheimlich Vertraut/The Uncanny Familiar. Bilder vom Terror/Images of Terror*, exh. cat. C/O Berlin (Cologne: Walter König, 2011).

2 Klaus Forster and Thomas Knieper, 'Das Blutbad von München', in Gerhard Paul (ed.), *Das Jahrhundert der Bilder*, vol. 2 (Göttingen: Vandenhoek und Ruprecht, 2008), pp. 434–14, here p. 436.

3 'Die Verantwortlichen sagen aus. Das Massaker von München', *Stern*, 39 (1972), p. C35.

4 According to Brigitte L. Nacos, an estimated 800 million people worldwide followed the tragedy on their television screens (Brigitte L. Nacos, *Mass-Mediated Terrorism: The Central Role of the Media in Terrorism and Counterterrorism*, 2nd edn (Plymouth: Rowman & Littlefield, 2007), p. 45).

5 Forster and Knieper, 'Das Blutbad von München', p. 439.

6 See among others 'Der Geheimbund "Schwarzer September"', *Stern*, 39 (1972), p. 224; 'Schwarzer September an Rhein und Ruhr', *Spiegel*, 38 (1972), p. 24.

7 Sybil Wagener, *Feindbilder. Wie kollektiver Hass entsteht* (Berlin: Quadriga, 1999), p. 28.

8 Christina Hellmich, 'Al-Qaeda – Terrorists, hypocrites, fundamentalists? The view from within', *Third World Quarterly*, 1 (2005), 39–54, here p. 48.

9 See Susanne Regener, 'Facial politics – Bilder des Bösen nach dem 11. September', in Petra Löffler and Leander Scholz (eds), *Das Gesicht ist eine starke Organisation* (Cologne: DuMont, 2004), pp. 203–24, here pp. 220–1.

10 Wagener, *Feindbilder*, p. 28.

11 James Der Derian, 'Imaging terror: Logos, pathos and ethos', in Fraser MacDonald, Rachel Hughes and Klaus Dodds (eds), *Observant States: Geopolitics and Visual Culture* (London: I.B. Tauris, 2010), pp. 23–40.

12 Eugene Robinson, 'Why I would've released the Bin Laden photos', *Washington Post* (4 May 2011), www.washingtonpost.com/blogs/post-partisan/post/why_i_wouldve_released_thc_bin_laden_photos/2011/03/04/AFztulpF_blog.html?wprss=post-partisan (accessed 11 December 2018).

13 See among others *Frankfurter Allgemeine Zeitung* (19 November 2015), front page and *The Times* (19 November 2015), p. 2. It is notable, however, that the French press treated the photograph with much more reservation. For example, neither *Le Monde* nor *Marianne* magazine published it.

14 Walter Laqueur, *A History of Terrorism,* expanded edn (New Brunswick: Transaction Publishers, 2016), p. 123. For a summary of the social profiles of politically motivated perpetrators, see Thomas Riegler, *Terrorismus. Akteure, Strukturen, Entwicklungslinien* (Innsbruck: StudienVerlag, 2009), pp. 171–223.

15 Christoph Reuter, *Die Schwarze Macht. Der Islamische Staat und die Strategen des Terrors* (Munich: Deutsche Verlags-Anstalt, 2015).
16 Diego Gambetta and Steffen Hertog, *Engineers of Jihad: The Curious Connection between Violent Extremism and Education* (Princeton, NJ: Princeton University Press, 2016), p. 158.
17 Tore Bjørgo, 'Conclusion', in Tore Bjørgo (ed.), *Root Causes of Terrorism: Myths, Reality and Ways Forward* (London: Routledge, 2005), pp. 256–64, here p. 257. A counter-position is held by the art historian Christian Saehrendt, who suggests that the motivation of young people who join terror organisations is more likely to be found in irrational longings and desires in a Romantic tradition (Christian Saehrendt, *Gefühlige Zeiten. Die zwanghafte Sehnsucht nach dem Echten* (Cologne: DuMont, 2015)).
18 Corey Robin, 'Primal fear', *Theory & Event*, 4 (2001), https://muse.jhu.edu/article/32656 (accessed 26 March 2019).
19 Sara Ahmed, 'Affective economies', *Social Text*, 2 (2004), 117–39. For an empirical long-term study of collective stereotypes in the context of Israeli perception of Arabs, see Daniel Bar-Tal and Yona Teichmann, *Stereotypes and Prejudice in Conflict: Representations of Arabs in Israeli Jewish Society* (Cambridge: Cambridge University Press, 2005).
20 Jens Jäger, 'Photography: A means of surveillance? Judicial photography 1850 to 1900', *Crime, History and Societies*, 1 (2001), 2–23; Marguerite de Marcillac (ed.), *Fichés? Photographie et identification 1850–1960* (Paris: Perrin, 2011).
21 Valentin Groebner, *Der Schein der Person. Steckbrief, Ausweis und Kontrolle im Mittelalter* (Munich: C.H. Beck, 2004); Gérard Noiriel (ed.), *L'identification. Genèse d'un travail d'État* (Paris: Belin, 2007).
22 Simon A. Cole, *Suspect Identities: A History of Fingerprinting and Criminal Identification*, 2nd edn (Cambridge, MA: Harvard University Press, 2001); Jane Caplan and John Torpey (eds), *Documenting Individual Identity: The Development of State Practices in the Modern World* (Princeton, NJ: Princeton University Press, 2001); Miloš Vec, *Die Spur des Täters. Methoden der Identifikation in der Kriminalistik 1879–1933* (Baden-Baden: Nomos Verlag, 2002); Jonathan Finn, *Capturing the Criminal Image: From Mug Shot to Surveillance Society* (Minneapolis, MN: University of Minnesota Press, 2009).
23 Pierre Piazza (ed.), *Aux origines de la police scientifique. Alphonse Bertillon, précurseur de la science du crime* (Paris: Karthala, 2011).

24 Susanne Regener, *Fotografische Erfassung* (Munich: Wilhelm Fink, 1999), pp. 111–18.
25 Jäger, 'Photography', p. 13.
26 Susanne Regener, 'Anarchistische Gewalttäter. Zur Mediengeschichte der RAF-Plakate', in Gerhard Paul (ed.), *Das Jahrhundert der Bilder*, vol. 2 (Göttingen: Vandenhoeck und Ruprecht, 2008), pp. 402–9, here p. 404.
27 *Ibid.*, p. 405.
28 *Ibid.*, p. 404.
29 On the Islamic Jihad Union in Germany, see Peter Wichmann, *Al-Qaida und der globale Djihad. Eine vergleichende Betrachtung des transnationalen Terrorismus* (Wiesbaden: Springer, 2014), pp. 311–14.
30 Sabine Schiffer, *Die Darstellung des Islams in der Presse. Sprache, Bilder, Suggestionen* (Würzburg: Ergon-Verlag, 2005).
31 Staff and agencies, 'Police shot Brazilian eight times', *Guardian* (25 July 2005), http://www.theguardian.com/uk/2005/jul/25/july7.uksecurity5 (accessed 1 April 2019).
32 Roland Barthes, *Camera Lucida: Reflections on Photography*, trans. Richard Howard (London: Jonathan Cape, 1982), p. 13.
33 The newspapers also published images of Ravachol that showed him being photographed according to Bertillon's method: *L'Illustration* (9 April 1882), p. 297; *Illustrirte Zeitung* (23 April 1892), p. 450.
34 Andreas Elter suggests that the decisive hint did not come from the police but from neighbours. It is also possible that the press inter cepted police radio transmissions; see Andreas Elter, *Propaganda der Tat. Die RAF und die Medien* (Frankfurt am Main: Suhrkamp, 2008), p. 129.
35 *Ibid.*, p. 129.
36 *Stern*, 45 (1980), pp. 20–9.
37 Charles Townshend, *Terrorism: A Very Short Introduction* (Oxford: Oxford University Press, 2002), p. 16.
38 Riegler, *Terrorismus*, p. 190.
39 *Stern*, 45 (1977), pp. 28–30.
40 Michael Sontheimer, 'Anfänge der RAF. Todesschüsse in der Seitenstraße', *Spiegel Online* (15 July 2011), http://www.spiegel.de/einestages/anfaenge-der-raf-a-947270.html#featuredEntry (accessed 21 April 2019).
41 *Stern*, 24 (1972), p. 20.
42 For a more comprehensive analysis of the reception of female RAF members in the West German press, see Clare Bielby, *Violent Women in Print: Representations in the West German*

Print Media of the 1960s and 1970s (Rochester: Camden House, 2012).

43 Eileen MacDonald, *Shoot the Women First* (London: Fourth Estate, 1991), p. 4.

44 Rhiannon Talbot summarised the patterns commonly used to explain female terrorists: 'they are (a) extremist feminists; (b) only bound to terrorism via a relationship with a man; (c) only acting in supporting roles within terrorist organizations; (d) mentally inept; (e) unfeminine in some way' (Rhiannon Talbot, 'Myths in the representation of women terrorists', *Eire-Ireland*, 3–4 (2000), 165–86, here p. 165). See also Sue Malvern, 'Femininity, feminism and the terrorist', in Sue Malvern and Gabriel Koureas (eds), *Female Transgressions: Gender and the Visual Culture of the Terrorist* (London: I.B. Tauris, 2014), pp. 39–55.

45 *Quick*, 25 (1972), front page.

46 Similar police images of Holger Meins and Brigitte Mohnhaupt, showing them grimacing, were published in the 1970s; see among others Meins after his arrest in *Der Spiegel*, 24 (1972), p. 22, and Mohnhaupt in *Stern*, 44 (1977), p. 28. Mohnhaupt had been released in February that same year and immediately went back underground; when she was wanted following the attacks of autumn 1977, the police were able to use their own photograph.

47 On Narodnaya Volya, see Rudolf Walther, 'Terror, Terrorismus', in Otto Brunner, Werner Conze and Reinhart Koselleck (eds), *Geschichtliche Grundbegriffe. Historisches Lexikon zur politisch-sozialen Sprache in Deutschland*, vol. 6 (Stuttgart: Klett-Cotta, 1990), pp. 323–444, here pp. 389–90. On the RAF, see Elter, *Propaganda der Tat*, pp. 108–18.

48 Jörg Requate, 'Die Faszination anarchistischer Attentate im Frankreich des ausgehenden 19. Jahrhunderts', in Klaus Weinhauer and Jörg Requate (eds), *Gewalt ohne Ausweg? Terrorismus als Kommunikationsprozess in Europa seit dem 19. Jahrhundert* (Frankfurt: Campus, 2012), pp. 99–122, here p. 100.

49 John Merriman, *The Dynamite Club: How Bombing in Fin-de-Siècle Paris Ignited the Age of Modern Terror* (London: JR Books, 2009), pp. 180–201.

50 Elter, *Propaganda der Tat*, pp. 99–100.

51 See among other sources *Der Spiegel*, 21 (1970), p. 100, and *Stern*, 23 (1970), p. 52.

52 Charlotte Klonk, 'Bildterrorismus. Von Meins bis Schleyer', in Inge Stephan and Alexandra Tacke (eds), *NachBilder der RAF* (Cologne: Böhlau, 2008), pp. 197–215, here p. 200.

53 See, for example, *Der Spiegel*, 24 (1972), p. 19.

54 Astrid Proll, *Hans und Grete. Bilder der RAF 1967–1977* (Göttingen: Steidl, 1998).

55 Niels Werber, 'Die Prada-Meinhof-Bande', *Literaturen*, 12 (2001), 28–31, here p. 31. On the pop-cultural appropriation of the RAF in literature, see Luise Tremel, 'Litterorisierung', in Wolfgang Kraushaar (ed.), *Die RAF und der linke Terrorismus*, vol. 2 (Hamburg: HIS Verlag, 2006), pp. 1117–54; on the pop-cultural appropriation of the RAF in literature, film and art, see Inge Stephan and Alexandra Tacke (eds), *Nachbilder der RAF* (Cologne: Böhlau, 2008); Norman Ächtler and Carsten Gansel (eds), *Ikonographie des Terrors. Formen ästhetischer Erinnerung in der Bundesrepublik 1978–2008* (Heidelberg: Universitätsverlag Winter, 2010); and Svea Bräunert, *Gespenstergeschichten. Der linke Terrorismus der RAF und die Künste* (Berlin: Kadmos, 2015).

56 For a comparison of the laws and ways of dealing with such images and recordings, see Bundesministerium der Justiz, *Gutachten zum Thema 'Ist das 1964 geschaffene Verbot von Bild- und Tonübertragungen aus Gerichtsverhandlungen noch zeitgemäß?'*, results of the meeting of 21–26 October 2013 in Waren an der Müritz, https://www.bmjv.de/SharedDocs/Downloads/DE/Service/StudienUntersuchungenFachbuecher/Gutachten_StrafrechtskommissionRichterbund_%C2%A7169.pdf?__blob=publicationFile&v=3 (accessed 26 March 2019).

57 Haus der Geschichte Baden-Württemberg (ed.), *RAF. Terror im Südwesten* (Stuttgart: Haus der Geschichte Baden-Württemberg, 2013), p. 68.

58 Robert Kahr, 'Der mediale Umgang mit dem Breivik-Prozess', *Bundeszentrale für politische Bildung* (24 September 2012), http://www.bpb.de/politik/hintergrund-aktuell/142949/der-mediale-umgang-mit-dem-breivik-prozess-24-08-2012 (accessed 21 April 2019).

59 Astrid Proll, *Hans und Grete. Bilder der RAF 1967–1977*, expanded new edn (Berlin: Aufbau-Verlag, 2004), p. 8.

60 Haus der Geschichte Baden-Württemberg, *RAF*, pp. 37–9.

61 *Stern*, 48 (1974), pp. 16–17.

62 Petra Terhoeven, 'Opferbilder – Täterbilder. Die Fotografie als Medium linksterroristischer Selbstermächtigung in Deutschland und Italien während der 70er Jahre', *Geschichte und Wissenschaft und Unterricht*, 7–8 (2007), 380–99, here p. 392.

63 Hans-Joachim Klein, *Rückkehr in die Menschlichkeit. Appell eines ausgestiegenen Terroristen* (Reinbek: Rowohlt, 1979), p. 281.

64 Stefan Wisniewski, *Wir waren so unheimlich konsequent. Ein Gespräch zur Geschichte der RAF*, 3rd edn (Berlin: ID-Verlag, 2003), p. 18.

65 *Stern*, 11 (1974), p. 152; *Spiegel*, 50 (1974), p. 28; Per A. Rosenberg, *Kärlek med förhinder. Texte der RAF* (Malmö: Bo Cavefors, 1977), p. 12.
66 Rosenberg, *Kärlek med förhinder*, pp. 5–11.
67 Bräunert, *Gespenstergeschichten*, p. 176.
68 For example, Anthony D. Buckley, *Symbols in Northern Ireland* (Liverpool: Institute of Irish Studies, 1998); Mahmoud Abu Hashhash, 'On the visual representation of martyrdom in Palestine', *Third Text*, 3–4 (2006), 391–403; Laleh Khalili, *Heroes and Martyrs of Palestine: The Politics of Commemoration* (Cambridge: Cambridge University Press, 2007); Rabih Mroué, *The Inhabitants of Images*, video, 2009; Maximilian Rapp, *Murals in Nordirland. Symbol der ethno-kulturellen Identität und Spiegel des politischen Wandels* (Baden-Baden: Nomos, 2014). In Palestine, however, the martyr posters showed not just attackers, but everyone who had lost their lives; see Lori A. Allen, 'The polyvalent politics of martyr commemoration in the Palestinian intifada', *History and Memory*, 18 (2006), 107–38.
69 Peter L. Bergen, *Holy War, Inc.: Inside the Secret World of Osama Bin Laden* (New York: Simon & Schuster, 2001), p. 100.
70 Peter L. Bergen, *The Osama Bin Laden I Know* (New York: Free Press, 2006), p. 209.
71 For a comprehensive account of the visual representation of Al-Qaida, see Abdelasiem El Difraoui, *Al-Qaida par l'image. La prophétie du martyre* (Paris: Presses Universitaires de France, 2013).
72 Bruce Hoffmann, *Inside Terrorism*, extended new edn (New York: Columbia University Press, 2006), p. 81.
73 Riegler, *Terrorismus*, p. 287.
74 *Ibid.*
75 Hoffman, *Inside Terrorism*, p. 197.
76 See Mohammed M. Hafez, 'Martyrdom mythology in Iraq: How jihadists frame suicide terrorism in videos and biographies', in John Horgan and Kurt Braddock (eds), *Terrorism Studies: A Reader* (London: Routledge, 2012), pp. 420–38; Joshua Simon, 'The aesthetics of terror in general and suicide bomber videos in particular', in Boris Groys and Peter Weibel (eds), *Medium – Religion – Faith – Geopolitics – Art*, exh. cat. ZKM Karlsruhe (Cologne: Walter König, 2011), pp. 58–84; Rabih Mroué, 'The fabrication of truth', in Groys and Weibel, *Medium*, pp. 78–85; Verena Straub, 'The making and gendering of a martyr: Images of female suicide bombers in the Middle East', in Jens Eder and Charlotte Klonk (eds), *Image Operations: Visual Media and*

Political Conflict (Manchester: Manchester University Press, 2017), pp. 137–50. On the martyr cult in Palestinian families, see Ahlam Shibli, *Phantom Home* (Ostfildern: Hatje Cantz, 2013).

77 On the videos in which the perpetrators of the 7 July 2005 attack took responsibility for the bombings, see Bruce Hoffman, 'The 7 July 2005 London bombings', in Bruce Hoffman and Fernando Reinares (eds), *The Evolution of the Global Terrorist Threat: From 9/11 to Osama bin Laden's Death* (New York: Columbia University Press, 2014), pp. 192–223.

78 'The Islamic State', https://www.youtube.com/watch?v=AUjHb4C7b94 (accessed 14 May 2019).

79 See Greg Miller and Scott Higham, 'Confronting the "Caliphate"', *Washington Post* (8 May 2011), www.washingtonpost.com/world/national-security/in-a-propaganda-war-us-tried-to-play-by-the-enemys-rules/2015/05/08/6eb6b732-e52f-11e4-81ea-0649268f729e_story.html (accessed 1 April 2019).

80 *Ibid.*

81 The best-known thus far is the 'Element Zero' series by the Jordanian cartoonist Suleiman Bakhit, which is also available as a game on Facebook.

82 Anne Speckhard and Ahmet S. Yayla, 'Eyewitness accounts from recent defectors from Islamic State: Why they joined, what they saw, why they quit', *Perspectives on Terrorism*, 9 (2015), http://www.terrorismanalysts.com/pt/index.php/pot/article/view/475/html (accessed 26 March 2019).

83 Sontheimer, 'Anfänge der RAF'.

84 See the database of the Combating Terrorism Center at West Point, 'The Islamic imagery project: Visual motifs in Jihadi internet propaganda' (March 2006), p. 86, https://www.hsdl.org/?abstract&did=236104 (accessed 6 May 2019).

85 See among others *Frankfurter Allgemeine Zeitung* (18 November 2015), p. 2; *Libération* (17 November 2015), p. 12; *Libération* (19 November 2015), front page; *Le Parisien* (20 November 2015), p. 2.

86 'From hypocrisy to apostasy: The extinction of the grayzone', *Dabiq*, 7 (n.d.). https://clarionproject.org/docs/islamic-state-dabiq-magazine-issue-7-from-hypocrisy-to-apostasy.pdf (accessed 8 May 2019). On IS's internet magazine, see Daniel H. Heinke and Hazim Fouad, 'Das Dabiq-Magazin als Rekrutierungswerkzeug des IS', in Janusz Biene and Martin Schmetz (eds), *Kalifat des Terrors. Interdisziplinäre Perspektiven auf den Islamischen Staat* (Frankfurt am Main: Security Policy Blog, 2015), pp. 7–12; and Christoph Günther, 'Der Islamische Staat und die Islamisierung

des Abendlandes', in Biene and Schmetz, *Kalifat des Terrors*, pp. 13–17, http://www.sicherheitspolitik-blog.de/files/2015/07/Kalifat-des-Terrors.pdf (accessed 26 March 2019); Christoph Günther, 'Presenting the glossy look of warfare in cyberspace: The Islamic State's magazine Dabiq', *CyberOrient*, 1 (2015), http://www.cyberorient.net/article.do?aricleID=9538 (accessed 26 March 2019).

87 On Al-Qaida's martyr images, see El Difraoui, *Al-Qaida par l'image*, pp. 297–399.

88 Charlotte Klonk, 'Warum wir trotzdem Bilder brauchen', *Frankfurter Allgemeine Zeitung* (14 May 2011), p. 34.

89 Louise Richardson, *What Terrorists Want: Understanding the Terrorist Threat* (London: John Murray, 2006), p. 253.

Chapter 4

1 Hans-Bernd Brosius, *Alltagsrationalität in der Nachrichtenrezeption. Ein Modell zur Wahrnehmung und Verarbeitung von Nachrichteninhalten* (Opladen: Westdeutscher Verlag, 1995); Gary Bente and Bettina Fromm, *Affektfernsehen. Motive, Angebotsweisen und Wirkungen* (Opladen: Leske und Budrich, 1997); Arvid Kappas and Marion G. Müller, 'Bild und Emotionen. Ein neues Forschungsfeld', *Publizistik*, 1 (2006), 3–23.

2 Thomas Schierl, 'Der Schein der Authentizität. Journalistische Bildproduktion als nachfrageorientierte Produktion scheinbarer Authentizität', in Thomas Knieper and Marion G. Müller (eds), *Authentizität und Inszenierung von Bildwelten* (Cologne: Herbert von Halem Verlag, 2003), pp. 150–67; Thomas Knieper, 'Die ikonologische Analyse von Medienbilder und deren Beitrag zur Bildkompetenz', in *ibid.*, pp. 193–212, here p. 194.

3 Roland Barthes, *Camera Lucida: Reflections on Photography*, trans. Richard Howard (London: Jonathan Cape, 1982), p. 5.

4 Judith Butler, 'Torture and the ethics of photography: Thinking with Sontag', in Judith Butler, *Frames of War: When Is Life Grievable* (London and New York: Verso, 2010), pp. 63–100.

5 Gottfried Boehm, *Wie Bilder Sinn erzeugen. Die Macht des Zeigens* (Berlin: Berlin University Press, 2007), p. 69.

6 Ludwig Jäger, 'Intermedialität, Intramedialität, Transkriptivität. Überlegungen zu einigen Prinzipien der kulturellen Semiosis', in Arnulf Deppermann and Angelika Linke (eds), *Sprache*

intermedial. Stimme und Schrift, Bild und Ton (Berlin: De Gruyter, 2009), pp. 301–24.

7 Robert Hariman and John Louis Lucaites, *No Caption Needed: Photographs, Public Culture, and Liberal Democracy* (Chicago, IL: University of Chicago Press, 2007).

8 On press photographs, see especially Marion G. Müller, who has developed an associative iconology in the tradition of Aby Warburg by looking closely at the context and distinguishing between the material image (*Abbild*) and the immaterial concept of an image (*Denkbild*). According to Müller, an image derives its power through the materialisation of a *Denkbild*, which in turn is structured by previous models: Marion G. Müller, 'Bilder – Visionen – Wirklichkeiten. Zur Bedeutung der Bildwissenschaft im 21. Jahrhundert', in Thomas Knieper and Marion G. Müller (eds), *Kommunikation visuell. Das Bild als Forschungsgegenstand. Grundlagen und Perspektiven* (Cologne: Herbert von Halem Verlag, 2001), pp. 14–25. See also Kappas and Müller, 'Bild und Emotionen'.

9 That picture agencies select images according to known schemata of interpretation has been shown by the anthropologist Zeynep D. Gürsel in a number of field studies: Zeynep D. Gürsel, *Image Brokers: Visualizing World News in the Age of Digital Circulation* (Berkeley, CA: University of California Press, 2016).

10 See, among others, Bertram Scheufele, *Frames – Framing – Framing-Effekte. Theoretische und methodische Grundlegung sowie empirische Befunde zur Nachrichtenreproduktion* (Wiesbaden: Westdeutscher Verlag, 2003).

11 Nicole Haußecker, *Terrorismusberichterstattung in Fernsehnachrichten. Visuelles Framing und emotionale Reaktionen* (Baden-Baden: Nomos, 2013).

12 Robert M. Entman, 'Framing: Toward clarification of a fractured paradigm', *Journal of Communication*, 4 (1993), 51–8.

13 Haußecker, *Terrorismusberichterstattung in Fernsehnachrichten*, p. 211.

14 *Ibid.*, p. 224.

15 Ben O'Loughlin, 'Images as weapons of war: Representation, mediation and interpretation', *Review of International Studies*, 1 (2011), 71–91.

16 Andrew Hoskins and Ben O'Loughlin, *War and Media: The Emergence of Diffused War* (Cambridge: Polity Press, 2010), p. 2.

17 Winfried Gerling, Susanne Holschbach, and Petra Löffler (eds), *Bilder verteilen. Fotografische Praktiken in der digitalen Kultur* (Bielefeld: Transcript, 2018).

18 Thomas Riegler, *Terrorismus. Akteure, Strukturen, Entwicklungslinien* (Innsbruck: StudienVerlag, 2009), p. 319.
19 Shane Kingston, 'Terrorism, the media, and the Northern Ireland conflict', *Studies in Conflict and Terrorism*, 3 (1995), 203–31.
20 Brigitte L. Nacos, *Mass-Mediated Terrorism: The Central Role of the Media in Terrorism and Counterterrorism*, 2nd edn (Plymouth: Rowman and Littlefield, 2007), pp. 163–4.
21 Jürgen Bermes, *Der Streit um die Presse-Selbstkontrolle. Der Deutsche Presserat* (Baden-Baden: Nomos, 1991), pp. 273–4.
22 Christian F. Buck, *Medien und Geiselnahmen. Fallstudien zum inszenierten Terror* (Wiesbaden: VS Verlag für Sozialwissenschaften, 2007), p. 60.
23 Ariella Azoulay has coined the term 'civil contract of photography' for such involuntary photographic collaborations; Ariella Azoulay, *The Civil Contract of Photography* (Cambridge, MA: MIT Press, 2012).
24 German Press Council, 'Guidelines for journalistic work as recommended by the German Press Council: Complaints procedure', 13.03.2013 version, https://www.presserat.de/fileadmin/user_upload/Downloads_Dateien/Pressekodex13english_web.pdf (accessed 10 June 2019).
25 Stefan Leifert, *Bildethik. Theorie und Moral im Bildjournalismus der Massenmedien* (Munich: Wilhelm Fink, 2007), p. 299.
26 *New York Times*, 12 September 2001, p. A7; *Süddeutsche Zeitung*, 13 September 2001, p. 15; *Die Welt*, 13 September 2001, p. 5.
27 Andrea D. Fitzpatrick, 'The movement of vulnerability: Images of falling and September 11', *Art Journal*, 4 (2007), 84–102; Godehard Janzing, 'The Falling Man', in Gerhard Paul (ed.), *Das Jahrhundert der Bilder*, vol. 2 (Göttingen: Vanderhoeck und Ruprecht, 2008), pp. 664–701.
28 Leifert, *Bildethik*, p. 188.
29 Deutscher Presserat (ed.), *Jahrbuch 2002. Mit der Spruchpraxis des Jahres 2001* (Konstanz: UVK, 2002), p. 87.
30 Hans Belting, *The Invisible Masterpiece*, trans. Helen Atkins (London: Reaktion Books, 2001), pp. 87–90.
31 Janzing, 'The Falling Man', p. 698.
32 Tom Junod, 'The Falling Man', *Esquire* (8 September 2003), http://archive.esquire.com/issue/20030901 (accessed 26 March 2019).
33 Susan Sontag, *Regarding the Pain of Others* (London: Hamish Hamilton, 2004), p. 102.

34 German Press Council, 'Guidelines for journalistic work', Guideline 8.2, p. 6, https://www.presserat.de/fileadmin/user_upload/Downloads_Dateien/Pressekodex13english_web.pdf (accessed 10 June 2019).
35 *Bild-Zeitung*, 9 September 2002, p. 6.
36 Deutscher Presserat (ed.), *Jahrbuch 2003. Mit der Spruchpraxis des Jahres 2002* (Konstanz: UVK, 2003), p. 146.
37 For a more extended discussion of the political use of images of terror victims in recent times and their ethical dimensions, see Charlotte Klonk, 'In whose name? Visualizing victims of terror', in Petra Terhoeven (ed.), *European History Yearbook*, 19 (2018), 103–16.
38 Andreas Elter, *Propaganda der Tat. Die RAF und die Medien* (Frankfurt: Suhrkamp, 2008), pp. 244–7.
39 See Carolin Emcke, *Stumme Gewalt. Nachdenken über die RAF* (Frankfurt: S. Fischer, 2008).
40 German Press Council, Guideline 8.1, Criminal reporting, 13.03.2013 version, https://www.presserat.de/fileadmin/user_upload/Downloads_Dateien/Pressekodex13english_web.pdf (accessed 10 June 2019).
41 Emcke, *Stumme Gewalt*, p. 135.
42 For a history of the acceptance of these images as evidence in US courts, see Louis-Georges Schwartz, *Mechanical Witness: A History of Motion Picture Evidence in U.S. Courts* (Oxford: Oxford University Press, 2009).
43 Jan Eckel, *The Ambivalence of Good: Human Rights in International Politics since the 1940s*, trans. Rachel Ward (Oxford: Oxford University Press, 2019), p. 171.
44 Meg McLagan, 'Human rights, testimony, and transnational publicity', in Michel Feher, Gaëlle Krikorian and Yates McKee (eds), *Nongovernmental Politics* (New York: Zone Books, 2007), pp. 304–17; Sam Gregory, 'Human rights made visible: New dimensions to anonymity, consent, and intentionality', in Meg McLagan and Yates McKee (eds), *Sensible Politics: The Visual Culture of Nongovernmental Activism* (New York: Zone Books, 2012), pp. 551–63.
45 Sam Gregory, 'Human rights in an age of distant witnesses: Remixed lives, reincarnated images and live-streamed co-presence', in Jens Eder and Charlotte Klonk (eds), *Image Operations: Visual Media and Political Conflict* (Manchester: Manchester University Press, 2017), pp. 184–96.
46 Video filmed by Imad Abu Shamsiyeh: 'Soldier executes Palestinian lying injured on ground after the latter stabbed a soldier in Hebron',

http://www.btselem.org/firearms/20160324_soldier_executes_palestinians_attaker_in_hebron (accessed 19 May 2016).

47 See among others *Los Angeles Times*, 26 March 2016, p. A3; *Frankfurter Allgemeine Zeitung*, 29 March 2016, p. 6; *Marianne*, 8–14 April 2016, pp. 44–6.

48 Hans-Christian Rößler, 'Der Schuss von Hebron', *Frankfurter Allgemeine Zeitung* (5 January 2017), p. 3.

49 In 1998, Israel passed such a law, which is known as the Good Samaritan Law. For international law, see for example the following penal codes: §323c of the German Strafgesetzbuch, §95 of the Austrian Strafgesetzbuch, §128 of the Swiss Strafgesetzbuch and §222–6 of the French Code Pénal.

50 Kari Anden-Papadopolous and Mervi Pantti (eds), *Amateur Images and Global News* (Chicago, IL: Chicago University Press, 2011); Stuart Allan and Thorsen Einar (eds), *Citizen Journalism: Global Perspectives, Global Crises and the Media* (New York: Peter Lang, 2014).

51 On non-professional camera use in recent times, see Asko Lehmuskallio, *Pictorial Practices in a 'Cam Era': Studying Non-professional Camera Use* (Tampere: Tampere University Press, 2012).

52 *Süddeutsche Zeitung*, 13 January 2016, front page; *Tagesspiegel*, 13 January 2016, front page.

53 Heidemarie Hanekop and Volker Wittke, 'Kollaboration der Prosumenten', in Birgit Blättel-Mink and Kai-Uwe Hellmann (eds), *Prosumer Revisited. Zur Aktualität einer Debatte* (Wiesbaden: VS Verlag für Sozialwissenschaften, 2010), pp. 96–113.

54 For a discussion of some of these examples, see an earlier essay by Charlotte Klonk, 'Image terror', in Eder and Klonk, *Image Operations*, pp. 128–36.

55 Charlotte Klonk, 'Wenn die Bilder Terror machen', *Frankfurter Allgemeine Zeitung* (19 January 2016), p. 12.

56 See among others the *Guardian*, 30 July 2005, p. 4, and *The Times*, 30 July 2005, front page.

57 See among others the *Daily Telegraph*, 12 July 2007, p. 6.

58 Else Frenkel-Brunswik, 'Intolerance of ambiguity as an emotional and perceptual personality variable', *Journal of Personality*, 1 (1949), 108–43.

59 Susan Sontag, *Regarding the Pain of Others* (London: Hamish Hamilton, 2004), p. 102.

60 *Ibid.*, p. 104.

61 Butler, 'Torture and the ethics of photography', p. 98.

62 Sontag, *Regarding the Pain of Others*, p. 104.

63 Horst Dreier, *Idee und Gestalt des freiheitlichen Verfassungsstaates* (Tübingen: Mohr Siebeck, 2014), pp. 109–10.
64 Michael Rosen, *Dignity: Its History and Meaning* (Cambridge, MA: Harvard University Press, 2012).
65 Dreier, *Idee und Gestalt*, p. 90.

Bibliography

Ächtler, Norman and Carsten Gansel (eds), *Ikonographie des Terrors. Formen ästhetischer Erinnerung in der Bundesrepublik 1978–2008* (Heidelberg: Universitätsverlag Winter, 2010).

Adelmann, Rolf and Rolf F. Nohr, '"Man versucht sich zu öffnen". Video und RAF – Eine abgeschlossene Geschichte', *Text und Kritik*, 108 (2000), 77–83.

Ahmed, Sara, 'Affective economies', *Social Text*, 2 (2004), 117–39.

Alexander, Yonah, *International Terrorism: National, Regional, and Global Perspectives* (New York: Praeger, 1976).

Allan, Stuart, 'Citizen journalism and the rise of "mass self-communication": Reporting the London bombings', *Global Media Journal*, Australian edn, 1 (2007), 1–20.

Allan, Stuart and Thorsen Einar (eds), *Citizen Journalism: Global Perspectives, Global Crises and the Media* (New York: Peter Lang, 2014).

Allen, Lori A., 'The polyvalent politics of martyr commemoration in the Palestinian intifada', *History and Memory*, 18 (2006), 107–38.

Altheide, David L., 'Iran vs. US TV news: The hostage story out of context', in William C. Adams (ed.), *Television Coverage of the Middle East* (Norwood, Ablex Publishing, 1981), pp. 128–57.

Ambos, Kai, 'What international law says about the killing of Bin Laden', *Der Spiegel*, 13 May 2011, www.spiegel.de/international/world/terrorists-have-rights-too-what-international-law-says-about-the-killing-of-bin-laden-a-762417.html (accessed 8 December 2018).

Anden-Papadopolous, Kari and Mervi Pantti (eds), *Amateur Images and Global News* (Chicago, IL: Chicago University Press, 2011).

Anderson, Terry, *Den of Lions: Memoirs of Seven Years* (New York: Random House, 1993).

Antokol, Norman and Mayer Nudell, *No One a Neutral: Political Hostage-Taking in the Modern World* (Medina: Alpha Publications, 1990).

Asad, Talal, *On Suicide Bombing* (New York: Columbia University Press, 2007).

Aston, Clive C., *A Contemporary Crisis: Political Hostage-Taking and the Experience of Western Europe* (New York: Greenwood Press, 1982).

Azoulay, Ariella, *The Civil Contract of Photography* (Cambridge, MA: MIT Press, 2012).

Baberowski, Jörg, *Der rote Terror. Die Geschichte des Stalinismus* (Munich: DVA, 2003).

Barnett, Brooke and Amy Reynolds, *Terrorism and the Press: An Uneasy Relationship* (New York: Peter Lang, 2009).

Bar-Tal, Daniel and Yona Teichmann, *Stereotypes and Prejudice in Conflict: Representations of Arabs in Israeli Jewish Society* (Cambridge: Cambridge University Press, 2005).

Barthes, Roland, *Camera Lucida: Reflections on Photography*, trans. Richard Howard (London: Jonathan Cape, 1982).

Belting, Hans, *The Invisible Masterpiece*, trans. Helen Atkins (London: Reaktion Books, 2001).

Benjamin, Walter, 'Small history of photography', in Walter Benjamin, *On Photography*, ed. and trans. Esther Leslie (London: Reaktion Books, 2015), p. 59–94.

Bente, Gary and Bettina Fromm, *Affektfernsehen. Motive, Angebotsweisen und Wirkungen* (Opladen: Leske und Budrich, 1997).

Bergen, Peter L., *Holy War, Inc.: Inside the Secret World of Osama Bin Laden* (New York: Simon & Schuster, 2001).

———, *The Osama Bin Laden I Know* (New York: Free Press, 2006).

Bermes, Jürgen, *Der Streit um die Presse-Selbstkontrolle. Der Deutsche Presserat* (Baden-Baden: Nomos, 1991).

Betancourt, Ingrid, *Même le silence a une fin* (Paris: Gallimard, 2010).

Bielby, Clare, *Violent Women in Print: Representations in the West German Print Media of the 1960s and 1970s* (Rochester, NY: Camden House, 2012).

Bjørgo, Tore, 'Conclusion', in Tore Bjørgo (ed.), *Root Causes of Terrorism: Myths, Reality and Ways Forward* (London: Routledge, 2005), pp. 256–64.

Bleicher, Joan Kristin, 'Lesarten des Wirklichen. Narrative Strukturen der Live-Übertragung vom 11. September 2001', in Michael Beuthner, Joachim Buttler, Sandra Fröhlich *et al.* (eds), *Bilder des Terrors – Terror der Bilder? Krisenberichterstattung am und nach*

dem 11. September (Cologne: Herbert von Halem Verlag, 2003), pp. 60–73.

Bloomfield, Keith, 'Hostage taking and government response', *RUSI Journal*, 4 (2001), 23–7.

Boehm, Gottfried, *Wie Bilder Sinn erzeugen. Die Macht des Zeigens* (Berlin: Berlin University Press, 2007).

Bräunert, Svea, *Gespenstergeschichten. Der linke Terrorismus der RAF und die Künste* (Berlin: Kadmos, 2015).

Bredekamp, Horst, *Das Beispiel Palmyra* (Cologne: Walther König, 2016).

Brosius, Hans-Bernd, *Alltagsrationalität in der Nachrichtenrezeption. Ein Modell zur Wahrnehmung und Verarbeitung von Nachrichteninhalten* (Opladen: Westdeutscher Verlag, 1995).

Bruce, Victoria and Karin Hayes, *Hostage Nation: Columbia's Guerrilla Army and the Failed War on Drugs* (New York: Alfred A. Knopf, 2010).

Buck, Christian F., *Medien und Geiselnahmen. Fallstudien zum inszenierten Terror* (Wiesbaden: VS Verlag für Sozialwissenschaften, 2007).

Buckley, Anthony D., *Symbols in Northern Ireland* (Liverpool: Institute of Irish Studies, 1998).

Buhite, Russell D., *Lives at Risk: Hostages and Victims in American Foreign Policy* (Wilmington, DE: Scholarly Resources, 1995).

Bundesministerium der Justiz, *Gutachten zum Thema 'Ist das 1964 geschaffene Verbot von Bild- und Tonübertragungen aus Gerichtsverhandlungen noch zeitgemäß?'*, results of the meeting of 21–26 October 2013 in Waren an der Müritz, www.bmjv.de/SharedDocs/Downloads/DE/Service/StudienUntersuchungenFachbuecher/Gutachten_StrafrechtskommissionRichterbund_%C2%A7169.pdf?__blob=publicationFile&v=3 (accessed 26 March 2019).

Burke, Edmund, *Reflections on the Revolution in France* (London: Dodsley, 1790).

Butler, Judith, 'Torture and the ethics of photography: Thinking with Sontag', in Judith Butler, *Frames of War: When Is Life Grievable?* (London and New York: Verso, 2010), pp. 63–100.

Butterworth, Alex, *The World That Never Was: A True Story of Dreamers, Schemers, Anarchists, and Secret Agents* (New York: Vintage, 2010).

Buttler, Joachim, 'Ästhetik des Terrors – Die Bilder des 11. September 2001', in Michael Beuthner, Joachim Buttler, Sandra Fröhlich *et al.* (eds), *Bilder des Terrors – Terror der Bilder? Krisenberichterstattung am und nach dem 11. September* (Cologne: Herbert von Halem Verlag, 2003), pp. 26–41.

Caplan, Jane and John Torpey (eds), *Documenting Individual Identity: The Development of State Practices in the Modern World* (Princeton, NJ: Princeton University Press, 2001).

Cappella, Joseph N. and Kathleen H. Jamieson, 'News frames, political cynicism, and media cynicism', *Annals of the American Academy of Political and Social Science*, 546 (1996), 71–84.

Chandrasekaran, Rajiv, 'Sole informant guided decision on Afghan strike', *Washington Post* (6 September 2009), front page and p. A12.

Chéroux, Clément, *Diplopie: L'image photographique à l'ère des médias globalisés: essai sur le 11 septembre 2001* (Paris: Le Point du Jour, 2009).

———, 'The déja vu of 11 September: An essay on intericonicity', http://eitherand.org/social-medium/deja-vu-september-11-essay-intericonicity (accessed 8 February 2019).

Clutterbuck, Lindsay, 'The progenitors of terrorism: Russian revolutionaries or extreme Irish Republicans?' *Terrorism and Political Violence*, 1 (2004), 154–81.

Cohen, Richard, 'The terrorism story – and how we blew it', *Washington Post* (4 October 2001), p. A31.

Cohen, William S., 'Preparing for a grave new world', *Washington Post* (26 July 1999), p. A19.

Cole, Simon A., *Suspect Identities: A History of Fingerprinting and Criminal Identification*, 2nd edn (Cambridge, MA: Harvard University Press, 2001).

Conrad, Joseph, *The Secret Agent: A Simple* Tale, first published 1907 (London, Penguin Books, 2012).

Cronin, Audrey Kurth and James M. Ludes (eds), *Attacking Terrorism: Elements of a Grand Strategy* (Washington, DC: Georgetown University Press, 2004).

Dahlgren, Will, 'Terror video reached 83% of British population', https://yougov.co.uk/news/2014/08/22/terror-video-reached-83-percent-british-people (accessed 28 March 2019).

Dahlke, Matthias, *Demokratischer Staat und transnationaler Terrorismus. Drei Wege zur Unnachgiebigkeit in Westeuropa 1972–1975* (Munich: Oldenbourg, 2011).

Dayan, Daniel and Elihu Katz, 'Medienereignisse', in Ralf Adelmann, Jan O. Hesse, Judith Keilbach *et al.* (eds), *Grundlagentexte zur Fernsehwissenschaft. Theorie – Geschichte – Analyse* (Konstanz: UTB, 2002), pp. 413–53.

Demandt, Alexander (ed.), *Das Attentat in der Geschichte* (Cologne: Böhlau, 1996).

de Marcillac, Marguerite (ed.), *Fichés? Photographie et identification 1850–1960* (Paris: Perrin, 2011).

Bibliography

Demmer, Ulrike, Markus Feldenkirchen, Ullrich Fichtner *et al.*, 'Ein deutsches Verbrechen', *Der Spiegel*, 5 (2010), pp. 34–57.

Der Derian, James, 'Imaging terror: Logos, pathos and ethos', in Fraser MacDonald, Rachel Hughes and Klaus Dodds (eds), *Observant States: Geopolitics and Visual Culture* (London: I.B. Tauris, 2010), pp. 23–40.

Deutscher Presserat (ed.), *Jahrbuch 2002. Mit der Spruchpraxis des Jahres 2001* (Konstanz: UVK, 2002).

———, *Jahrbuch 2003. Mit der Spruchpraxis des Jahres 2002* (Konstanz: UVK, 2003).

'Deutsch- und englischsprachige Monographien, Sammelbände und Themenhefte zum 11. September 2001', compiled by Jonas Brendebach, last updated 15 August 2011, *Zeithistorische Forschungen/Studies in Contemporary History*, 8 (2011), 463–74, www.zeithistorische-forschungen.de/sites/default/files/medien/material/Bibliographie_11_09_2001.pdf (accessed 26 March 2019).

Dreier, Horst, *Idee und Gestalt des freiheitlichen Verfassungsstaates* (Tübingen: Mohr Siebeck, 2014).

Ebetkar, Massoumeh and Fred Reed, *Takeover in Teheran: The Inside Story of the 1979 U.S. Embassy Capture* (Vancouver: Talonbooks, 2000).

Eckel, Jan, *The Ambivalence of Good: Human Rights in International Politics since the 1940s*, trans. Rachel Ward (Oxford: Oxford University Press, 2019).

Eder, Jens, 'Affective image operations', in Jens Eder and Charlotte Klonk (eds), *Image Operations: Visual Media and Political Conflict* (Manchester: Manchester University Press, 2017), pp. 63–78.

Eder, Jens and Charlotte Klonk, 'Introduction', in Jens Eder and Charlotte Klonk (eds), *Image Operations: Visual Media and Political Conflict* (Manchester: Manchester University Press, 2017), pp. 1–22.

Edwards, Aaron, *The Northern Ireland Troubles: Operation Banner 1969–2007* (Oxford: Osprey Publishing, 2011).

El Difraoui, Abdelasiem, *Al-Qaida par l'image. La prophétie du martyre* (Paris: Presses Universitaires de France, 2013).

Elter, Andreas, *Propaganda der Tat. Die RAF und die Medien* (Frankfurt: Suhrkamp, 2008).

Emcke, Carolin, 'Dankrede anlässlich der Verleihung des Johann-Heinrich-Merck-Preises der Deutschen Akademie für Sprache und Dichtung 2014', (2014), http://deutscheakademie.de/de/auszeichnungen/johann-heinrich-merck-preis/carolin-emcke/dankrede (accessed 26 March 2019).

——, *Stumme Gewalt. Nachdenken über die RAF* (Frankfurt: Fischer, 2008).

Entman, Robert M., 'Framing: Toward clarification of a fractured paradigm', *Journal of Communication*, 4 (1993), 51–8.

Enzensberger, Hans Magnus, 'Ausblicke auf den Bürgerkrieg', *Der Spiegel*, 25 (1993), p. 174.

Fahmy, Shahira, *Filling Out the Frame: Transnational Visual Coverage and News Practitioners' Attitudes. Towards the Reporting of War and Terrorism* (Saarbrücken: VDM Verlag, 2007).

Farhi, Paul, 'How to show Bin Laden is dead', *Washington Post* (4 May 2011), p. C10.

Finn, Jonathan, *Capturing the Criminal Image: From Mug Shot to Surveillance Society* (Minneapolis, MN: University of Minnesota Press, 2009).

Fitzpatrick, Andrea D., 'The movement of vulnerability: Images of falling and September 11', *Art Journal*, 4 (2007), 84–102.

Fly, Claude, *No Hope But God* (Portland, OR: Hawthorn Books, 1973).

Forster, Klaus and Thomas Knieper, 'Das Blutbad von München', in Gerhard Paul (ed.), *Das Jahrhundert der Bilder*, vol. 2 (Göttingen: Vandenhoek und Ruprecht, 2008), pp. 434–41.

Frenkel-Brunswik, Else, 'Intolerance of ambiguity as an emotional and perceptual personality variable', *Journal of Personality*, 1 (1949), 108–43.

'From hypocrisy to apostasy: The extinction of the Grayzone', *Dabiq*, 7 (n.d.). https://clarionproject.org/docs/islamic-state-dabiq-magazine-issue-7-from-hypocrisy-to-apostasy.pdf (accessed 8 May 2019).

Fyfe, Paul, 'Illustrating the accident: Railways and the catastrophic picturesque in the Illustrated London News', *Victorian Periodicals Review*, 1 (2013), 61–91.

Gambetta, Diego and Steffen Hertog, *Engineers of Jihad: The Curious Connection between Violent Extremism and Education* (Princeton, NJ: Princeton University Press, 2016).

Gerhards, Jürgen, Mike S. Schäfer, Ishtar Al-Jabiri *et al.*, *Terrorismus im Fernsehen. Formate, Inhalte und Emotionen in westlichen und arabischen Sendern* (Wiesbaden: VS Verlag, 2011).

Gerling, Winfried, Susanne Holschbach and Petra Löffler, *Bilder verteilen. Fotografische Praktiken in der digitalen Kultur* (Bielefeld: Transcript, 2018).

German Press Council, 'Guidelines for journalistic work as recommended by the German Press Council: Complaints procedure', 13.03.2013 version, www.presserat.de/fileadmin/user_upload/Downloads_Dateien/Pressekodex13english_web.pdf (accessed 10 June 2019).

Glück, Antje, *Terror im Kopf. Terrorismusberichterstattung in der deutschen und arabischen Elitepresse* (Berlin: Frank und Timme, 2008).

Gombrich, Ernst H., 'The evidence of images: The variability of vision', in C.S. Singleton (ed.), *Interpretation: Theory and Practice* (Baltimore, MD: Johns Hopkins University Press, 1969), pp. 35–68.

———, *The Image and the Eye: Further Studies in the Psychology of Pictorial Representation* (London: Phaidon, 1994).

Goodmann, Walter, 'Of television images and hostage realities', *New York Times* (10 August 1989), p. 18.

Grabowski, Klaus H., 'Die Stimmen der Intellektuellen und ihr Echo', in Felicitas von Aretin and Bernd Wannenmacher (eds), *Weltlage. Der 11. September, die Politik und die Kulturen* (Opladen: Leske und Budrich, 2002), pp. 195–208.

Gregory, Sam, 'Human rights in an age of distant witnesses: Remixed lives, reincarnated images and live-streamed co-presence', in Jens Eder and Charlotte Klonk (eds), *Image Operations: Visual Media and Political Conflict* (Manchester: Manchester University Press, 2017), pp. 184–96.

———, 'Human rights made visible: New dimensions to anonymity, consent, and intentionality', in Meg McLagan and Yates McKee (eds), *Sensible Politics: The Visual Culture of Nongovernmental Activism* (New York: Zone Books, 2012), pp. 551–63.

Grimonprez, Johan, *Dial H-I-S-T-O-R-Y*, DVD (Ostfildern: Hatje Cantz, 2003).

Groebner, Valentin, *Der Schein der Person. Steckbrief, Ausweis und Kontrolle im Mittelalter* (Munich: C.H. Beck, 2004).

Gugerli, David, *Suchmaschinen. Die Welt als Datenbank* (Frankfurt: Suhrkamp, 2009).

Günther, Christoph, 'Der Islamische Staat und die Islamisierung des Abendlandes', in Janusz Biene and Martin Schmetz (eds), *Kalifat des Terrors* (Frankfurt: Sicherheitspolitik-Blog Fokus, 2015), pp. 13–17, www.sicherheitspolitik-blog.de/files/2015/07/Kalifat-des-Terrors.pdf (accessed 26 March 2019).

———, 'Presenting the glossy look of warfare in cyberspace: The Islamic State's magazine Dabiq', *CyberOrient*, 1 (2015), www.cyberorient.net/article.do?articleId=9538 (accessed 26 March 2019).

Gürsel, Zeynep D., 'Framing Zarqawi: Afterimages, headshots, and body politics in a digital age', in Olga Shevchenko (ed.), *Double Exposure: Memory and Photography* (Piscataway, NJ: Transaction, 2014), pp. 65–90.

———, *Image Brokers: Visualizing World News in the Age of Digital Circulation* (Berkeley, CA: University of California Press, 2016).

Hachmeister, Lutz, *Schleyer. Eine deutsche Geschichte* (Munich: DTV, 2007).

Hacht, Anne Marie (ed.), *Gale Encyclopedia of U.S. History*, vol. 2 (Detroit, MI: Gale, 2008).

Hafez, Mohammed M., 'Martyrdom mythology in Iraq: How jihadists frame suicide terrorism in videos and biographies', in John Horgan and Kurt Braddock (eds), *Terrorism Studies: A Reader* (London: Routledge, 2012), pp. 420–38.

———, 'The origins of sectarian terrorism in Iraq', in Bruce Hofman and Fernando Reinares (eds), *The Evolution of the Global Terrorist Threat: From 9/11 to Osama bin Laden's Death* (New York: Columbia University Press, 2014), pp. 436–60.

Hamill, Sean D., 'A Sept. 11 photo brings out the conspiracy theorists', *New York Times* (11 September 2007), p. A20.

Hanekop, Heidemarie and Volker Wittke, 'Kollaboration der Prosumenten', in Birgit Blättel-Mink and Kai-Uwe Hellmann (eds), *Prosumer Revisted: Zur Aktualität einer Debatte* (Wiesbaden: VS Verlag für Sozialwissenschaften, 2010), pp. 96–113.

Harclerode, Peter, *Secret Soldiers: Special Forces in the War against Terrorism* (London: Cassell, 2001).

Hardy, Deborah, *Land and Freedom: The Origins of Russian Terrorism* (New York: Greenwood Press, 1987).

Hariman, Robert and John Louis Lucaites, *No Caption Needed: Iconic Photographs, Public Culture, and Liberal Democracy* (Chicago, IL: Chicago University Press, 2007).

Harris, Neil, 'Iconography and intellectual history: The halftone effect', in John Higham and Paul K. Conkin (eds), *New Directions in American Intellectual History* (Baltimore, MD: John Hopkins University Press, 1979), pp. 196–211.

Hashhash, Mahmoud Abu, 'On the visual representation of martyrdom in Palestine', *Third Text*, 3–4 (2006), 391–403.

Haus der Geschichte Baden-Württemberg (ed.), *RAF: Terror im Südwesten* (Stuttgart: Haus der Geschichte Baden-Württemberg, 2013).

Haußecker, Nicole, *Terrorismusberichterstattung in Fernsehnachrichten. Visuelles Framing und emotionale Reaktionen* (Baden-Baden: Nomos, 2013).

Heinke, Daniel H. and Hazim Fouad, 'Das Dabiq-Magazin als Rekrutierungswerkzeug des IS', in Janusz Biene and Martin Schmetz (eds), *Kalifat des Terrors. Interdisziplinäre Perspektiven*

auf den Islamischen Staat (Frankfurt: Sicherheitspolitik-blog, 2015), pp. 7–12.

Hellmich, Christina, 'Al-Qaeda: Terrorists, hypocrites, fundamentalists? The view from within', *Third World Quarterly*, 1 (2005), 39–54.

Herman, Edward S., *The Real Terror Network: Terrorism in Fact and Propaganda* (Boston, MA: South End Press, 1982).

Hess, Henner, 'Die neue Herausforderung. Von der RAF zu Al Qaida', in Wolfgang Kraushaar (ed.), *Die RAF und der linke Terrorismus*, vol. 1 (Hamburg: Hamburger Edition, 2006), pp. 103–22.

———, 'Terrorismus und Terrorismus-Diskurs', in Henner Hess, Martin Moerings and Dieter Paas (eds), *Angriff auf das Herz des Staates. Soziale Entwicklung und Terrorismus*, vol. 1 (Frankfurt: Suhrkamp, 1988), pp. 55–74.

Höffe, Ottfried, *Ethik. Eine Einführung* (Munich: C.H. Beck, 2013).

Hoffman, Bruce, *Inside Terrorism*, revd and exp. edn (New York: Columbia University Press, 2006).

———, 'The 7 July 2005 London bombings', in Bruce Hoffman and Fernando Reinares (eds), *The Evolution of the Global Terrorist Threat: From 9/11 to Osama bin Laden's Death* (New York: Columbia University Press, 2014), pp. 192–223.

Hoffmann, Felix (ed.), *Unheimlich Vertraut/The Uncanny Familiar. Bilder vom Terror/Images of Terror*, exh. cat. C/O Berlin (Cologne: Walter König, 2011).

Hoskins, Andrew and Ben O'Loughlin, *War and Media: The Emergence of Diffused War* (Cambridge: Polity Press, 2010).

Hüppauf, Bernd, *Fotografie im Krieg* (Munich: Fink, 2015).

Jackson, Geoffrey, *People's Prison* (London: Faber, 1973).

Jäger, Jens, 'Photography: A means of surveillance? Judicial photography 1850 to 1900', *Crime, History and Societies*, 1 (2001), 2–23.

Jäger, Ludwig, 'Intermedialität, Intramedialität, Transkriptivität. Überlegungen zu einigen Prinzipien der kulturellen Semiosis', in Arnulf Deppermann and Angelika Linke (eds), *Sprache intermedial. Stimme und Schrift, Bild und Ton* (Berlin: De Gruyter, 2009), pp. 301–24.

Janzing, Godehard, 'The falling man', in Gerhard Paul (ed.), *Das Jahrhundert der Bilder*, vol. 2 (Göttingen: Vanderhoeck und Ruprecht, 2008), pp. 664–701.

Jenkins, Brian, *International Terrorism: A New Kind of Warfare* (Santa Monica, CA: Rand, 1974).

Jenkins, Philip, *Images of Terror: What We Can and Can't Know about Terrorism* (New York: de Gruyter, 2003).

Jensen, Richard Bach, *The Battle against Anarchist Terrorism: An International History, 1878–1934* (Cambridge: Cambridge University Press, 2014).

Joll, James, *The Anarchists* (London: Methuen, 1964).

Jordan, Hamilton, *Crisis: The Last Year of the Carter Presidency* (New York: Putnam, 1982).

Juergensmeyer, Mark, *Terror in the Mind of God: The Global Rise of Religious Violence* (Berkeley, CA: University of California, 2000).

———, *The New Cold War? Religious Nationalism Confronts the Secular State* (Berkeley, CA: University of California, 1993).

Junod, Tom, 'The falling man', *Esquire* (8 September 2003), http://archive.esquire.com/issue/20030901 (accessed 26 March 2019).

Jussim, Estelle, *Visual Communication and the Graphic Arts: Photographic Technologies in the Nineteenth-Century* (New York: Bowker, 1974).

Kahr, Robert, 'Der mediale Umgang mit dem Breivik-Prozess', *Bundeszentrale für politische Bildung* (24 September 2012), www.bpb.de/politik/hintergrund-aktuell/142949/der-mediale-umgang-mit-dem-breivik-prozess-24–08–2012 (accessed 21 April 2019).

Kappas, Arvid and Marion G. Müller, 'Bild und Emotionen. Ein neues Forschungsfeld', *Publizistik*, 1 (2006), 3–23.

Keenan, Brian, *An Evil Cradling* (London: Vintage, 1993).

Keller, Ulrich, *The Ultimate Spectacle: A Visual History of the Crimean War* (New York: Routledge, 2001).

Khalili, Laleh, *Heroes and Martyrs of Palestine: The Politics of Commemoration* (Cambridge: Cambridge University Press, 2007).

Khomami, Nadia, 'Marcy Borders, 9/11's "dust lady", dies of stomach cancer', *Guardian* (26 August 2015), www.theguardian.com/us-news/2015/aug/26/911s-dust-lady-marcy-borders-dies-of-stomach-cancer (accessed 26 February 2019).

Kinder, Hermann and Werner Hilgemann (eds), *Von der Französischen Revolution bis zur Gegenwart* (Munich: DTV, 2009).

Kingston, Shane, 'Terrorism, the media, and the Northern Ireland conflict', *Studies in Conflict and Terrorism*, 3 (1995), 203–31.

Klein, Hans-Joachim, *Rückkehr in die Menschlichkeit. Apell eines ausgestiegenen Terroristen* (Reinbek: Rowohlt, 1979).

Klonk, Charlotte, 'Bildterrorismus. Von Meins bis Schleyer', in Inge Stephan and Alexandra Tacke (eds), *NachBilder der RAF* (Cologne: Böhlau, 2008), pp. 197–215.

———, 'Die Entführung von Hanns Martin Schleyer oder die Entdeckung des Mediums Gesicht im terroristischen Bilderkampf', *Kritische Berichte*, 2 (2008), 49–58.

———, 'Image terror', in Jens Eder and Charlotte Klonk (eds), *Image Operations: Visual Media and Political Conflict* (Manchester: Manchester University Press, 2017), pp. 128–36.

———, 'Image terror', in Sue Malvern and Gabriel Koureas (eds), *Terrorist Transgressions: Gender and the Visual Culture of the Terrorist* (London: I.B. Tauris, 2014), pp. 15–37.

———, 'Macht der Bilder – Attentate als Medienereignisse', *Aus Politik und Zeitgeschichte*, 45–6 (2013), 30–9.

———, 'Warum wir trotzdem Bilder brauchen', *Frankfurter Allgemeine Zeitung* (14 May 2011), p. 34.

———, 'Wenn die Bilder Terror machen', *Frankfurter Allgemeine Zeitung* (19 January 2016), p. 12.

Kluge, Alexander, 'Die Macht der Bewußtseinsindustrie und das Schicksal unserer Öffentlichkeit', in Klaus von Bismarck, Günter Gaus, Alexander Kluge *et al.* (eds), *Industrialisierung des Bewußtseins. Eine kritische Auseinandersetzung mit den 'neuen' Medien* (Munich: Piper, 1985), pp. 51–129.

Knieper, Thomas, 'Die ikonologische Analyse von Medienbilder und deren Beitrag zur Bildkompetenz', in Thomas Knieper and Marion G. Müller (eds), *Authentizität und Inszenierung von Bildwelten* (Cologne: Herbert von Halem Verlag, 2003), pp. 193–212.

Laqueur, Walter, *A History of Terrorism*, exp. edn (New Brunswick: Transaction Publishers, 2016).

———, *The New Terrorism: Fanaticism and the Arms of Mass Destruction* (New York: Oxford University Press, 1999).

Lehmuskallio, Asko, *Pictorial Practices in a 'Cam Era': Studying Non-professional Camera Use* (Tampere: Tampere University Press, 2012).

Leifert, Stefan, *Bildethik. Theorie und Moral im Bildjournalismus der Massenmedien* (Munich: Wilhelm Fink, 2007).

Maasri, Zeina, *Off the Wall: Political Posters of the Lebanese Civil War* (London: I.B. Tauris, 2009).

MacCarthy, John and Jill Morrell, *Some Other Rainbow* (London: Bantam Press, 1993).

MacDonald, Eileen, *Shoot the Women First* (London: Fourth Estate, 1991).

McLagan, Meg, 'Human rights, testimony, and transnational publicity', in Michel Feher, Gaëlle Krikorian and Yates McKee (eds), *Nongovernmental Politics* (New York: Zone Books, 2007), pp. 304–17.

Magnum Photographers (eds), *New York, September 11* (New York: powerHouse Books, 2001).

Maitron, Jean, *Ravachol et les anarchistes*, first published 1973 (Paris: Gallimard, 1992).

Malvern, Sue, 'Femininity, feminism and the terrorist', in Sue Malvern and Gabriel Koureas (eds), *Female Transgressions: Gender and the Visual Culture of the Terrorist* (London: I.B. Tauris, 2014), pp. 39–55.

Merriman, John, *The Dynamite Club: How Bombing in Fin-de-Siècle Paris Ignited the Age of Modern Terror* (London: JR Books, 2009).

Miller, Greg and Scott Higham, 'Confronting the "Caliphate"', *Washington Post* (8 May 2015), www.washingtonpost.com/world/national-security/in-a-propaganda-war-us-tried-to-play-by-the-enemys-rules/2015/05/08/6eb6b732-e52f-11e4–81ea-0649268f729e_story.html (accessed 1 April 2019).

Möllers, Martin H. W. and Robert Chr. van Ooyen, *NSU-Terrorismus. Ergebnisse der parlamentarischen Untersuchungsausschüsse und Empfehlungen für die Sicherheitsbehörden* (Frankfurt: Verlag für Polizeiwissenschaft, 2015).

Monahan, Brian A., 'The fabrication of truth', in Boris Groys and Peter Weibel (eds), *Medium – Religion – Faith – Geopolitics – Art*, exh. cat. ZKM Karlsruhe (Cologne: Walter König, 2011), pp. 78–85.

———, *The Shock of the News: Media Coverage and the Making of 9/11* (New York: New York University Press, 2010).

Müller, Marion G., 'Bilder – Visionen – Wirklichkeiten. Zur Bedeutung der Bildwissenschaft im 21. Jahrhundert', in Thomas Knieper and Marion G. Müller (eds), *Kommunikation visuell. Das Bild als Forschungsgegenstand. Grundlagen und Perspektiven* (Cologne: Herbert von Halem Verlag, 2001), pp. 14–25.

Münkler, Herfried, *The New Wars*, trans. Patrick Camiller (London: Polity, 2004).

Nacos, Brigitte L., *Mass-Mediated Terrorism: The Central Role of the Media in Terrorism and Counterterrorism*, 2nd edn (Plymouth: Rowman & Littlefield, 2007).

———, *Terrorism and the Media: From the Iran Hostage Crisis to the World Trade Center Bombing* (New York: Columbia Press, 1994).

Nagarajan, Chitra, '#Bringbackourgirls hasn't brought back Chibok's Girls, but it has changed Nigeria's politics', *Guardian* (14 April 2015), www.theguardian.com/commentisfree/2015/apr/14/nigeria-women-activists-boko-haram (accessed 8 December 2018).

Nead, Lynda, *Victorian Babylon: People, Streets, and Images in Nineteenth-Century London* (New Haven, CT: Yale University Press, 2000).

Noiriel, Gérard (ed.), *L'identification. Genèse d'un travail d'État* (Paris: Belin, 2007).

Nye, David, *American Technological Sublime* (Cambridge, MA: MIT Press, 1994).

O'Loughlin, Ben, 'Images as weapons of war: Representation, mediation and interpretation', *Review of International Studies*, 1 (2011), 71–91.

Parker, Philip, *World History* (London: Dorling Kindersley, 2010).

Paul, Gerhard, *Bilder des Krieges – Krieg der Bilder. Die Visualisierung des modernen Krieges* (Paderborn: Schöningh, 2004).

———, *BilderMacht. Studien zur Visual History des 20. und 21. Jahrhunderts* (Göttingen: Wallstein, 2013).

———, *Der Bilderkrieg. Inszenierungen, Bilder und Perspektiven der 'Operation Irakische Freiheit'* (Göttingen: Wallstein, 2005).

Piazza, Pierre (ed.), *Aux origines de la police scientifique. Alphonse Bertillon, précurseur de la science du crime* (Paris: Karthala, 2011).

Presse- und Informationsamt der Bundesregierung, *Zu den Ereignissen und Entscheidungen im Zusammenhang mit der Entführung von Hanns Martin Schleyer und der Lufthansa-Maschine 'Landshut'*, 2nd edn (Munich: Goldmann, 1977).

Proll, Astrid, *Hans und Grete. Bilder der RAF 1967–1977* (Göttingen, Steidl, 1998).

———, *Hans und Grete. Bilder der RAF 1967–1977*, rev. new edn (Berlin: Aufbau-Verlag, 2004).

Quinlivan, Patrick and Paul Rose, *The Fenians in England, 1865–1872* (London: John Calder, 1982).

Quintana, Aldina and Rolf Kailuweit, '"De Madrid al cielo". (De) Kontextualisierung des 11-M durch Popmusik und Videoclips im Internet', in Ursula Hennigfeld and Stephan Packard (eds), *Abschied von 9/11? Distanznahmen zur Katastrophe* (Berlin: Frank und Timme, 2013), pp. 213–44.

Randal, Jonathan C., 'Hostages to be held until at least 1989, PLO official asserts', *Washington Post* (21 February 1987), p. A13.

Ranstorp, Magnus, 'Hizbollah's command leadership: Its structure, decision-making, and relationship with Iranian clergy and institutions', in John Horgan and Kurt Braddock (eds), *Terrorism Studies: A Reader* (London: Routledge, 2012), pp. 147–73.

Rapoport, David, *Assassination and Terrorism* (Toronto: CBC, 1971).

———, 'The four waves of modern terrorism', in Audrey Kurth Cronin and James Ludes (eds), *Attacking Terrorism: Elements of a Grand Strategy* (Washington, DC: Georgetown University Press, 2004), pp. 46–73.

Rapp, Maximilian, *Murals in Nordirland. Symbol der ethnokulturellen Identität und Spiegel des politischen Wandels* (Baden-Baden: Nomos, 2014).

Reed, David, *The Popular Magazine in Britain and the United States 1880–1960* (London: British Library, 1997).

Reemtsma, Jan Philipp, 'Terroristische Gewalt. Was klärt die Frage nach den Motiven?' in Michael Beuthner, Joachim Buttler, Sandra Fröhlich *et al.* (eds), *Bilder des Terrors – Terror der Bilder. Krisenberichterstattung am und nach dem 11. September* (Cologne: Herbert von Halem Verlag, 2003), pp. 330–49.

Regener, Susanne, 'Anarchistische Gewalttäter. Zur Mediengeschichte der RAF-Plakate', in Gerhard Paul (ed.), *Das Jahrhundert der Bilder*, vol. 2 (Göttingen: Vandenhoeck und Ruprecht, 2008), pp. 402–9.

———, 'Facial politics – Bilder des Bösen nach dem 11. September', in Petra Löffler and Leander Scholz (eds), *Das Gesicht ist eine starke Organisation* (Cologne, DuMont, 2004), pp. 203–24.

———, *Fotografische Erfassung* (Munich: Wilhelm Fink, 1999).

Requate, Jörg, 'Die Faszination anarchistischer Attentate im Frankreich des ausgehenden 19. Jahrhunderts', in Klaus Weinhauer and Jörg Requate (eds), *Gewalt ohne Ausweg? Terrorismus als Kommunikationsprozess in Europa seit dem 19. Jahrhundert* (Frankfurt: Campus, 2012), pp. 99–122.

Reuter, Christoph, *Die Schwarze Macht. Der Islamische Staat und die Strategen des Terrors* (Munich: Deutsche Verlags-Anstalt, 2015).

Richardson, Louise, *What Terrorists Want: Understanding the Terrorist Threat* (London: John Murray, 2006).

Riegler, Thomas, *Terrorismus. Akteure, Strukturen, Entwicklungslinien* (Innsbruck: StudienVerlag, 2009).

Robin, Corey, 'Primal fear', *Theory & Event*, 4 (2001), https://muse.jhu.edu/article/32656 (accessed 26 March 2019).

Robinson, Eugene, 'Why I would've released the bin Laden photos', *Washington Post* (4 May 2011), www.washingtonpost.com/blogs/post-partisan/post/why_i_wouldve_released_the_bin_laden_photos/2011/03/04/AFztulpF_blog.html?wprss=post-partisan (accessed 11 December 2018).

Rosen, Michael, *Dignity: Its History and Meaning* (Cambridge, MA: Harvard University Press, 2012).

Rosenberg, Per A., *Kärlek med förhinder. Texte der RAF* (Malmö: Bo Cavefors, 1977).

Rößler, Hans-Christian, 'Der Schuss von Hebron', *Frankfurter Allgemeine Zeitung* (5 January 2017), p. 3.

Rote Armee Fraktion, *Konzept Stadtguerilla* (Amsterdam: Niemec, 1971).

———, *Texte und Materialien zur Geschichte der RAF* (Berlin: ID-Verlag, 1997).

Runkle, Benjamin, *Wanted Dead or Alive* (New York: Palgrave, 2011).
Saehrendt, Christian, *Gefühlige Zeiten. Die zwanghafte Sehnsucht nach dem Echten* (Cologne: DuMont, 2015).
Scarry, Elaine, 'Who defended the country', in Daniel J. Sherman and Terry Nardin (eds), *Terror, Culture, Politics. Rethinking 9/11* (Bloomington, IN: Indiana University Press, 2006), pp. 184–205.
Scheufele, Bertram, *Frames – Framing – Framing-Effekte. Theoretische und methodische Grundlegung sowie empirische Befunde zur Nachrichtenreproduktion* (Wiesbaden: Westdeutscher Verlag, 2003).
Schierl, Thomas, 'Der Schein der Authentizität. Journalistische Bildproduktion als nachfrageorientierte Produktion scheinbarer Authentizität', in Thomas Knieper and Marion G. Müller (eds), *Authentizität und Inszenierung von Bildwelten* (Cologne: Herbert von Halem Verlag, 2003), pp. 150–67.
Schiffer, Sabine, *Die Darstellung des Islams in der Presse. Sprache, Bilder, Suggestionen* (Würzburg: Ergon-Verlag, 2005).
Schuurman, Bart, 'Topics in terrorism research: Reviewing trends and gaps, 2007–2016', *Critical Studies on Terrorism* (2019) DOI: 10.1080/17539153.2019.1579777.
Schwarte, Ludger, *Pikturale Evidenz. Zur Wahrheitsfähigkeit der Bilder* (Paderborn: Wilhelm Fink, 2015).
Schwartz, Louis-Georges, *Mechanical Witness: A History of Motion Picture Evidence in U.S. Courts* (Oxford: Oxford University Press, 2009).
Seehaus, Christine, 'Terrorismus in Bildern. Die Grenzen des rechtlich Zulässigen', in Sonja Glaab (ed.), *Medien und Terrorismus. Auf den Spuren einer symbiotischen Beziehung* (Berlin: Berliner Wissenschafts-Verlag, 2007), pp. 115–38.
Seeßlen, Georg and Markus Metz, *Krieg der Bilder – Bilder des Krieges. Abhandlung über die Katastrophe und mediale Wirklichkeit* (Berlin: Edition Tiamat, 2002).
Seitz, Clemens J., 'Das grelle Herz der Finsternis', *Die Zeit* (25 September 2014), pp. 47–8.
Shibli, Ahlam, *Phantom Home* (Ostfildern: Hatje Cantz, 2013).
Simon, Joshua, 'The aesthetics of terror in general and suicide bomber videos in particular', in Boris Groys and Peter Weibel (eds), *Medium – Religion – Faith – Geopolitics – Art*, exh. cat. ZKM Karlsruhe (Cologne: Walter König, 2011), pp. 58–84.
Sinnema, Peter W., *Dynamics of the Pictured Page: Representing the Nation in the Illustrated London News* (Aldershot: Ashgate, 1998).
Short, Kenneth R. M., *The Dynamite War* (Dublin: Gill and Macmillan, 1979).

Snyder, Joel and Neil W. Allen, 'Photography, vision, and representation', *Critical Inquiry*, 2 (1975), 143–69.

Sontag, Susan, *Regarding the Pain of Others* (London: Hamish Hamilton, 2004).

Sontheimer, Michael, 'Anfänge der RAF. Todesschüsse in der Seitenstraße', *Spiegel Online* (15 July 2011), http://www.spiegel.de/einestages/anfaenge-der-raf-a-947270.html#featuredEntry (accessed 21 April 2019).

Speckhard, Anne and Ahmet S. Yayla, 'Eyewitness accounts from recent defectors from Islamic State. Why they joined, what they saw, why they quit', *Perspectives on Terrorism*, 9 (2015), www.terrorismanalysts.com/pt/index.php/pot/article/view/475/html (accessed 26 March 2019).

Staff and agencies, 'Police shot Brazilian eight times', *Guardian* (25 July 2005), www.theguardian.com/uk/2005/jul/25/july7.uksecurity5 (accessed 1 April 2019).

Steinseifer, Martin, '"Fotos wie Brandwunden"? Überlegungen zur deontischen Bedeutung von Pressefotografien am Beispiel von Hanns Martin Schleyer als Opfer der Roten Armee Fraktion', in Dietrich Busse, Thomas Niehr and Martin Wengeler (eds), *Brisante Semantik. Neuere Konzepte und Forschungsergebnisse einer kulturwissenschaftlichen Linguistik* (Tübingen: Niemeyer, 2005), pp. 269–90.

Stephan, Inge and Alexandra Tacke (eds), *Nachbilder der RAF* (Cologne: Böhlau, 2008).

Sterling, Claire, *The Terror Network: The Secret War of International Terrorism* (New York: Holt, Rinehart, and Winston, 1981).

Störer, Bernd, *United States of America. Geschichte und Kultur* (Munich: C.H. Beck, 2012).

Straub, Verena, 'The making and gendering of a martyr: Images of female suicide bombers in the Middle East', in Jens Eder and Charlotte Klonk (eds), *Image Operations: Visual Media and Political Conflict* (Manchester: Manchester University Press, 2017), pp. 137–50.

Talbot, Rhiannon, 'Myths in the representation of women terrorists', *Eire-Ireland*, 3–4 (2000), 165–86.

Terhoeven, Petra, 'Opferbilder – Täterbilder. Die Fotografie als Medium linksterroristischer Selbstermächtigung in Deutschland und Italien während der 70er Jahre', *Geschichte und Wissenschaft und Unterricht*, 7–8 (2007), 380–99.

'The Islamic imagery project: Visual motifs in jihadi internet propaganda' (March 2006), *Homeland Security Digital Library*, 86,

https://www.hsdl.org/?abstract&did=236104 (accessed 6 May 2019).
'The Islamic State', https://www.youtube.com/watch?v=AUjHb4C7b94 (accessed 14 May 2019).
Torke, Hans-Joachim, 'Die Narodniki und Zar Alexander II. (1881). Ein Vorspiel zur Revolution', in Alexander Demandt (ed.), *Das Attentat in der Geschichte* (Frankfurt: Suhrkamp, 1999), pp. 298–316.
Townshend, Charles, *Terrorism: A Very Short Introduction* (Oxford: Oxford University Press, 2002).
Tremel, Luise, 'Litterorisierung', in Wolfgang Kraushaar (ed.), *Die RAF und der linke Terrorismus*, vol. 2 (Hamburg: HIS Verlag, 2006), pp. 1117–54.
van den Heuvel, Gerd, 'Terreur, Terroriste, Terrorisme', in Hans Ulrich Gumbrecht, Rolf Reichardt and Gerd van den Heuvel (eds), *Handbuch politisch-sozialer Grundbegriffe in Frankreich 1680–1820*, vol. 3 (Munich: De Gruyter, 1985), pp. 89–132.
Varennes, Henrie, *De Ravachol à Caserio, notes d'audience* (Paris: Farnier frères, 1895).
Vec, Miloš, *Die Spur des Täters. Methoden der Identifikation in der Kriminalistik 1879–1933* (Baden-Baden: Nomos, 2002).
Viehoff, Reinhold and Kathrin Fahlenbrach, 'Ikonen der Medienkultur. Über die (verschwindende) Differenz von Authentizität und Inszenierung der Bilder in der Geschichte', in Michael Beuthner, Joachim Buttler, Sandra Fröhlich *et al.* (eds), *Bilder des Terrors – Terror der Bilder? Krisenberichterstattung am und nach dem 11. September* (Cologne: Herbert von Halem Verlag, 2003), pp. 42–59.
von Dewitz, Bodo, 'Zur Geschichte der Kriegsphotographie des Ersten Weltkrieges', in Rainer Rother (ed.), *Die letzten Tage der Menschheit. Bilder des Ersten Weltkrieges* (Berlin: Ars Nicolai, 1994), pp. 163–76.
Vowinckel, Annette, *Flugzeugentführungen. Eine Kulturgeschichte* (Göttingen: Wallstein, 2011).
Wagener, Sybil, *Feindbilder. Wie kollektiver Hass entsteht* (Berlin: Quadriga, 1999).
Waite, Terry, *Taken on Trust* (San Diego, CA: Harcourt Brace, 1993).
Waldmann, Peter, *Terrorismus. Provokation der Macht* (Munich: Gerling Akademie, 1998).
Walther, Rudolf, 'Terror, Terrorismus', in Otto Brunner, Werner Conze and Reinhart Koselleck (eds), *Geschichtliche Grundbegriffe. Historisches Lexikon zur politisch-sozialen Sprache in Deutschland*, vol. 6 (Stuttgart: Klett-Cotta, 1990), pp. 323–444.

Warburg, Aby, 'Dürer and Italian antiquity', in Aby Warburg, *The Renewal of Pagan Antiquity*, ed. Kurt W. Forster, trans. David Britt (Los Angeles, CA: Getty Publications, 1999), pp. 553–8.

Weinhauer, Klaus, 'Terrorismus und Kommunikation. Forschungsstand und -perspektiven zum bundesdeutschen Linksterrorismus der 1970er Jahre', in Nicole Colin, Beatrice de Graaf, Jacco Pekelder *et al.* (eds), *Der 'Deutsche Herbst' und die RAF in Politik, Medien und Kunst. Nationale und internationale Perspektiven* (Bielefeld: Transcript, 2008), pp. 109–23.

Weller, Christoph, 'Die massenmediale Konstruktion der Terroranschläge am 11. September 2001. Eine Analyse der Fernsehberichterstattung und ihre theoretischen Grundlagen', *INEF-Report*, 63 (2002), 1–105, http://edoc.vifapol.de/opus/volltexte/2013/4544/pdf/report63_1.pdf (accessed 26 March 2019).

Werber, Niels, 'Die Prada-Meinhof-Bande', *Literaturen*, 12 (2001), 28–31.

Werckmeister, Otto Karl, 'Ästhetik der Apokalypse', in Bazon Brock and Gerlinde Koschik (eds), *Krieg und Kunst* (Munich: Wilhelm Fink, 2002), pp. 195–207.

Wichmann, Peter, *Al-Qaida und der globale Djihad. Eine vergleichende Betrachtung des transnationalen Terrorismus* (Wiesbaden: Springer, 2014).

Wiegel, Michaela, 'Ohne Strategie. Die französische Regierung verengt die Terrorismus-Debatte auf Sicherheitspolitik', *Frankfurter Allgemeine Zeitung* (5 April 2016), p. 8.

Wigg, Richard, 'Envoy writes from Tupamaros cell', *The Times* (27 March 1971), p. 5.

Wisniewski, Stefan, *Wir waren so unheimlich konsequent. Ein Gespräch zur Geschichte der RAF*, 3rd edn (Berlin: ID-Verlag, 2003).

Woodcock, George (ed.), *The Anarchist Reader* (Glasgow: Fontana, 1977).

Zelin, Aaron Y., 'Picture or it didn't happen: a snapshot of the Islamic State's official media output', *Perspectives on Terrorism*, 9 (2015), 85–97.

Index

Index

Index

Index

Index